Animal Characters

A volume in the Haney Foundation Series,
established in 1961 with the generous support
of Dr. John Louis Haney

Animal Characters

Nonhuman Beings in Early Modern Literature

Bruce Thomas Boehrer

PENN

UNIVERSITY OF PENNSYLVANIA PRESS

PHILADELPHIA • OXFORD

Published by
University of Pennsylvania Press
Philadelphia, Pennsylvania 19104-4112

Printed in the United States of America on acid-free paper

10 9 8 7 6 5 4 3 2 1

Library of Congress Cataloging-in-Publication Data
Boehrer, Bruce Thomas.
   Animal characters : nonhuman beings in early modern literature /
Bruce Thomas Boehrer.
      p. cm. — (Haney Foundation series)
   Includes bibliographical references and index.
   ISBN 978-0-8122-4249-2 (acid-free paper)
   1. Animals in literature. 2. Characters and characteristics in
literature. 3. English literature—Early modern, 1500–1700—History
and criticism. 4. European literature—Renaissance, 1450–1600—
History and criticism. 5. Symbolism in literature. 6. Animals,
Mythical, in literature. 7. Animals in art. I. Title.
PR149.A7B64 2010
820.9'374—dc22

                                                    2010004557

Contents

Animal Studies and the Problem
of Character

In February 1944, having just completed the manuscript of *Animal Farm*, George Orwell submitted to one of the most melancholy rituals to darken any professional writer's life: finding a publisher for his newly finished book. While making the usual rounds, he had the misfortune to send his novel to the American offices of Dial, whose response he recalled two years later in a letter to his agent, Leonard Moore: "I am not sure whether one can count on the American public grasping what [*Animal Farm*] is about. You may remember that the Dial Press had been asking me for some years for a manuscript, but when I sent the MS of *AF* in 1944 they returned it, saying shortly that 'it was impossible to sell animal stories in the USA.' Just recently they wrote saying that 'there had been some mistake' and that they would like to make another offer for the book. I rather gather they had at first taken it for a bona fide animal story" (Orwell 4:110). For Orwell (who never had much use for the United States), this incident reflects on the obtuseness of the American reading public; for me, it says more about the failures of the literary profession. In addition, it says something about the uncomfortable relationship between nonhuman animals and modern notions of literary character.

This book deals with a period of literary history—the fifteenth to the seventeenth centuries—that substantially predates *Animal Farm*. Still, one way to understand Orwell's novel is to place it within the European tradition of beast fable, poetry, and prose narrative that stretches back to Aesop and encompasses works directly germane to the present study: for example, the *Roman de Renart* (twelfth and thirteenth centuries), Chaucer's Nun's Priest's Tale (1396-1400), Skelton's "Speke, Parrot" (c. 1525), and the fables of La

Fontaine (1668). However, this tradition has largely gone fallow over the past two centuries, with the result that modern literary works foregrounding animal subjectivity usually tend to be marginalized as genre fiction: for instance, children's literature (*The Wind in the Willows*, *Winnie the Pooh*) or fantasy (*His Dark Materials*, *The Chronicles of Narnia*).[1] It is in this general spirit that Dial's reader understood and dismissed Orwell's novel as an animal story. Granted, one may also make sense of modern works dealing with animal characters by classifying them as exercises in allegory or surrealism or experimental fiction (Kafka's "Report to an Academy" and "Investigations of a Dog" come to mind). Indeed, the real failure of the reader for Dial Press is that she misidentified a work we tend to locate in the latter of these categories (allegorical and experimental) as belonging to the former (naive genre fiction). However, even literary works in the second category end up outside the literary mainstream, defined either as retrograde (for example, allegory) or idiosyncratic (for example, experimental fiction). In any case, what Dial Press called "animal stories" seem to require a special dispensation for their continued existence in the modern literary world. They stand as deviations from the norm, to be tolerated rather than encouraged.

John Ruskin offers us a way of understanding this development when he introduces his notion of the pathetic fallacy in *Modern Painters* (1843). For Ruskin, the pathetic fallacy is "always the sign of a morbid state of mind" (368) while also managing to be "eminently characteristic of the modern mind" (369)—observations that, taken together, lead inevitably to a debased and pathological view of modernity. Indeed, the pathetic fallacy's fallaciousness and its morbidity consist in the very same thing: "a falseness in . . . our impressions of external things," which results from "a mind and body . . . too weak to deal fully with what is before them" (364, 365) and which invests the natural world with the observer's own passions. Weakness of temperament (we might say weakness of character) generates the error, which leads the afflicted individual to invest brute nature with emotions she experiences but which, by virtue of its very brutishness, nature cannot share. The self is so overwhelmed with itself that it imprints itself on the rest of the world.

Ruskin's examples of this phenomenon are all drawn carefully from nonsentient nature: shivering crocuses, dancing leaves, "raging waves," "remorseless floods," "ravenous billows," and so forth (367). However, a moment's reflection shows that nonhuman animals may serve as a marginal case of the same mental event: their obvious ability to react to their surroundings complicates matters since it supplies proof of sentience, but their inner life—their susceptibility to what we might call human passion—remains inscrutable. So what does one do with raging lions or timorous lambs, with stubborn mules or proud peacocks, or with any of the innumerable other commonplaces whereby traditional language assumes a continuity between human and nonhuman animal experience? What, in the broader sense, does one do with the impulse to think of nonhuman animals as subjects—as characters—in their own right?

From the standpoint of the pathetic fallacy, one must concede that this impulse looks suspicious. Even granting that nonhuman animals are in some sense aware, we remain a long way indeed from endowing them with the mental and emotional furniture of human experience. To do so—especially in light of our proved tendency to extend this endowment to rocks and trees and other nonsentient natural entities—looks very much like a first step in the direction of sentimental anthropomorphism. In this respect, to allow that animals are more like us than like stones seems to entail a rich panoply of cultural silliness, ranging from pet cemeteries to childish fantasies about talking pigs. Indeed, when considered from the standpoint of the pathetic fallacy, animals appear particularly noxious. They are, as it were, the thin end of the wedge.

Humanity, Modernity, Character

Ruskin's work brings pressure to bear on the notion of modernity, which he considers especially susceptible to the silliness at the heart of the pathetic fallacy. The following pages, by contrast, focus on animal character in the *early* modern period, for it is the span from about 1400 to about 1700 that witnesses the birth of the intellectual dispensation Ruskin takes for granted. At heart, one could describe the present book as a set of interrelated zooliterary histories, or perhaps less pretentiously, as a series of character studies of early modern animals. It concentrates on animal character, in turn, because I consider this crucial to the development of notions of literary character in general. My underlying argument here is simple: that the problem of literary character may best be understood from the standpoint of animal studies, as an instance of broader philosophical and scientific problems in theorizing the human-animal divide.

That the concept of literary character *is* a problem—or at least entails problems—I take as axiomatic. It was certainly so for L. C. Knights when, in 1933, he published his classic essay "How Many Children Had Lady Macbeth?"[2] A brief for New Critical formalism, Knights's article also mounts an attack on the methods of character analysis that dominated earlier critical practice as exemplified by the study of Shakespeare: "The habit of regarding Shakespeare's persons as 'friends for life,' or, maybe, 'deceased acquaintances,' is responsible for most of the vagaries that serve as Shakespeare criticism. . . . It is responsible for all the irrelevant moral and realistic canons that have been applied to Shakespeare's plays, for the sentimentalizing of his heroes (Coleridge and Goethe on Hamlet) and his heroines. And the loss is incalculable" (30). Knights's critique has produced a kind of queasy ambivalence in more recent literary criticism, which remains attached to the notion of character without really wanting to be; as Elizabeth Fowler summarized matters in 2003, "Literary scholarship . . . speaks of characters as if they were real people and, just as frequently, warns us that they are not" (5). The resulting dilemma receives fine comic expression at the hands of David Lodge, an author with credentials both as a theorist and as a writer of fiction. In the 1988 academic novel *Nice Work*, Lodge's narrator is awkwardly obliged to introduce a character who "doesn't herself believe in the concept of 'character'"—one "Robyn Penrose, Temporary Lecturer in English Literature at the University of Rummidge" (21). Penrose's objections to the concept— that is, "that 'character' is a bourgeois myth, an illusion created to reinforce the ideology of capitalism," obscuring the crucial insight that "[t]here are no selves, only production, and we produce our 'selves' in language" (21–22)— attest to the role of Marxist and postmodernist theory in assailing the legitimacy of character as a literary construct.

However, the Marxist-postmodernist critique of literary character did not develop in a vacuum; it runs parallel to a broader assault on the category of the human. This broader line of argument is typified by the poststructuralist tradition in current animal-studies theory, which objects to the Benthamite and Kantian schools of animal-rights philosophy, represented by Peter Singer and Tom Regan respectively, on the grounds that these seek to protect nonhuman animals by extending to them a notion of human rights (or in Singer's case, human ethical subjectivity) that is intellectually untenable.[3] Thus, Derrida refuses "to assign, interpret, or project" meaning onto the animal other (this being, I take it, the impulse of traditional animal-rights theory) while likewise resisting the Cartesian reflex to "suspend . . . one's compassion and . . . depriv[e] the animal of every power of manifestation" (387). Gilles Deleuze and Félix Guattari replace the notion of being with one of becoming, located in "an objective zone of indetermination or uncertainty . . . 'that makes it impossible to say where the boundary between the human and animal lies'" (273). Giorgio Agamben, arguing that "[i]n our culture, the decisive political conflict . . . is that between the animality and the humanity *of man*," concludes that "what is decisive here is only the 'between,' the interval . . . between the two terms, their immediate constellation in a non-coincidence" (80, 83; my italics). Each of these positions assumes that to ground political or ethical action on notions of the human is to perpetuate the very inequities that politics and ethics are intended to remedy; hence the deconstruction of the human emerges as a philosophical imperative.

There can be no doubt that literary criticism's discomfort with the concept of character is related to this growing theoretical impulse to deconstruct the human-animal divide. After all, if a given philosophical category (the human) proves defective, it follows that the category's major literary manifestation (character) should share in its inadequacies. In what follows, I argue that the notion of character develops in English writing as an early effort to evade this very philosophical crisis: as a means of manufacturing and perpetuating the distinction between people and animals.

This is not how the turn to character and character criticism has usually been understood. Knights explains it in classic New Critical fashion, as a failure of linguistic engagement—in the case of Shakespeare scholars, "an inability to appreciate the Elizabethan idiom and a consequent inability to discuss Shakespeare's plays as poetry" (26). Lodge's Robyn Penrose, for her part, follows the Brechtian aperçu that literary illusionism aims to transform audiences into "the passive consumer[s] of a finished, unchangeable art object offered to them as 'real'" (Eagleton 64); thus, for her, "the rise of the novel (the literary genre of 'character' *par excellence*) in the eighteenth century coincided with the rise of capitalism" and its endless search for pliable markets (21). For scholars following Ian Watt, the rise of literary character derives from the eighteenth-century tendency to "pa[y] greater attention to the particular individual than had been common before" (Watt 18), a tendency deriving from the philosophical skepticism of figures such as Descartes, Locke, and Hume. While these narratives trace the ascendancy of literary character to different historical events (the development of new language practices, the birth of capitalism, the rise of scientific empiricism), they agree by locating it in the eighteenth century and identifying the novel as its exemplary genre.

Still, if one takes at face value the eighteenth-century passion for Shakespeare as a creator of characters, it challenges both the chronological focus on the eighteenth century and the generic focus on prose fiction. In any case, as Fowler's recent work with Chaucer has shown, it is patently silly to suppose that pre-Enlightenment authors had no literary characters, if one defines these simply—in Fowler's preferred way—as "social persons" (27). Moreover, even the term "character," as applied to the "description, delineation, or detailed report of a person's qualities" (*Oxford English Dictionary* [hereafter *OED*], s.v. "character," sb. 14), predates the eighteenth century. The *OED*'s earliest recorded instance of this usage comes from James Howell's *Letters* of 1645, but even this is unfairly belated; with the publication of Joseph Hall's Theophrastan *Characters* in 1608, the English already possessed a fully formed literary exemplar of the definition. Indeed, Theophrastus's works play a central role in establishing the noun "character" as an English literary term, and in the process they reveal the word's embeddedness in an ancient tradition of philosophical meditation on the nature of human identity.

Theophrastus is best remembered for treatises in the fields we would now call biology and psychology.[4] These works span the disciplinary divide—between "the representation of nonhumans" and "the representation of citizens" (Latour 28)—that Bruno Latour identifies with modernity's "separation of natural and political powers" (13). In this regard, they preserve the cross-disciplinary focus of Theophrastus's master, Aristotle, whom he succeeded in 322 B.C.E. as head of the Peripatetic school in Athens. Indeed, if readers of Theophrastus have detected a "botanical" impulse in his *Characters* (Boyce 5), that is because Theophrastus was working squarely within an Aristotelian tradition in which "[t]he methodical treatment of *poiesis* in the *Poetics* is similar to the orderly classification of the body in the *History of Animals*" (Craik 158). In this tradition the study of rhetoric and the study of natural history, the study of people and the study of animals emerge as parallel expressions of the same taxonomic impulse.

It may be objected that this is merely a matter of form, that in substance the two undertakings differ considerably. Perhaps, but the most recent translators of Theophrastus's *Characters* have traced its antecedents back to the lengthiest surviving verse fragment by Semonides of Amorgos (seventh century B.C.E.), consisting of character sketches of women whose "various vices (e.g. filthiness, cunning, extravagance) are explained by their creation from animals (e.g. the pig, fox, horse)" (Rusten and Cunningham 17). If, as these same editors aver, "the notion that individual good or bad traits of character may be isolated and studied separately" is "basic" to the philosopher's "whole enterprise" (13), then the *Characters* participates in an ethical project that encompasses the world of nonhuman animals as well. That, at least, is a major assumption of the bestiarists, those other heirs to Aristotle, when they identify the behavior of the halcyon hen as "an unexpected celebration of kindness" (White 124) or attribute to horses the capacity "to weep for man and feel the emotion of sorrow" (86) or expound upon "[t]he merciful nature of lions" (Barber 25). As quaintly familiar as such language may be, it points to the historical investment of character study in observation of the nonhuman world.

Thus, from the standpoint of animal studies, it becomes appropriate to view the bestiary entry as a particular variety of character study and to view the Theophrastan character as a particular variant of the bestiary entry. In terms of early modern English literary history, this linkage becomes especially visible in the "birds of prey"—Voltore, Corbaccio, and Corvino—who populate Ben Jonson's *Volpone* (1605; 1.2.89), as well as in Nano's claim, in the same play, to have passed former lives as an "*ox and asse, cammell, mule, goat, and brock*" (1.2.22). *Volpone*'s characterological bestiary draws simultaneously on the traditional figures of beast fable and epic, deriving from post-Aristotelian animal lore, and on the stock figures of New Comedy, based on post-Aristotelian psychology. In the latter respect, the linkage to Theophrastus again seems clear enough; Menander is said to have been one of the philosopher's students (Diogenes Laertius 485; 5.36–37). Later English usage retains the affinity between human and animal traits in the sense of "character" as denoting "the distinguishing features of a species or genus" (*OED*, s.v. "character," sb. 8b).

Jonson's carrion birds by no means exhaust the characterological possibilities of the animal in early modern literature. If we accept Fowler's working definition of literary characters as "social persons" compounded from overlapping "legal," "civic," "corporate," "economic," "kinship," and "literary" identities (16–17), the heavy integration of animals into all these aspects of early modern society makes it hard to see how one could reasonably deny them status as literary characters in their own right. Consider Montaigne's *Apology for Raymond Sebonde* (1576), which, apart from its inscrutable cat, abounds with sentient beasts: a magpie who, after "a profound study and withdrawal within herself," learns to mimic the sound of trumpets (341); elephants who help each other escape from traps (342); cranes and swallows with "the faculty of divination" (345); and so on. Or consider Baiardo in Lodovico Ariosto's *Orlando Furioso* (1516), a steed so cunning and faithful to Rinaldo that he refuses to let the latter mount him lest his master might call off the horse's steadfast pursuit of Rinaldo's beloved Angelica (Caretti, ed., 2.20–23). Or consider the beginning of Sir Philip Sidney's *Defense of Poesy* (1580–85), where John Pietro Pugliano praises the horse as "a peerless beast . . . , the only serviceable courtier without flattery, the beast of most beauty, faithfulness, courage, and such more . . . that I think he would have persuaded me to have wished myself a horse" (3).

One might protest that for Sidney, Pugliano serves as an object of derision, an exponent of "unbelieved" opinions, who defends these with "strong affection and weak arguments" (3). However, this fact speaks precisely to my broader point: that in early modern culture, the literal and figurative proximity of nonhuman to human animals elicited anxiety, generating what René Girard has called a "crisis of distinctions" (49). Pugliano's character as a horseman (or horse-man) inspires Sidney's disapproval, and yet Pugliano also provides Sidney with the model and motive—"self-love" (3)—for the latter's defense of verse. In fact, Sidney's relation to Pugliano is far too close for comfort. It is the archetypal relation of "scholar" to "master" (4), fraught with tension and ambivalence, which qualities receive figuration across the species barrier. Thus it stands as a further irony that in Sidney's case, "self-love" is the love of Philip, *phil-hippos*, bearing within itself the trace of the anathematized other.

This "crisis of distinctions" can be presented more broadly in Kuhnian terms, as an emerging dilemma in the early modern discourse of species—in effect, as a philosophical problem for which Descartes and his followers presented a paradigm-shifting solution.[5] Erica Fudge has traced this dilemma to inconsistencies within the early modern understanding of how and when a human being may be regarded as truly rational and therefore truly human: on one hand, "infants are not fully human, insofar as human status can only be designated truly by the actions that evidence the possession of a rational soul" (*Brutal Reasoning* 48); on the other hand, "a human can literally become an animal when acting without reason" (66); and various subaltern categories of humanity (for example, women, slaves, ethnic others) present further challenges to a conventional understanding of humanity as grounded in reason. In sum, "There are natural born humans who can only be human because they possess the rational soul. Then there are humans in possession of the rational soul who require education to become truly human. Finally, there are humans who possess rational souls, can be educated, but are still less human than the human. Thus the category begins to collapse into absurdity" (58). Descartes solved this problem with mathematical elegance by elevating human reason to the status of a first principle, requiring no proof outside the philosopher's own inference. The way was thus clear to discount the apparent sentience of other animals by dismissing it as an anthropomorphic projection, so that how beasts behaved no longer told us anything about what they thought or felt.

To this extent, the Cartesian cogito is itself a product of the inward turn, an application of skepticism to the philosopher's own beliefs and instincts until what remains—skepticism itself—becomes the ground of his identity as a rational being. Appropriately enough, this inward turn takes the confessional mode as its proper form of literary expression: "I judged that I was as prone to error as anyone else, and I rejected as false all the reasoning I had hitherto accepted as valid proof. Finally, . . . I resolved to pretend that everything that had ever entered my head was no more true than the illusions of my dreams. But immediately afterwards I noted that, while I was trying to think of all things being false in this way, it was necessarily the case that I, who was thinking them, had to be something" (Descartes 28, 4.32). In effect, the Cartesian self arises from and entails the exploration of a new notion of character: not an Aristotelian taxonomy of shared attributes, but rather a sense of personal identity as singular and doubtful, consisting in particularity and observation, privileging mind over body and interior over exterior. This, of course, is the mode of character celebrated in the grand literary achievements of the late seventeenth, eighteenth, and nineteenth centuries: the novel, the illusionistic theater, the cult of sentiment, and the critical veneration of Shakespeare.

Hence we may recognize this notion of character, in its originary Cartesian moment, as an instrument for defining and maintaining the species barrier. It is no accident that the *Discourse on Method* (1637) remains almost equally famous for two distinct philosophical postulates: the cogito and the *bête-machine*. These principles emerge hand in hoof from Descartes's meditations, in symbiotic and mutually reinforcing relation: the former crafts a notion of humanity composed of inwardness and speculation, while the latter denies such qualities to the nonhuman. Taken together, these philosophical constructs offer a response to earlier notions of human character that had come by the early modern period to appear increasingly untenable. In the process Descartes's principles also paved the way for new literary techniques of representing the human, techniques that in turn proved essential in consolidating the species distinction on which they were based.

But to return to more conventionally literary writing, what then of

Shakespeare? How is this very pre-Cartesian playwright conscripted so durably into the Enlightenment project of literary character construction? We might start to answer this question by noting how haunted Shakespeare is by the relationship between people and other animals. From Launce and Crab to the asinine Bottom, from the "inexecrable dog" Shylock (*Merchant of Venice* [1596–97] 4.1.128) to Banquo's currish murderers (*Macbeth* [1606] 3.1.91–104), from Lear's "pelican daughters" (3.4.75) to the man-fish Caliban, the poet's work seems like nothing so much as a protracted, uneasy meditation on the ties that bind species together and the traumas that tear them apart. From this standpoint, Shakespeare's particular claim to fame may lie not so much in the characters he created as in the discomfort he expressed through them: that is to say, in the resonance and clarity with which he lent voice to the problem of distinctions that preceded the Cartesian moment. Perhaps there is something a bit complacent, even self-infatuated, in recent efforts to celebrate Shakespeare as the inventor of the human. Perhaps we should remember him instead as the poet of humanity in crisis.

Character and Premodernity

Hence my core argument: Shakespeare and his contemporaries inherit a crisis of distinctions that expresses itself through a fixation on the human-animal relationship; Descartes resolves this same crisis a priori, by granting humanity exclusive access to consciousness via the ability "to use words or other signs . . . to declare our thoughts to others" (46); and in the process, he also creates a new purpose for literary activity—that of drawing and redrawing the species boundary through the elaboration of literary character as defined by the revelation in words of a distinctive personal interiority. This, of course, is the very same mode of revelation through which Descartes confirms humanity's unique access to the exercise of reason, and its presumed absence in nonhuman animals leads him to conclude that they, by contrast, "have no mental powers whatsoever" (48).

By no accident, this notion of the species boundary conforms to Bruno Latour's "modern Constitution" (29): that grand division of the map of knowledge into two zones—a "scientific" one for "representing things" and a "political" one for "representing subjects" (29)—that Latour regards as distinctive of society in its modernized western form. Insofar as literature, the arts, and the humanities count for anything at all in this dispensation, they belong squarely within the second of these two zones. Thus it makes perfect sense that they should be charged with the task of representing, defining, and refining the human through the creation and exploration of character. Likewise, it makes equal sense that the assignment of human attributes to nonhuman beings—the problem that Ruskin calls the pathetic fallacy—should emerge as a compound form of category confusion, not only confusing people with nonpeople but simultaneously confusing the modes of discourse proper to the understanding of each. On this logic the humanities should rightly declare that *Nihil humanum mihi alienum est*, whereas the pathetic fallacy drops the first adjective.

To this extent we might, in fact, take the pathetic fallacy as an error peculiar to the arts and humanities; in any case, that is certainly how Ruskin presents it. Latour's critique of the modern constitution, however, suggests something very different: that despite the most rigorous attempts to suppress them in the name of modern disciplinarity, such modes of category confusion have become more the rule than the exception. For Latour, the modern constitution must be understood as a mode of false consciousness, seeking an unattainable ideal of "analytic continuity" (7) consistent with the distinction between scientific and sociopolitical modes of understanding. However, its efforts in this direction are forever frustrated by the appearance of "entirely new types of beings, hybrids of nature and culture" (10), of which Ruskin's pathetic fallacy, with its distinctively modern morbidity, may be seen as only an initial instance. For Latour, indeed, this is the very tragedy of the modern: that its dream of discursive purity lies forever out of reach, that "the more we forbid ourselves to conceive of hybrids, the more possible their interbreeding becomes" (12).

One may therefore find it instructive to discover a parallel to the language of pathetic fallacy operating not in the disciplinary regime of the humanities but rather in that of the biological sciences. Here again questions of animal consciousness throw the problem into relief. Surveying the vocabularies of zoological and ethological observation, Eileen Crist concludes that differing scientific idioms generate very different ways of understanding the inner life of animals. On one hand, the "Cartesian verdict of an unbridgeable hiatus between humans and animals" (1) produces "a technical and causal language" of scientific observation that "leads to the portrayal of animals as objects," "blind to the meaning and significance of their activities and interactions" (5). On the other hand, "the Darwinian affirmation of evolutionary continuity" (1) elicits a very different model of discourse, which "deliver[s] subjectivity to the world of animals" by presenting their actions "as *meaningful, authored, and continuous*" (4). In both cases there is a sense in which the scientific methodology in question actually invents the conclusions it is ostensibly designed to discover, so that "divergent portrayals of animals as subjects, on the one hand, and as objects, on the other, form the conceptual foundations that, respectively, allow the emergence of animal mentality or prescind its very possibility" (6).

Crist's narrative is rich with irony. To begin with, it yields the spectacle of a Darwinian theory apparently grounded in Cartesian empiricism yet nonetheless producing a view of "animal mentality" at odds with that proposed by Descartes. (Darwin draws on scientific observation to argue for the development of certain species out of others through a process of adaptation and natural selection; adaptation, in turn, argues for some kind of individual agency; however, to attribute agency to animals is to endow them with the beginnings of a mental life, despite the fact that Descartes insists they have "no mental powers whatsoever.") This, in turn, leads to the further ironic possibility that Descartes's empiricism might prove less rigorous than it at first appears, since it is grounded on the a priori assumption that the human-nonhuman species barrier is defined by "mental powers" or their lack. This suspicion, in turn, gives way to yet another layer of irony, if one agrees with Crist that *neither* the Cartesian nor the Darwinian position can be accepted as rigorously empirical, insofar as the language of observation employed by each tends to predetermine the significance of what is being observed. From Latour's perspective, both Cartesianism and Darwinianism are hybrid constructs, aspiring to an "analytic continuity" they can never possess. From the perspective of Ruskin, both are forms of the pathetic fallacy, projecting onto the nonhuman world the mental environment of its human observers.

So far, I have spent a good deal of time here defining and investigating the emergence of modern attitudes toward animal mentality and its relation to human character. However, my purpose in doing so is to move beyond these attitudes, in effect by moving behind them to the issues and developments that preceded them. My instrument for doing so is character study, that most downtrodden and disrespected of critical tools, which I shall reconfigure so as to render it amenable to the treatment of nonhuman animals. In so adapting the notion of character, I return it to its pre-Cartesian status as elaborated in the Aristotelian and Theophrastan tradition of nature writing and animal writing that dominated western philosophy from classical times well into the early modern period. Since this tradition diverges sharply from its successor on certain points while on other points the two systems retain a surprising consistency, the major differences and similarities at stake here should be clarified.

Let us begin with terminology. As is well known, the English noun "character," which by the seventeenth century refers to the artificial human beings created by writers in writing, originally refers to the act of writing.[6] Theophrastus's *charactaeres* is a plural substantive formed from the Attic *charassein* , "to engrave, carve," "inscribe," or "simply, write" (Liddell and Scott "*charasso*" v. III.1), and in its Theophrastan application the noun thus refers simultaneously to the "distinctive mark, characteristic, character" that has been "impressed (as it were) on a person" (Liddell and Scott "*charactaer*" sb. II.4) and to the act of impression or inscription. In this respect, the noun *charactaer* is similar to the *historia* of Aristotle's *Historia Animalium*, which refers to "information obtained through investigation" (Peck 1:v). In both cases we encounter from the outset a hybrid of object and subject: a catalog of observable qualities fabricated by the observer's stylus. However, in their English *Nachleben* the two terms part company. English "history" emphasizes the objective nature of reportage so relentlessly that Hayden White's rediscovery of the narrative element in historical writing could become a major twentieth-century intellectual event.[7] Literary "character," on the other hand, comes to denote invention rather than reportage, fiction rather than fact. Thus both words are subjected to a sort of spurious purification, consistent with their original reference to nonhuman and human subject matter, respectively.

This false purification furthers the efforts of history to distinguish itself as the most scientific of the humanities—efforts that arguably reach their apex late in the 1800s with the alliance of history and economics under the banner of historical materialism. However, from the standpoint of the study of character, this same purification still invests contemporary approaches to Theophrastus, which generally seek to identify his *Characters* as a study in "moral behavior" (Rusten and Cunningham 13). On this view, Theophrastus's work finds its closest Aristotelian relative in the *Nicomachean Ethics*, and in this spirit Theophrastus's most recent translators remind us that the title of the *Characters* is really a misnomer of sorts—that "the Greek word for character is usually *ethos*" (Rusten and Cunningham 13). All of this is very true but also quite misleading: it implies that Aristotle and Theophrastus distinguish the ethical from the scientific in ways that they do not, and that instead typify more modern forms of disciplinary thinking.

In fact, Aristotle declares early on in the *Historia Animalium* that this work, too, is much concerned with character. After three opening pages on comparative anatomy, the philosopher proceeds to other points of interest: "Further differences exhibited by animals are those which relate to their manner of life, their activities and their dispositions *[kai ta ethae]*, as well as their parts" (1:6–7; 487a10–12). Aristotle promises to give special attention to each of these categories, and later sections of the *Historia* repeatedly engage questions of animal character or disposition or temperament:

> The characters of the animals *[Ta d'ethae ton zoon]* are less obvious to us by perception in the case of the less developed and shorter-lived ones, but more obvious in the longer-lived. (3:215; 608a1–3)

> The females are softer, more vicious, less simple, more impetuous, . . . while the males on the contrary are more spirited, wilder, simpler, less cunning. There are traces of these characters *[ton ethon]* in virtually all animals, but they are all the more evident in those that are more possessed of character *[en tois echousi mallon ethos]* and especially in man. (3:218–19; 608a34–608b7)

> The animals' characters *[ta d'ethae ton zoon]*, as we have said earlier, differ both in respect of cowardice, mildness, courage, tameness, and also in mind and ignorance. (3:235; 610b20–22)

> Just as it comes about for all animals that their activities accord with their occasional bodily states, so again their characters too change *[ta ethae metaballousi]* according to their activities. (3:397; 631b5–7)

> The animals change their forms and character *[kai to ethos]* not only, in certain cases, according to their ages and the seasons, but also through being castrated. (3:399; 631b19–21)

On the basis of word choice alone we must grant that the *Historia Animalium* is in some significant degree an ethical treatise, concerned with questions of character, temperament, and/or disposition. In this respect it sets an important precedent for the bestiarists' quaint concern with similar matters, and the behavior traits on which it focuses very much include the sort that interest Theophrastus in his *Characters*:

Some [animals] are mischievous and wicked, e.g., the fox; others are spirited and affectionate and fawning, e.g., the dog; some are gentle and easily tamed, e.g., the elephant; others are bashful and cautious, e.g., the goose; some are jealous and ostentatious, like the peacock. (Aristotle, *Historia* 1:19; 488b20–24)

[Animals] are seen to have a certain natural capability in relation to each of the soul's affections—to intelligence and stupidity, courage and cowardice, to mildness and ferocity, and the other dispositions of this sort. Certain animals at the same time are receptive of some learning and instruction, some from each other, some from humans. (Aristotle, *Historia* 3:215; 608a14–19)

Aristotle's word for "cowardice" (*deilia*) in the second of these passages also provides the title for one of Theophrastus's *Characters* (25); the fawning behavior Aristotle associates with dogs receives treatment in not one but two Theophrastan characters (2 [Flattery], 5 [Obsequiousness]); and Aristotle's word for "wickedness" in the former of these two passages (*kakourgia* literally "evildoing," or "bad behavior") could arguably serve as an organizing rubric for all of the traits explored in Theophrastus's treatise.

Consistent with *De Anima*'s assignment of an inorganic rational soul to humanity alone, as distinct from the lower creation,[8] the *Historia Animalium* insists on a sharp difference between the mental capacities of human beings and those of other animals: "The only animal which is deliberative is man. Many animals have the power of memory and can be trained; but the only one which can recall past events at will is man" (1:19; 488b24–30). However, this distinction coexists uncomfortably with the notion that human beings and other animals share the same basic components of character—"intelligence and stupidity, courage and cowardice, . . . mildness and ferocity," and so forth. It is a nice question, for instance, to what extent intelligence and stupidity may be gauged independently of the deliberative faculty, and thus by the seventeenth century it had become a popular topic of academic debate to argue whether or not dogs can form syllogisms.[9] Elsewhere, Aristotle claims, "In general, with regard to their lives, one may observe many imitations of human life in the other animals" (3:251; 612b18–20). Moreover, Aristotle's argument that physical conditions—castration, for instance, or procreation— can affect animal character carries over to human beings as well, suggesting that despite the supposedly inorganic nature of the rational soul, human character too can have a physiological basis. Thus on the predictable issue of gender difference Aristotle remarks that "a wife is more compassionate than a husband and more given to tears, but also more jealous and complaining and more apt to scold and fight" (3:219; 608b9–11). On the subject of human facial features, he maintains, "Persons who have a large forehead are sluggish, those who have a small one are fickle; those who have a broad one are excitable, those who have a bulging one, quick-tempered" (1:39; 491b11–14). The former of these observations points to a causal relationship whereby anatomy influences character, whereas the latter assumes the opposite: that character expresses itself in the lineaments of the body, and especially the face. It is in this latter capacity, of course, that Marlowe's Tamburlaine can refer to the "characters graven in [Theridamas's] brows" (1.2.169), thus exploiting the semantic duality of the Greek *charactaer* while also reading character anatomically, in a manner we can trace directly to the *Historia Animalium*.

Thus we can understand the notion of character in Aristotle and Theophrastus as a complex of ethical qualities or predispositions (for example, courage and cowardice, generosity and jealousy, calmness and irascibility), shared by human and nonhuman animals alike to a greater or lesser extent, related to the body in both a causal and an expressive manner, and susceptible to classification just as are the physical qualities that distinguish one class or species of being from another. This sense of character is readily available to European writers of the fifteenth to seventeenth centuries, many if not most of whom were well trained in the Aristotelian-Theophrastan tradition. Furthermore, this sense of character exists in tension both with Aristotle's insistence on human uniqueness (as registered by the possession of a rational soul) and with later notions of literary character grounded in exercise of the distinctively human rational faculties.

So, is the difference between human and nonhuman animals one of kind or of degree? At heart the two theories of human-animal relation that have contended most fiercely to replace Aristotle's as the dominant model—the Cartesian and the Darwinian—offer different answers to this question, with Descartes insisting on difference in kind and Darwin favoring difference in degree. Aristotle anticipates both positions while trying to have the argument both ways; his "conflicting comments about animals . . . reflect Aristotle's recognition of a continuum between human beings and animals while seeking to distinguish human beings on the basis of their rational capacities" (Steiner 76). In other words, both Descartes and Darwin may be seen to adopt and develop certain tendencies in the Aristotelian tradition. Most famously,

Descartes inherits the notion of the rational soul, which he transforms into the cogito through the process of inner-directed skepticism described above. As is well known, this process accords with Descartes's Thomist Catholicism, which regards the immortal soul as an exclusively human property;[10] in this respect, Cartesian philosophy may be understood as an effort to resolve the inconsistencies in Aristotle's theory of animals while also preserving the species barrier. The Darwinian tradition, although less directly indebted to Aristotle, nonetheless insists on a notion of relationality across the species barrier—what Gary Steiner calls "a continuum between human beings and animals"—that conflicts with the insistence on difference in kind.

The model of literary character explored in the following chapters derives expressly from Aristotle's notion of the interspecies continuum, as this is manifested in his zoological treatises and remains implicit in the ethical work of his successor Theophrastus. This latter work helps convey the term "character" into English as a word for the fictional persons created by writers, but even before the term becomes thus established, the sense of character that underwrites it is available for literary exploration. This sense of character openly creates a space for the interaction of human and nonhuman species. Aristotle describes the latter as generating "imitations of human life" (*mime matu . . . taes anthropinaes zoaes*) [3:251; 612b19–20]), but it takes little effort to imagine this mimetic impulse as reversing course, in which case nonhuman animals put pressure on the development of human personality as well. Indeed, this is just how Theophrastus presents the figures in his *Characters*: for instance, the boor "stands in rapt attention at the sight of a cow, an ass, or a goat" (4.8); the obsequious man "is apt to keep a pet monkey" (5.9); the garrulous man "appear[s] to chatter more than the swallows" (7.7). Here, too, lies one arguable reason for the preoccupation of Enlightenment authors with creating singular human personalities in their work: earlier notions of literary personhood take species mixing for granted, developing in a dynamic and indefinite space for which Leviticus reserves the special name of "confusion" (Leviticus 18.23). Under the circumstances some clarification might seem in order.

The Immediate Field of Study

Starting with the model of pre-Cartesian literary character delineated above, the rest of this book is devoted to a series of what might be called brief literary biographies—if we accept that the subjects of these minibiographies are nonhuman rather than human and that they are the creations, rather than the creators, of literature. In terms of genre choice, distant antecedents here thus include Theophrastus, Pliny, the bestiarists, and (in a different way) Plutarch, Aubrey, Hall, and Sir Thomas Overbury. The main literary evidence on which I base my character portraits comes from European works produced between 1400 and 1700. Given my own training, it is inevitable (if perhaps regrettable) that English-language materials should take up the lion's share of the bibliography. However, I also discuss selected relevant works from France, Italy, Spain, Portugal, the Low Countries, and the Holy Roman Empire.

In keeping with the Aristotelian-Theophrastan tradition, these character portraits focus on broad groups rather than singular beings; in other words, they presume that character exists primarily as an instrument of class taxonomy rather than as a mode of individuation. Particular traits help to define broad affinities, and these, in turn, do not simply distinguish one species or genus of animal from another; they also trace modes of similitude and affiliation between different species and genera. As a result, each of the animals studied in the following chapters displays particular qualities that find a complement of sorts in human behavior and human social groupings. Given early modern European culture's well-attested fixation on issues of religious practice and social rank, it should come as no surprise that the animals studied here all interact with these variables in especially suggestive ways.

As for the particular species of animal I have chosen for study, I have chosen these in part because they represent each of the three principal uses to which early modern Europeans put the beasts in their lives: haulage, companionship, and food. For the latter two of these categories, two chapters apiece are devoted to beasts with high and low social associations, respectively. In the first case, that of haulage, a single, exceptionally lengthy chapter focuses on the horse. This seems appropriate given that horses assume such preeminent material and symbolic importance in early modern culture, given that different breeds of horses acquire very different rank-specific associations during the period from 1400 to 1700, and also—most important—given that the precise nature of the horse's elite social significance undergoes an important shift during the same period.

The unmanageable breadth of equestrian reference in early modern European literature also prompts me to pursue a limited authorial focus in these two opening chapters. Rather than seeking to produce a thick description of horses in European culture from the fifteenth to the seventeenth centuries—a topic worthy of many volumes—I have attempted a reading of equine character as manifest in the works of the period's principal writers of continental romance—Pulci, Boiardo, Ariosto, and Tasso—and its influence on the two dominant English authors of the same age: Shakespeare and Milton. One could portray the resulting story, in its English dimension at least, as a contrast between secular and sacred idioms, or between Tory and Whig politics. For his part, Shakespeare invokes equine character in ways that recall the horse's traditional chivalric associations, while also registering the English gentry's incipient transformation from a warrior class to a leisure class. What emerges is a conflicted vision of horse character: one drawn nostalgically to conventional models of equestrian heroism while also recognizing the limitations of these models in an era of courtly display and administrative intrigue. As for Shakespeare's dramatic representatives of this new era, they figure either in the comic mode, as effete ninnies, or in the tragic mode, as figures out of step with the world of sixteenth-century courtiership and the Machiavellian political theory that underwrites it.

Milton, by contrast, seems to feel no nostalgia at all for the age of knight-errantry. His epic references to chivalric lore and classical horse culture are extraordinarily consistent, reflecting a wholesale rejection of the martial values endemic to traditional heroic verse. However, if Milton turns his back on the age of classical and medieval equestrian exploit, he also turns inward, to a spiritual realm that serves as a prior and superior model for the debased heroism of the classical epic tradition. Here, in the heaven of *Paradise Lost* (1667), one encounters another sort of steed entirely: fiery angelic coursers through which the Father's transcendent power manifests itself in something like animal form. This reconstitution of the equine within the field of the spiritual marks a particularly fascinating moment in the history of literary character and its accommodations to the nonhuman.

If the western world's most important species of animal transportation, the horse, undergoes a change of character between the fifteenth and seventeenth centuries, the same is also true of certain key species of companion animal. Dating as it does to ancient times, the practice of pet keeping is by no means an early modern innovation; however, the early modern period witnesses an explosion in both the number of animals and the range of different animal species kept as pets. Likewise, the nature and intensity of human intimacy with companion animals seems to undergo a transformation during the same period. In England, as Keith Thomas has remarked, "it was in the sixteenth and seventeenth centuries that pets seemed to have really established themselves as a normal feature of the middle-class household" (*Man* 110); indeed, the noun "pet," as a referent for companion animals, first enters English usage in the early 1500s.[11] In the growth of pet culture, as in other ways, English practice lags a bit behind that of the Mediterranean nations, where household animals and private menageries begin their proliferation about a century earlier.

When it comes to the pets of distinguished individuals, I focus on an order of birds I have had occasion to write about before and which leaves a far less extensive trail of documentary evidence in the early modern period than do horses: the order Psittaciformes, consisting of parrots and cockatoos. Here I trace the emergence of parrots as conventional figures of mindless mimicry in European satire and comedy. As it happens, this familiar model of animal character evolves directly from the association of exotic birds with the sacred and secular Catholic nobility of the late Quattrocento. As the Reformation gains head in early sixteenth-century Europe, its exponents increasingly employ these birds—which initially served as markers of authority and distinction—in a countersignifying capacity, to represent the vacuous extravagance of the Catholic elite who owned them and to epitomize the mindlessness of prayer in ancient languages and set forms. Once parrots had thus acquired a new sort of literary character, in keeping with the sectarian tensions of the Reformation, that new character could be further translated—as it is by writers such as Shakespeare and Jonson—into a generic, secular model of empty-headed silliness that remains common even today.

On a humbler level, it is in the 1500s and 1600s that cats make the transition from tolerated household scavengers to beloved animal companions. In examining this shift, I concentrate on the semiotic residue of earlier social practices as these inform a tradition of cat torture that survives even into the late nineteenth and early twentieth centuries. Again, this tradition speaks to an early understanding of the cat as character—marginal, tricky, inscrutable, opportunistic, associated with demonic or diabolical forces. In this vein, the practice of cat torture develops in pre-Christian times as a means to ward off evil by punishing its representatives, and medieval Catholicism assimilates such pre-Christian practices to its own spiritual agenda via calendar festivals and witch lore. However, during the Reformation such practices become representative of Catholic superstition more generally, and here the tale takes its most ironic turn. Rather than rejecting the superstitious devices of its despised enemy, the Protestant faith actually adopts them, but with a difference, translating cat torture from an efficacious ritual to an insulting sign of

Catholic ignorance. Thus, even as the rise of Protestant belief makes possible a culture of sentiment in which house pets notably participate, it also keeps alive the bloody practices of an earlier spiritual dispensation, which serve now as an index of the reformed faith's relative enlightenment.

When it comes to the relationship between people and food animals, we approach a subject of primary anthropological significance, a centerpiece of the emerging discipline of food studies. For early modern Europeans, it is also a subject deeply embedded in complex systems of social precedence and spiritual significance. In the three centuries from 1400 to 1700 it undergoes a rapid series of changes as new food animals become available to European diners, new modes of culinary preparation and consumption come to the fore, and regimens of diet and health undergo a major shift. As Robert Appelbaum has put it, "The early modern period . . . constituted a unique chapter in the history of food and food practices" (xv). In the process it also changed the way people treated and viewed the animals they ate.

From the standpoint of what we might call the food of privilege, I see this change embodied in the most important new animal foodstuff to reach the Old World from the Americas: the turkey. While it participates, over the course of two centuries, in a broad transformation of western culinary practices, this fowl at first gains European acceptance by being assimilated to traditional medieval models of courtly dining. Indeed, the turkey gradually claims for itself the traditional spectacular position reserved on the medieval table for grand banqueting birds. In the process, as successful domestication leads to an increase in their numbers and a decline in their cost, turkeys also make it possible for a form of the grand banqueting fowl to appear more frequently and on humbler tables, in ways that force a reconception of the idea and character of elite dining.

Thus the turkey begins its western existence as a culinary marker of aristocratic culture but gradually metamorphoses into something more modest. In a reversal of this pattern, one of the commonest and most humble of European food animals, the sheep, acquires symbolic preeminence through its association with the Eucharist and the figure of Christ as Agnus Dei. However, this is only one of many narrative figurations through which sheep acquire significance as characters in early modern writing; one may mention as well their association with the pastoral mode, with emergent literatures of animal husbandry and georgic nationalism, with debates over enclosure and engrossing, and with the conflict between carnival indulgence and Lenten abstinence. In exploring the various relations between these forms of meaning, I

conclude that animal character is always necessarily figurative, a result of so-
cially generated patterns of meaningful action that ethologists have arguably
discerned within animal behavior, prior to its contamination by the human.
To this extent—and despite Erica Fudge's exhortation that we attend to "the
literal meaning of animals" in early modern texts (*Brutal Reasoning* 4)—one
emerges with a sense of animal character as that which arises through group
interaction, in the space between individuals. Whether the groups in question are intraspecies or cross-species, they generate a sense of social being that
cannot be reduced, as it were, to a literal notion of the *Tier an sich*.

From Chapter 1 forward, this book draws on an eclectic variety of cultural materials with the aim of showing readers how particular kinds of animals acquire a distinct set of attributes and meanings within the framework
of early modern society. To that end, discussion includes the romances of
Renaud de Montaubon, Luigi Pulci, Matteo Boiardo, Lodovico Ariosto, and
Torquato Tasso; the verse of John Skelton and Jean Lemaire de Belges; the
prose fiction of François Rabelais and William Baldwin, Miguel de Cervantes
and Sir Thomas More and the *Roman de Renart*; paintings by Jan van Eyck
and Andrea Mantegna, Hans Baldung Grien and Vittore Crivelli; husbandry
manuals by such writers as Gervase Markham and Leonard Mascall and
Conrad von Heresbach; natural histories by the likes of Edward Topsell and
Gonzalo Fernandez de Oviedo; plays by William Shakespeare, Ben Jonson,
Thomas Middleton, and others; as well as travel narratives, cookbooks, theological treatises, and more. My aim is not to provide a thorough treatment of
any of these genres of cultural production but rather to draw from them all,
as necessary and appropriate, to illustrate the character of the animals that
are my more immediate concern. The book concludes with a brief coda addressing the work of Margaret Cavendish, Duchess of Newcastle, and most
particularly her *Blazing World* (1666). Coming as it does toward the end of
the three centuries of cultural activity surveyed here, this peculiar narrative
helps to summarize many of the concerns of this book as a whole, while also
providing a sense of the new character dispensation that enters European
experience with the Cartesian revolution.

The Species Divide and Theories of Literary Personhood

This book traces notions of literary character, and animal character in particular, through the Aristotelian and Theophrastan tradition of classifying

types by their shared attributes. This tradition manifests itself both in works on human behavior such as Theophrastus's *Characters* and in the conventions of natural history as these developed from Aristotle's *Historia Animalium* through Pliny, the Physiologus, and the bestiarists. This model of character study has the advantage of participating in a well-recognized, influential school of ancient philosophical practice, and it also forges etymological (and therefore conceptual) links between classical thought and modern literary conventions. But such an approach to character also deserves to be situated amid more recent scholarship on the subject of literary character.

The scholarly discussions of literary character to appear since 1970 exhibit predictable differences of methodology and nuance, but they share certain emphases worth mentioning here. For one thing, they are frequently committed to a notion of character that privileges interiority—a notion I have presented as consistent with Cartesian definitions of the human. This focus is perhaps most clear in works such as Dorrit Cohn's *Transparent Minds*, which casts itself as a study of literary "modes for rendering consciousness" (11): the techniques whereby an author creates "beings whose inner lives he can reveal at will" (4). This premium on the inner life of literary personages leads Cohn to a heavy concentration on the nineteenth-century novel. Similarly, Martin Price locates literary character in "that stream of images, feelings, ideas, and fantasies that make up mental life" (38). For him, too, literary character is largely invested in "intellectual history" (39), thus producing a kind of "(virtual) being" that encourages one to speculate "about what characters think and feel" (64). Unsurprisingly, Price, too, finds his test cases of literary character in the realm of the novel: Austen, Stendhal, Dickens, Eliot, James. Using a more varied and idiosyncratic vocabulary, Amélie Oksenberg Rorty marshals a series of related terms—for example, character, figure, person, self—to distinguish different modes of literary personage; however, in the process she, too, repeatedly privileges the inward turn, emphasizing "dispositional characteristics" (80), "insight" (91), and "the tensions within selves" (92) in a critical lexicon that presents "the idea of a person [a]s the idea of a unified center of choice and action" (85). For Rorty, too, novelists such as Dickens, Dostoevsky, Austen, James, and Woolf provide illustrative material.

This focus on inner being, privileging unseen mental processes as these are relayed through literary conventions such as free indirect discourse, comprises a mainstay of recent character theory, and as the foregoing examples illustrate, it is usually regarded as arising in eighteenth- and nineteenth-century novels. Katharine Eisaman Maus, on the other hand, argues for a model of the inner-directed character that predates the Enlightenment and that privileges the drama. For Maus, 1980s-era critics "who . . . claimed that the Renaissance lacked a conception of inwardness" had it wrong (32); on the contrary, "in late-sixteenth and early-seventeenth-century England the sense of discrepancy between 'inward disposition' and 'outward appearance' seems unusually urgent and consequential for a large number of people" (13). As I hope is already clear, neither Maus's position nor the more conventional one presents any particular problem for the present study. On the contrary, I have no interest in denying an inner life to citizens of pre-Enlightenment Europe, and my own reading of late Renaissance culture as marked by a crisis of species distinctions bears some broad resemblance to Maus's view that the period was subject to ongoing "crises of authenticity" (Maus 32). For Maus, the disjunction between inner life and outer life serves as the source of these crises; in my judgment, it comes closer to supplying the solution. That is to say, discrepancies between the inner self and its outward manifestations become increasingly representative of *human* experience, in proportion as an inner self is denied to *nonhuman* experience. With interiority or its lack thus foregrounded as the prime determinant of human identity, the stage is set for the introspective, self-absorbed characters of Enlightenment and post-Enlightenment fiction.

While expressing interest in the interior function of literary character, scholars have also remained mindful of the Aristotelian commitment to character as a delineation of general "ethical types" (Lynch 39). For instance, Deidre Shauna Lynch has recalled the persistence of the Theophrastan character study into eighteenth-century literature (39–55), while noting that the Aristotelian system for "thinking about typicality as such" existed in tension with the impulse to endow characters with "individuated, psychological meanings" (9). Distinguishing between the mimetic, synthetic, and thematic functions of character—that is, character's simultaneous impulse to reproduce living beings, to fabricate nonexistent beings, and to delineate exemplary figures—James Phelan has likewise acknowledged that "the distinction between the mimetic and thematic components of character is a distinction between characters as individuals and characters as representative entities" (13). Most recently Elizabeth Fowler has opted for a model of character as "social persons" or "sets of personae" (2) that seem particularly indebted to the Aristotelian tradition: "abstract figurations" such as "alewife, merchant, and buyer, . . . Moor, Scythian, and Briton" or "senex amans, author, and allegorical personification" (16–17). While I agree with Phelan that character as individuation—the mimetic function—and character as ethical or social type—the thematic function—may and often do coexist in literary character depiction, I adopt a fairly conventional view of the history of literary character as marked by a gradual impulse to privilege the former over the latter, an impulse that gains unprecedented strength in the seventeenth and eighteenth centuries.

Concurrent with their focus on interiority and typicality, recent theorists of literary character exhibit one other trait worth mentioning at the outset of this book: they usually—and most of the time quite casually—assume that characters are by their very nature human. Martin Price ends the first paragraph of his book on character by defining the term as "the spectrum of attitudes and feelings we loosely call human" (xi). Dorrit Cohn speaks of character as "revealing the hidden side of the human beings who inhabit" a fictional world (5). More suspicious of the humanist project than these authors, Deidre Lynch still ties eighteenth-century character writing to the project of "anthologiz[ing] and . . . sum[ming] up human nature" (55). Elizabeth Fowler's study *Literary Character* is subtitled *The Human Figure in Early English Writing*. The common assumption here is obvious enough, and on the surface it seems reasonable enough as well: literary character is an imitation of the human that tells us something about what it means to be human.

However, as James Phelan observes with particular acuity, there are "messy problems" underlying any such assumption: "[A]ll this talk about characters as plausible or possible persons presupposes that we know what a person is. But the nature of the human subject is of course a highly contested issue among contemporary thinkers. . . . [To explore this issue properly would] require lengthy excursions into biological, philosophical, psychological, sociological, and economic territories" (11). The present study addresses this issue from one limited perspective: the perspective of animal studies that questions how well the human may be understood as a category qualitatively distinct from nonhuman animal life. To that end, it is worth returning briefly to Elizabeth Fowler's sense of characters as social persons, for Fowler is operating in the same chronological and conceptual universe to be explored in the following chapters: the Aristotelian and pre-Cartesian universe, in which character functions primarily as a categorization of types. One thing to note about the type categories Fowler invokes is that some of them—for instance, "allegorical personification," or, as Foucault has shown, the "author" (Fowler 17)—can be called "human" only in the most capacious and indeed figurative sense of the term, whereas others—for instance, "Scythian" and "Briton"—

are geographical or racial designations that extend just as properly to kinds of nonhuman animals (Scythian horses, British bulldogs) as they do to kinds of people.

This is not a frivolous objection. Fowler offers us a sophisticated way "to make sense of pre-modern ideas of person" (249), and her system for doing so is grounded on commonly recognized social types: figures of kinship, civic entities, economic agents, legal entities, and so forth. However, premodern society admits nonhuman animals into these categories on a regular basis, in ways that modern or postmodern analysis has trouble accommodating. When it comes to kinship, the term "family" originates in Roman legal thinking as a means of classifying property, including livestock,[12] and as late as the 1800s at least one English writer could still call the pig "an important member of the family" (quoted in Harrison 63). As mascots, commodities, and emblems, animals were indissolubly associated with civic and economic life. On the legal level, "[d]omestic beasts were often treated as morally responsible" (Thomas, *Man* 97), with the result that they—and wild animals as well—were notoriously liable to prosecution and punishment in European courts of law.[13] As Keith Thomas has observed, "In the towns of the early modern period, animals were everywhere. . . . Dwelling in such proximity to men, these animals were often thought of as individuals. . . . Shepherds knew the faces of their sheep as well as those of their neighbors. . . . [D]omestic beasts . . . were . . . frequently spoken to, for their owners, unlike Cartesian intellectuals, never thought them incapable of understanding" (*Man* 95–96). To neglect this aspect of early modern life is not only to misunderstand the nature of early modern animals; it is also to misunderstand the nature of early modern personhood.

Of the animal characters studied in the following chapters, some have been endowed by their creators with a semblance of inner life: for instance, Lodovico Ariosto's Baiardo, William Baldwin's Mouse-slayer, John Skelton's Parrot, Jean Lemaire de Belges's Amant Vert, and Tybert from *The History of Reynard the Fox*. Others, such as the theatrical sheep of Middleton and Shakespeare and *The Second Shepherds' Pageant* (c. 1475), seem innocent of interiority. In one instance—the "Cherubic shapes" that motivate "The Chariot of Paternal Deitie" in Milton's *Paradise Lost* (6.753, 750)—we seem to encounter an amalgam of animal and divinity whose consciousness transcends not just the human but species distinction of any sort. In every case, however, we meet with figures that speak to the nature of personhood, that provide models for significant behavior across the species boundary, and that attest in the process to the interrelation of the human and the nonhuman.

In pointing this out, I do not seek to make broad claims for the politically or ethically ameliorative power of this book. I agree with Cary Wolfe that "there is no longer any good reason to take it for granted that the theoretical, ethical, and political question of the subject is automatically coterminous with the species distinction between *Homo sapiens* and everything else" (1). However, I see no reason to claim that this book therefore helps detach "a properly postmodern pluralism from the concept of the human with which progressive political and ethical agendas have traditionally been associated," or, more grandly, that it offers "a posthumanist and transdisciplinary theory of the relation between . . . species, ethics, and language, conceived in its exteriority and materiality" (9, 11). While I sympathize with these objectives, I cannot help tempering them with the comic realism of David Lodge, one of whose fictional characters exclaims that the rituals of academic discourse have "no point, . . . [i]f by point you mean the hope of arriving at some certain truth. . . . [W]hen did you ever discover *that* in a question-and-discussion session?" (*Small World* 32). Bearing in mind the inherent limitations of the scholarly idiom (not least of which is its reliable tendency to take itself too seriously), I have here sought to write a book of modest aims, one that simply seeks to sketch in a bit of western literary history by studying the development of concepts of literary character from the standpoint of interspecies relations. That is the book's sole purpose and the sole aim in light of which it should be evaluated.

Chapter 1

Baiardo's Legacy

Lodovico Ariosto's *Orlando furioso* (1516) begins with an encounter arranged by a horse. Having lost her protector to an onslaught of heathen warriors, the princess Angelica escapes the fray on her palfrey and falls into the company of the horseless Sacripante, King of Circassia, who has loved her long and unrequitedly. As the two make their way together, they are startled by an uproar in the nearby undergrowth, from which emerges the riderless Baiardo, steed of another suitor to Angelica, Rinaldo. Sacripante attempts to mount Baiardo, but the stallion submits only at the behest of Angelica, whom he greets, literally, "with human gesture" ["con . . . gesto umano" (1.75.2)]. Then, as the couple fare forward once more, Rinaldo appears, on foot, challenging Sacripante to combat for the theft of his horse and his lady.

Sacripante, astride Baiardo, turns to attack the disadvantaged Rinaldo, but the horse will have none of it:

> The beast did know thus much by nature's force,
> To hurt his master were a service bad.
> The pagan could not nor with spur nor hand
> Make him unto his mind to go or stand.

> [(I)l destrier per instinto naturale ·
> non volea fare al suo signore oltraggio:
> né con man né con spron potea il Circasso
> farlo a volontà sua muover mai passo.]
>
> (2.6.4–8)

Thus obliged to dismount and fight hand to hand, Sacripante falls to blows with Rinaldo, and Angelica once more uses the confusion of battle as a cover for escape. As the episode concludes, Rinaldo regains his horse and sets off in pursuit of his beloved, and Ariosto's narrator pauses to explain Baiardo's bizarre behavior:

> The horse (that had of humane wit some tast)
> Ran not away for anie jadish knacke.
> His going only was to this intent
> To guide his maister where the Ladie went.
> . . . .
> He followed her through valley, hill, and plaine,
> Through woods and thickets for his maisters sake
> Whom he permitted not to touch the raine
> For feare lest he some other way should take.
>
> [Fece il destrier, ch'avea intelletto umano,
> non per vizio seguirsi tante miglia,
> ma per guidar dove la donna giva,
> il suo signor, da chi bramar l'udiva.
> . . . .
> Bramoso di ritrarlo ove fosse ela,
> per la gran selva inanzi se gli messe;
> né lo vlea lasciar montare in sella,
> perché ad altro camin non lo volgesse.]
>   (2.20.1–8, 22.1–4)

Only when the horse is satisfied that Rinaldo will indeed follow Angelica does he permit his master to mount him once again.

This sequence of events, comprising canto 1 and the first part of canto 2 of Ariosto's poem, can occur only because Baiardo, the horse, makes a series of calculated decisions: to abandon Rinaldo and pursue Angelica; by doing so to lead Rinaldo to Angelica; to refuse to engage in unequal combat against his master; and to reunite with his master when circumstances appear to warrant it. In the process, Baiardo reveals himself to possess what Ariosto calls "intelletto umano" (2.20.5). He distinguishes between persons, responds to certain ones with loyalty and intimacy, and confronts others with willful resistance.

He occasionally differs in opinion even with his intimates, and he is prepared to translate this difference into uncooperative behavior. He is self-aware, acts on personal motives, reaches considered judgments concerning the motives and behavior of others, and engages in hypothetical reasoning. By all of these measures, Baiardo is a fully drawn literary character: an agent, a subject, a person.

Baiardo is not unique, either within Ariosto or to Ariosto. Other Ariostan horses—Orlando's Brigliadoro, for instance, and Astolfo's Rabicano—are endowed with their own literary personalities. And more generally, the *Furioso* unfolds in a quasi-Ovidian universe characterized by highly unstable species boundaries, in which nonhuman animals can exhibit the indicia of human character while human beings, on the other hand, can devolve into nonhuman forms. Thus, for instance, just four cantos after the opening encounter between Angelica, Sacripante, Rinaldo, and Baiardo, another of Ariosto's heroes tethers his mount to a myrtle tree, only to hear the tree cry out in pain. As the hero, Ruggiero, questions the tree, it identifies itself as a former knight named Astolfo, imprisoned in arboreal form by the Circe-like enchantress Alcina, who has likewise transformed other knights-errant into streams and animals ("altri in liquido fonte, alcuni in fiera" [6.51.7]). However, such scenarios prove so endemic to the genre of courtly romance as to exceed the purview of any single author.

Indeed, it is the generic legacy, as this meets its English demise in the works of Shakespeare and Milton, with which the present chapter concerns itself. My interest here engages the fate of animal characters such as Baiardo—the extraordinary yet also typical fauna of the romance tradition—at the hands of England's two greatest Renaissance poets. Equally responsive to this tradition, both Shakespeare and Milton repudiate it in different ways, the former with a certain Tory wistfulness, the latter with a Whiggish contempt. In doing so, both these authors arguably respond and contribute to the intellectual tensions that enable the Cartesian moment. In the process, they also lay the groundwork for future literary conventions that will strive for new rigor in distinguishing between human and nonhuman life by depriving the latter of any claim to sentience or conscious agency.

Horse-Sense and Chivalry

I begin with Ariosto's Baiardo for two reasons: because the *Orlando furioso*, more than any other literary work, may claim to stand as the apotheosis of the courtly romance tradition; and because within the *Furioso*, Baiardo offers a particularly rich example of that tradition's approach to the character potential of nonhuman animals. Like much else in Ariosto's poem, Rinaldo's horse carries with him the weight of history—a history that in his case encompasses some three and a half centuries of literary portrayal. In effect, he embodies a specific legacy of equine representation, one that derives from a chivalric culture centered on the relationship between warriors and horses and which, as a result, tends to assign enhanced subjectivity to certain privileged exemplars of both groups. Indeed, one might object that the very qualities which render Baiardo a fitting subject of chivalric song—his preternatural intelligence, loyalty, strength, and speed—prevent him from serving as an illustration of medieval attitudes toward horses or nonhuman animals in general. That, however, in a sense is the point. Baiardo is a literary product of a highly and self-consciously stratified social order. He appears in courtly romance for the same reason as do the genre's human protagonists: because he is distinctive, superior, exceptional—in a word, heroic. In this respect he embodies the ideals of the courtly elite that romance as a genre is designed to celebrate. To this extent one could argue that in *Orlando furioso*—and more broadly within the romance tradition it epitomizes—rank trumps species as a marker of difference between persons.

On this view, Baiardo would, in fact, appear to be more suitable as a companion and peer for Rinaldo than would the vast mass of humanity. Certainly the romance tradition insists on a special linkage. Baiardo first appears, as Bayard, in the early thirteenth-century *Quatre fils Aymon*, traditionally attributed to Renaud de Montauban, and here the horse already possesses the qualities that distinguish him as a literary figure. On one occasion, for instance, Renaud and Bayard compete in a grand horse race whose prize includes the crown of Charlemagne. Before the race commences, both horse and rider have been subjected to insults by other members of the field, so pride is particularly at stake. When the starting trumpets sound, Bayard and his master quickly find themselves at the rear of the field, and Renaud takes time to give his horse a pep talk:

> [W]han Reynawde saw that it was tyme for to renne after the other: he spurred his horse, & said to bayarde, we been ferre behynde ye myght wel abide. For if ye be not soone afore: ye shall be blamed, whan Bayarde heard his master speake thus: he understoode him as well as thoughe he had been a man. Than he grylled his nosethrels

and bare his head up and made a long necke, and tooke his course so fast that it semed the erthe should haue sonken under hym, and within a whyle he was passed all the other horses a ferre waye. (*Right plesaunt . . . historie*, fol. 49v)

["Baiart, ce dist Renaus, trop uos alons tarjant.
Se cil i vont sans nos, blasme i averons grant;
Reprovés vos sera à trestot vo vivant."
Baiart oï Renaut, si va le cief dreçant;
Ensement l'enten li com mere son enfant.
Il fronce des narines, le cief vait escoant.
Renaus lache les regnes, Baiart s'en va bruiant,
Tot à col estendu, le terre (porprennant);
En trois arpens de terre en a trespassé tant,
Que trestot le plus cointe se tient por (recreant).]
                                                        (4927–36)

Here the bond between horse and knight manifests itself in a common language and a harmony of interest, with the former acting as an expression of the latter. The La Vallière Manuscript of the *Quatre fils* has Bayard understand Renaud "com mere son enfant," that is, as a mother does her child; William Caxton's 1489 English translation, perhaps drawn from a different copy text, renders the same line as "he understood him as well as thoughe he had been a man." Like Renaud, Bayard is concerned with honor, his own and his master's, and the two figures base their claim to heroism on the determination to maintain their good name through exploits of the sort described in this episode. In the process, however, the *Quatre fils Aymon* also celebrates resistance to authority, situating itself within the tradition of the Old French "epics of revolt" (Calin 113), which take feudal injustice and rightful disobedience as their subject matter. From this standpoint the poem retails the exploits of Renaud in resisting the persecution of Charlemagne, whose nephew Renaud has slain after quarreling over a game of chess. In the action that follows, Bayard and Renaud emerge as equally resourceful opponents of Charlemagne, and when the two human antagonists are finally reconciled, it is at the expense of the horse, who effectively takes Renaud's place as the object of Charlemagne's punishment:

[Charlemagne] made be brought afore hym the good horse of Reynawde Bayarde. And whan he saw him: he began for to saye in this wyse. Ha Bayarde, bayarde, thou hast often angred me, but I am come to ye poynt, god gramercy for to auenge me. . . . And whan the kyng had sayd so: he made a great milstone to be fastened at the necke of bayard, and than made him to be cast from the brydge downe into the water, & whan Bayarde was thus tombled into the ryuer . . . the kynge . . . made great Ioye and so said. Ha bayarde nowe haue I that I desyred and wysshed so lo[n]g For ye be now dead. . . . And whan the fre[n]che men sawe the greate cruelnes of Charlemayne that auenged himself upon a poore beast: they were yll co[n]tent. (*Right plesaunt . . . historie*, fol. 146v)

[Puis (Charlemagne) fist mander Baiart que Renau li fist rendre.
"Baiart, dist Charlemagnes, ta vigor m'(as) fait vandre
Maint jor m'as (fait corrout), maint povre, disner, prendre."
. . . .
    Li rois fist Baiart penre iluecques maintenant.
Une mu(e)le li pent à son col par devant,
Et il fu sor le pont, si lo bota avant.
. . . .
(Quant le voit Charlemaignes, si en ot joie grant.
"Baiart, ce dist li rois, or ai quanque demant.")
. . . .
Quant François l'ont oï, si en ont mautalent.]
(15296–98, 303–5, 308–9, 12)

In the event the horse not only functions as "the *pharmakos*, the sacrificial victim immolated to ensure the others' happiness" (Calin 95), but in the process he also throws into further relief the injustice of the oppression under which he and his master have suffered. Moreover, in representing his master for the purpose of punishment, Bayard also reaffirms his own heroic status as equivalent to that of Renaud: smashing the millstone that weighs him down, the horse escapes his tormentors to live out his life at ease in the forest of the Ardennes.

The *Quatre fils Aymon* proved highly popular in the late medieval and early modern periods, surviving in numerous manuscripts, translations, and adaptations.[1] It spawned verse continuations in thirteenth-century Spain and fourteenth-century Italy and received mention in England in the early thirteenth century. However, the work's influence on later chivalric verse culminated with the Italian romances of the fifteenth and early sixteenth centuries. Luigi Pulci's *Morgante* (1483), for instance, revisits the exploits of Rinaldo and Baiardo, again remarking on the intimacy of the relationship between man and horse. Thus, for example, when Pulci's Rinaldo finds himself beset by a band of giants, Baiardo fights as furiously as he, prompting one of the giants to exclaim, "[G]o on your road, / for this your horse is better than a friend" ["piglia il tuo cammino, / ché questo tuo destriere è buon compagno" (16.103, 3–4)]. Taking his advice, Rinaldo finds rest in a shepherd's hut, but as soon as the knight falls asleep, his host steals Baiardo and conveys him to the nearest city, where he offers the horse for sale to the city hangman. Before committing to the purchase, the hangman asks for a display of riding, and predictable mayhem ensues:

> [M]ost eager to comply, the shepherd spurred
> Baiardo, who could feel who'd mounted him:
> Quickly, therefore, into midair he leapt.
> The shepherd, who knew not the art of riding,
> fast found himself upon the barren ground
> with two ribs broken.

> [(Q)uel pastor di spron détte al cavallo.

> Baiardo conosceva a chi egli é sotto:
> Subitamente prese in aria un salto,
> onde il pastor, ch'a l'arte non è dotto
> so ritrovò di fatto in su lo smalto
> e del petto due costole s'ha rotto.]
> (16.108.8–16.109.5)

Here, as in the *Quatre fils Aymon*, Baiardo operates as a figure of calculated resistance who possesses the functional equivalent of human intelligence. In the *Quatre fils* he understands Renaud's conversation; in the *Morgante* he recognizes when an unfit rider climbs onto his back; in both cases he exhibits self-awareness and intellectual discrimination while casting his lot with his master and opposing his master's enemies. More than a well-trained animal in the modern understanding of the phrase, he emerges from these poems as a "buon compagno," already possessing the distinctive personality he will retain in Ariosto as well. Moreover, these same qualities also characterize Rinaldo's horse in Ariosto's immediate precursor, the *Orlando innamorato* of

Matteo Boiardo (1483). The key scene here unfolds when Baiardo, who has become separated from Ranaldo (Boiardo's spelling) and has passed through the hands of several caretakers in the process, finds himself bearing Orlando into combat, ironically, against Orlando's cousin and the horse's own true master, Ranaldo himself:

Valiant Orlando and Aymone's
strong son converged: both violent,
each thought he'd knock the other down.
Now listen to what's strange and new.
The good Baiardo recognized
its master when it saw Ranaldo.

. . . .

[A]nd that horse, as if he could think,
had no desire to go against
Ranaldo, so he swerved, despite
Orlando, to avoid the clash.

. . . .

At the same time, [Orlando] yanked the reins,
believing he would turn Baiardo,
but the horse moved no more or less
than if it stood to graze on grass.

[Il franco Orlando e il forte fio d'Amone
Se vanno addosso con tanto flagella,
Che profondar l'un l'altro ha opinione.
Ora ascoltare che strana novella:
Il bon Baiardo cognobbe di saldo,
Come fu gionto, il suo patron Ranaldo.

. . . .

E quel destrier, come avesse intelletto,
Contra Ranaldo non volse venire;
Ma voltasi a traverso a mal disperto

De Orlando, proprio al contro del ferire.

. . . .

Ed a quel tempo ben ricolse il freno,
Credendolo a tal guisa rivoltare;
Non si muove Baiardo più di meno,
Come fosse nel prato a pascolare.

(1.26.26.2–8, 27.3–6, 30.1–4)

In sum, from his first appearance in the *Quatre fils Aymon* through his appropriations by the Italian romances of the fifteenth and sixteenth centuries, the figure of Baiardo maintains a distinctive and steady character profile consonant with his intelligence and ability to engage in considered acts of disobedience. In the *Quatre fils*, Bayard already understands human language and successfully opposes the tyranny of Charlemagne; in Pulci, the horse serves as a "buon compagno" to Rinaldo, resisting his enemies in combat and refusing to obey when they seek to command him; in Boiardo, the horse behaves "come avesse intelletto," refusing to engage in combat with his master; and in Ariosto, Baiardo expressly possesses "intelletto umano," which he exercises in part by refusing to obey Rinaldo's enemies and in part by refusing to obey Rinaldo himself. Moreover, the various poets who develop Baiardo's character do so through consistent narrative gestures—topoi deployed after the manner of a Wagnerian leitmotif to serve, in effect, as the literary signature of the character in question. Baiardo's repeated human behavior—his "gesto umano"—provides a case in point, but perhaps the most distinctive such feature of the horse's presentation is what I would call the topos of equine civil disobedience: Baiardo's set-piece refusal to comply with commands or submit to conditions that he considers unjust or misguided. This refusal already appears in the *Quatre fils*, where, among other exploits, Bayard carries Charlemagne without his consent into Renaud's castle of Montaubon and then later escapes the emperor's persecution. However, the topos reaches its most distinctive form in Boiardo and Ariosto, in the horse's flat refusal to enter into combat against his master.

As I have argued above, this refusal—together with the broader qualities of character it presupposes—serves to ally Baiardo with Rinaldo, establishing a cross-species bond between the two companions that is grounded in their shared heroism and nobility and that serves to distinguish them from lesser human beings and lesser horses. However, this distinction does not prevent Baiardo from also serving as a symbolic referent for all horses everywhere. Indeed, the extreme popularity of the romances that deal with Baiardo, coupled with Baiardo's own status in those romances as the paragon of equine nobility, virtually assures that he will enter into late medieval popular culture as a synecdoche for horses in general. In England, for instance, the noun "bayard" becomes established in the mid-1300s as referring to "a bay horse"—in homage, the *OED* declares, to "the bright-bay-coloured magic steed given by Charlemagne to Renaud"; thereafter the term generalizes as "a kind of mock-heroic name for any horse" (s.v. "Bayard," sb. 1, 2). Yet even in this downscale popularization, the character of Baiardo can assert itself in complex fashion across the species barrier. That, at least, is what it does in Chaucer's *Troilus and Criseyde* (1380–88), where a humble namesake of Renaud's horse offers a figurative referent for Troilus's sudden and irresistible infatuation:

> As proude Bayard gynneth for to skippe
> Out of the weye, so pryketh him his corn,
> Til he a lasshe have of the longe whippe—
> Than thynketh he, "Though I praunce al byforn
> First in the trays, ful fat and newe shorn,
> Yet am I but an hors, and horses lawe
> I moot endure, and with my feres drawe"—
>
> So ferde it by this fierse and proude knyght.
>
> (1.218–25)

Even as it marks boundaries and specifies limits, Chaucer's simile expands into an interspecies *mise-en-abîme*, tracing discriminations and affiliations in the same moment. For all his pride, Bayard discovers that a horse is a horse, that even the most exemplary specimen of the kind must endure "horses lawe" and draw in the traces with his companions, and yet this discovery is made possible by the unhorselike fact that Bayard—like his descendants in Boiardo and Ariosto—"thinketh." His hard-won self-awareness thus traces a bond between horse and man, especially the love-captivated Troilus, with whom he shares both consciousness of his situation and an inability to escape its constraints. In this case, at least, the human-animal boundary seems especially significant for the differences it *fails* to mark.

On the other hand, Baiardo's literary legacy does seem to inspire at least one English writer to draw the boundary between species with a firmer hand. Ariosto's great early modern translator, Sir John Harington, appears determined to distance Rinaldo's horse from human capacities and human character; at any rate, Harington consistently downplays the moments in Ariosto's narrative that endow the horse with intelligence and agency. When, for instance, Baiardo greets Angelica in canto 1, Ariosto describes him as going "mansueto alla donzella, / con umile sembiante e gesto umano, / come intorno al padrone il can saltella, / che sia duo giorni o tre stato lontano" (1.75.1–4)—that is, approaching "the damsel gently, with humble appearance and human gesture, as a dog dances about its master when he has been absent for two or three days." Harington's version of these lines suppresses the phrase "gesto umano," leaving the horse much more firmly situated within a subordinate and separate order of creation:

> But to the damsell gently he doth go
> In humble manner and in lowly sort,
> A spaniell after absence fauneth so
> And seekes to make his master play and sport.
>
> (1.75.1–4)

Likewise, when Ariosto excuses Baiardo's disobedience of Rinaldo by explicitly crediting the horse with human understanding, Harington lessens the force of the attribution. Ariosto's phrase "il destrier, ch'avea intelletto umano, / non per vizio seguirsi tante miglia" ["the horse, which had human intellect, did not follow such a course out of vice" (2.20.5–6)] reappears in the Elizabethan version as "The horse (that had of humane wit some tast) / Ran not away for anie jadish knacke" (2.20.5–6). And as if it were not enough to reduce "intelletto umano" to "some tast" of "humane wit," the edition of 1591 supplies a wholly misleading marginal note at this point, likening Baiardo's mental abilities to those not of any human being but of another horse: "Bayardo is compared with Bucephalus for wit." In fact, Ariosto draws no explicit comparison between Baiardo and Bucephalus, here or anywhere else in his vast romance, nor does Alexander's horse appear by name anywhere in the *Orlando furioso*. Even so, Harington goes out of his way at this particular moment to introduce the parallel. It seems to derive from Aulus Gellius's *Attic Nights* (c. 169), which offers the following description of Bucephalus's death in battle against the Rajah Porus:

> It is . . . related that Alexander, in the war against India, mounted upon that horse and doing valorous deeds, had driven him, with dis-

regard of his own safety, too far into the enemies' ranks. The horse had suffered deep wounds in his neck and side from the weapons hurled from every hand at Alexander, but though dying and almost exhausted from loss of blood, he yet in swiftest course bore the king from the midst of the foe; but when he had taken him out of range of the weapons, the horse at once fell, and satisfied with having saved his master breathed his last, with indications of relief that were almost human.

[Id etiam de isto equo memoratum est, quod, cum insidens in eo Alexander bello Indico at facinora faciens fortia, in hostium cuneum non satis sibi providens inmisisset, coniectisque undique in Alexandrum telis, vulneribus altis in cervice atque in latere equus perfossus esset, moribundus tamen ac prope iam exanguis e medies hostibus regem vivacissimo cursu retulit atque, ubi eum extra tela extulerat, ilico concidit et, domini iam superstitis securus, quasi cum sensus humani solacio animam expiravit. (5.2.4)]

It is a stirring picture of equine fidelity, and like Ariosto's depiction of Baiardo and Rinaldo, it speaks to a form of heroic companionship that transcends the species barrier. As Gellius remarks just prior to this anecdote, Bucephalus "would never allow himself to be mounted by any other than the king" ["haud umquam inscendi sese ab alio nisi ab rege passus sit" (5.2.3)]; under the circumstances, it seems right to speak of the horse as literally giving up the ghost ["animam expira(rens)"], for he and his master share a very particular spiritual bond. Likewise, in the conventional Aristotelian vocabulary of species difference, it appears reasonable to suppose that the "animam" Bucephalus surrenders is, in fact, something like the immaterial "anima rationalis" that supposedly distinguishes human from nonhuman animals.[2] Yet even so, to credit Baiardo with "intelletto umano" seems a far more capacious claim than to endow Bucephalus "quasi cum sensus humani solacio" [literally, "with relief of an almost human character"], and at any rate Harington's marginal gloss reroutes Ariosto's original comparison of horse and human being into a comparison of horse and horse. By contrast, when Ariosto declares that Baiardo refuses, out of "instinto naturale," to fight Rinaldo (2.6.5), Harington faithfully preserves this explanation: "The beast did know this much by natures force, / To hurt his maister were a service bad" (2.6.7–8).

The general purpose of these peculiar renderings becomes clearer if we consult the interpretive endnotes appended to each canto of Harington's 1591 translation. At the conclusion to canto 1 (and again after canto 2) the endnote on "Allegorie" fits Baiardo into an emblematic tradition stretching back to Plato whereby Rinaldo's mount, "a strong horse without rider or governour, is likened to the desire of man that runnes furiously after *Angelica* as it were after pleasure or honor or whatsoever man doth most inordinately affect" (1.Allegorie). Standing here for "mans fervent and furious appetite"—his "unbridled desire" (2.Allegorie)—Baiardo is in manifest need of rational—that is, human—governance, and Harington's local renderings of specific lines from Ariosto help to fit the verse, as it were, to this particular construction. In so inclining Ariosto's poem, Harington integrates it into a popular mode of Platonic allegoresis, grounded originally in the *Phaedrus*, to which I shall return soon. However, he does so at the cost of Baiardo's own claims to rational motivation, which have led other readers of Ariosto to view "the wise horse" as "a sly pun on 'Boiardo,' whom Ariosto is 'following' much as Rinaldo pursues his (apparently errant, actually purposeful) steed" (Ascoli 28n52). Harington's translation and glosses open up the former line of interpretation at the same time that they foreclose the latter, and apparently all because Harington was comfortable assigning instinctive motivation to Baiardo's behavior but drew the line (or tried to, at any rate) when it came to endowing the beast with a human mind.

Of course, drawing the line between species was not a concern for Harington alone in the early modern period. As Erica Fudge has observed, the conventional early modern discourse of species difference was riddled with conundrums, exceptions, contradictions, and downright absurdities— a set of "logical breakdowns" that "the reemergence of skepticism" in the late sixteenth and seventeenth centuries, particularly via the philosophy of Descartes, "offers . . . a way of thinking through" (Fudge, *Brutal Reasoning* 122). In this broad cultural context, the persistence of animal characters like Baiardo—endowed with the capacity for language, with self-awareness and awareness of others, with the ability to reason in the abstract, with personal and political agency, and with a privileged position in complex social networks that cut across the boundaries of species—emerges as one aspect of a much larger philosophical dilemma. Simply put, horses like Rinaldo's make it impossible to think of humanity as a distinct category with exclusive attributes. Baiardo's legacy puts the question, as it were, to humanism, suggesting on the intuitive level what Giorgio Agamben has asserted more directly: that "the humanist discovery of man is that he lacks himself, the discovery of his irremediable lack of *dignitas*" (30). Form does not differ from emptiness; emptiness does not differ from form.

It remains finally impossible to demonstrate beyond any doubt that Harington's decisions as a translator of Ariosto were driven by discomfort with the Italian poet's implicit challenge to human *dignitas*. Harington has left no express declaration on the subject, and his position on it can be inferred only from his interpretive practices. However, these practices all move in the same direction, all seeking, in their way, to reaffirm the categorical distinction between human and nonhuman animals. To this extent it seems reasonable to read Harington's translation as participating in broad cultural anxieties concerning the character of humanity, anxieties that were also coming to the fore in the philosophical discourse of Harington's contemporaries. Beyond Harington, moreover, other writers of the late sixteenth and seventeenth centuries clearly found Baiardo's legacy ever more untenable and reacted to it in a variety of consistently negative ways. In England, Shakespeare and Milton provide the most prominent cases in point.

Chivalry's End

Among the available studies of Shakespeare's horses, the paradigm-setting work may be an essay on the first tetralogy produced some twenty-five years ago by Robert N. Watson.[3] There, in typically meticulous fashion, Watson argues that "literal and figurative references to horsemanship serve to connect the failure of self-rule in such figures as Richard II, Hotspur, Falstaff, and the Dolphin with their exclusion from political rule," while parallel references "connect Henry IV's and Henry V's self-mastery with their political mastery of England" ("Horsemanship" 274). For Watson, the equation of horsemanship with self-mastery and, by extension, with political authority finds its locus classicus in Plato's *Phaedrus*, with its metaphor of the human soul as a winged chariot ideally governed by the charioteer Reason.[4] As Watson demonstrates, this text was widely dispersed in the early modern period, generating responses and adaptations in contemporary verse, iconography, and even riding manuals. The running allusions to horsemanship in Shakespeare's second tetralogy arguably participate in this pattern of metaphorical reference. More broadly, one could also argue that Shakespeare's equestrian references speak to the early modern English gentry's ongoing translation from a warrior class to a leisure class by associating horsemanship with the "defunct ideology" of chivalry (Ralph Berry 105).[5]

Without doubt, Plato's metaphorical association of self-mastery with horsemanship has left its mark on Shakespeare's work, as it has done on early modern culture more broadly. Albert Ascoli, for one, has also traced its influence on the equestrian symbolism of *Orlando furioso* (382–83), and as we have seen, Sir John Harington was pleased to detect its influence there as well, some centuries before Ascoli. However, Plato's metaphor offers little scope for the exercise of animal agency, which it understands only as a set of appetitive impulses in need of rational governance. As a result, this metaphor remains in certain ways hostile to the equine characters of chivalric romance, horses like Baiardo and Bucephalus who provide their masters not just with unquestioning obedience but with something closer to considered and selective collaboration. For Shakespeare, at least, that may well be the point. The poet's work unfolds in a universe broadly uncongenial to the sentient animals of the romance tradition, a universe in which the actual beasts that now and then wander onto the Shakespearean stage—most notably Crab in *Two Gentlemen of Verona*—function as nontheatrical singularities, excluded from the logic of mimesis and the social interaction it enables. By the same token, Shakespeare's figurative references to beasts are riddled with the anxiety that accompanies composite forms: Caliban the fish-man, Shylock the cur-man, Bottom the ass-man, Othello and Desdemona making the beast with two backs. All of this taken in aggregate suggests a Shakespearean sensibility with little sympathy for the chivalric ethos or for the peculiar relationship between human and nonhuman nature that it presupposes.

This is not to say, however, that Shakespeare ignores the world of chivalry: on the contrary, he gestures toward it through a variety of equestrian references that participate in the romance tradition and that resist the binary of dominance and servitude deriving from Plato's *Phaedrus*. Take, for instance, *Henry V*'s Dolphin. An anti-Gallic caricature redolent with aristocratic snobbery, he lavishes extravagant praise on his horse, describing it in ways that echo the Ariostan idiom: "I will not change my horse with any that treads but on four [pasterns]. *Ça,* ha! He bounds from the earth, as if his entrails were hairs; *le cheval volant,* the Pegasus, *chez les narines de feu!* When I bestride him, I soar, I am a hawk; he trots the air. . . . It is a beast for Perseus. He is pure air and fire, and the dull elements of earth and water never appear in him. . . . He is indeed a horse, and all other jades you may call beasts"

(3.7.11–24). With his allusion to Pegasus, the Dolphin places his horse within a mythic lineage that extends through *Orlando furioso*'s hippogriff, "un gran destriero alato" (4.4.7), trained by the enchanter Atlante to convey his ward Ruggiero to the far ends of the earth, while also encompassing Baiardo, who in Ariosto's sixteenth canto flies toward the pagan besiegers of Paris as if he had wings ["il destrier volta / tanto leggier, che fa sembrar ch'abbia ale" (16.49.1–2)]. The associations here are, of course, literary and figurative, rather than biological and literal, but the Dolphin uses them to insist that a difference of degree (his horse is better than other horses) is, in fact, a difference of kind: "He is indeed a horse, and all other jades you may call beasts." It is a familiar rhetorical gesture, participating in the chivalric ethos that conceives distinctions of rank to be irreducible, unalterable, and fundamental determinants of identity.

Of course, to say "My horse is not a beast as other horses are" comes very close to saying "My horse is more like to me than to other horses," which in turn raises the possibility of saying "My horse is more like to me than are other men." This is the extreme implication of the chivalric premise that differences of degree can confound those of species, and the Dolphin wastes no time in hastening toward it: "It [the Dolphin's horse] is the prince of palfreys: his neigh is like the bidding of a monarch, and his countenance enforces homage. . . . 'Tis a subject for a sovereign to reason on, and for a sovereign's sovereign to ride on; and for the world, familiar to us and unknown, to lay apart their particular functions and wonder at him. I once writ a sonnet in his praise and began thus: 'Wonder of nature'— (3.7.27–40). The Dolphin's kinsman, the Duke of Orleance, listens to this blather with increasing annoyance. When the Dolphin likens his horse's whinnying to human speech (and worse than that, to royal speech), further suggesting that the animal's "countenance enforces homage" (that is, that a mere look at the beast should compel inferior beings to revere him), Orleance calls time: "No more, cousin" (3.7.30). And when the Dolphin, not to be discouraged by lesser mortals, segues into poetic effusions, Orleance responds with deflating humor: "I have heard a sonnet begin so to one's mistress" (3.7.40–41).

From here the scene devolves into a series of off-color jokes based on confusion of the species barrier: for instance, "Your mistress bears well" (3.7.45; this from Orleance to the Dolphin) or "I tell thee, Constable, my mistress wears his own hair" (3.7.60–61; this from the Dolphin to the Constable of France, who has entered the fray in support of Orleance). One could dismiss such stuff as coarse fare for the groundlings, but it arises out of tensions created by a specifically aristocratic discourse: that is, by the Dolphin's efforts to present himself and his mount in heroic terms derived from the chivalric romance tradition. It makes particular sense that Orleance, of all characters, should find this self-presentation most irritating; after all, a human member of the royal family has most to lose from the proposition that animals, too, can be human and royal. Responding with erotic innuendo, he invokes the language of sexism to reaffirm the logic of speciesism.

As it happens, this gesture—whereby difference of gender is conceived in terms of difference of species, and vice versa—occurs so often in Shakespeare as to comprise a signature motif of sorts. Moreover, it assumes its definitive form in the equation of women to horses. To Petruchio, Katharina becomes "My horse, my ox, my ass, my anything" (*Taming of the Shrew* 3.2.232). Puck promises the sleeping Lysander that "Jack shall have Jill; / . . . / The man shall have his mare again" (*Midsummer Night's Dream* 3.2.461–63). Hotspur assures his wife that "when I am a' horseback, I will swear / I love thee infinitely" (*1 Henry IV* 2.3.101–2). Cleopatra wishes she could be a horse so as "to bear the weight of Antony" (1.5.21). Antigonus responds to the possibility of an unchaste Hermione by exclaiming, "I'll keep my stables where / I lodge my wife" (*The Winter's Tale* 3.1.134–35). Such moments may derive in part from the obvious sexual suggestiveness of the horse-and-rider configuration, in part from the shared dynamics of dominance and submission that traverse both gender and species relations, in part from the traditional status of both women and horses as property within the legal *patrimonium* of a Roman paterfamilias.[6] However, beyond all these considerations, the conflation of women with horses provides Shakespeare with a powerful antichivalric image, an antidote to the heroic dyad of Rinaldo and Baiardo, hero and steed. This is why Orleance invokes it to counter the Dolphin's grandiose claims for the preeminence of his horse. This is arguably also why Shakespeare contrasts the pretentious nonsense of *Henry V*'s horsey Frenchmen with a hardscrabble vision of the English cavalry at Agincourt:

> The [English] horsemen sit like fixed candlesticks,
> With torch-staves in their hand; and their poor jades
> Lob down their heads, dropping the hides and hips,
> The gum down-roping from their pale-dead eyes,
> And in their pale dull mouths the [gimmal'd] bit
> Lies foul with chaw'd-grass, still and motionless.
>
> (4.2.45–50)

In this context, Henry's victory marks not only the triumph of England over France and yeomanly virtues over aristocratic preciosity; it also entails the conquest of one literary idiom by another and a transition between the models of nature these literary idioms presuppose. The possibility of Baiardo—to put it more broadly, the possibility of animal character and perhaps even that of a sentient nature in general—emerges as one casualty of this transition.

In the Dolphin's case, anti-Gallic prejudice combines with a selective sort of antiaristocratic contempt to produce a mockery of the chivalric tradition. However, when not inflected by nationalism and racial prejudice, Shakespeare's equestrian depictions of aristocratic privilege can take widely varied forms, ranging in quality from regal triumphalism to tragic ambivalence. Even Richard II, perhaps the most famously flawed royal horseman in the Shakespeare canon, emerges from his play less as an effete ninny than as an object of pathos and a source of national guilt. This difference in tone derives in large part from Richard's intensely voiced sense of sympathetic connection to his kingdom, a connection he figures repeatedly as a kind of communion with the fabric of nature. His "senseless conjuration" (3.2.23) at Barkloughly Castle provides a classic, if typically extreme, example:

> Dear earth, I do salute thee with my hand,
> Though rebels wound thee with their horses' hoofs.
> . . . .
> Feed not thy sovereign's foe, my gentle earth,
> Nor with thy sweets comfort his ravenous sense,
> But let thy spiders, that suck up thy venom,
> And heavy-gaited toads lie in their way,
> Doing annoyance to the treacherous feet,
> Which with usurping steps do trample thee.
> Yield stinging nettles to mine enemies;
> And when they from thy bosom pluck a flower,
> Guard it, I pray thee, with a lurking adder.
> (3.2.6–20)

As Gabriel Egan has observed, "Throughout the drama of Shakespeare, characters speak of the world around them as though it is alive" (22), and Richard's speech provides an exemplary instance of this habit. Its logic derives from the Piconian assumption that "God has sown and planted" throughout the fabric of nature a "harmony of the universe which the Greeks with greater aptness of terms called *sumpatheia*" (Pico 57). On Richard's view, the same divine will that ordained the natural order also ordained his own privileged position within that order. Thus any act of rebellion against Richard is equivalent to rebellion against nature itself, and the way is cleared, in Richard's imagination, for spiders, toads, and adders to fight on his behalf. Putting the same idea more directly to Bullingbrook and his allies, Richard elsewhere frames it in epidemiological terms:

> [T]hough you think that all, as you have done,
> Have torn their souls by turning them from us,
> And we are barren and bereft of friends,
> Yet know my master, God omnipotent,
> Is mustering in his clouds on our behalf
> Armies of pestilence, and they shall strike
> Your children yet unborn and unbegot.
>
> (3.3.82–88)

Elsewhere still Richard urges the very same notion via an astronomical analogy:

> [W]hen this thief, this traitor Bullingbrook
> Who all this while hath revell'd in the night,
> Whilst we were wandering with the antipodes,
> Shall see us rising in our throne, the east,
> His treasons will sit blushing in his face,
> Not able to endure the sight of day.
>
> (3.2.47–52)

Nonhuman animals, plagues, heavenly bodies—Richard imagines himself as intimately aligned with all of these by virtue of their common status as expressions of the divine purpose. Within this context his own royal nature emerges as an object of revelation rather than attainment: something to be displayed and admired, not maintained and contested.

It should be immediately evident that the chivalric bond between horse and master with which this chapter is concerned—what I have called Baiardo's legacy—relates to Richard's general self-presentation as does species to genus. If, that is, the king's preeminence is written into the fabric of nature, it should be recognizable not just by toads and adders but by more exalted beasts as well, and chivalric equestrian culture lends special importance to the horse as a case in point. That is why the Alexander romances insist that Bucephalus would admit only one rider;[7] in a universe imbued with divine harmony, the prince of horses instinctively recognizes the prince of men and submits to him and him alone. Likewise, Baiardo's refusal—in both Ariosto and Boiardo—to do battle with his master speaks to the same model of sympathetic nature; the extraordinary horse, understanding himself as such, recognizes his counterpart in the extraordinary man and obeys no other. In a sense, Shakespeare's Richard II can be understood as an extreme embodiment of this model of the universe: a dramatic figure whose governing principle is the law of universal harmony, a character created to take this law seriously and tease out its implications for all to see.

Understood in this way, Richard opens his play by enacting a problem intrinsic to his mode of self-apprehension: if the king stands preeminent within the order of nature, to what extent may he preempt that order? Has the divine will fashioned royal privilege as a principle of self-negation empowered to suspend, supersede, reconfigure, or simply ignore its other manifestations? Richard's own view of the question is made clear by his conduct of the dispute between Mowbray and Bullingbrook with which his play begins. "We were not born to sue, but to command" (1.1.196), he tells the quarreling peers and then prepares to adjudicate their differences via the definitive ritual of courtly romance, the trial by joust:

> Be ready, as your lives shall answer it,
> At Coventry upon Saint Lambert's day.
> There shall your swords and lances arbitrate
> The swelling difference of your settled hate.
> Since we cannot atone you, we shall see
> Justice design the victor's chivalry.
> (1.1.198–203)

Of course, this is not how things turn out. Instead, Richard aborts the trial by combat, replaces it with royal fiat, and thus fashions himself into the first and most ominous antichivalric principle in his own play:

> Let them lay by their helmets and their spears,
> And both return back to their chairs again.

Withdraw with us, and let the trumpets sound
While we return these dukes what we decree.

(1.3.119–22)

One may argue endlessly (and, in my opinion, pointlessly) whether Richard's behavior justifies Bullingbrook's rebellion; to my mind, *Richard II* concerns itself less with what should be than with what is. To this extent, the opening disruption of chivalric ritual sets the tone for everything that follows, placing the play's events in a world at odds with the logic and gestures of courtly romance. In this world even the most vocal advocate of the chivalric ethos, Richard himself, lacks the courage of his convictions. Unwilling to rely on trial by combat as an instrument of divine justice, he replaces it with royal decree. At Barkloughly Castle his extreme assertions of divine right prove so patently out of step with circumstances that he feels obliged to defend them, both to his companions and to himself:

Mock not my senseless conjuration, lords,
This earth shall have a feeling, and these stones
Prove armed soldiers, ere her native king
Shall falter under foul rebellion's arms.

(3.2.23–26)

Of course, the defense is vain, even when taken on its own terms. Richard's hopeful expectation that "[t]his earth shall have a feeling" in itself admits the contrary: that Egan's notion of a living, feeling world exists in this play, even for Richard, only as a function of the hypothetical subjunctive. Richard does falter, the stones do not rise up, and the chivalric ideal of a monarch at one with his environment yields to the image of a resistant natural world, figured through a flawed relationship between horse and rider:

Down, down I come, like glist'ring Phaëton,
Wanting the manage of unruly jades.

(3.3.178–79)

Critics have long read these lines as a glance at "Richard's failures of self-rule," which "have already deposed him from the solar chariot" (Watson, "Horsemanship" 284). However, at its heart, the tale of Phaethon is one of disharmony between man and nature: not just the ecological catastrophe of a sun-scorched earth but the more intimate strife between horse and rider locked in a fruitless contest of wills. As such, it marks the opposite of the Rinaldo-Baiardo dyad, horse and man in a harmony beyond dominance and submission.

If *Richard II* opens by invoking yet disabling the conventional expectations and topoi of chivalric romance, it ends in the same way. Indeed, Richard's final conversation is focused on the failure of the horse-rider relationship as exemplified in Boiardo and Ariosto by what I have called the topos of equine civil disobedience. Shakespeare conjures up a nameless groom of Richard's stable to visit the deposed king and condole with him over his straitened circumstances, and perhaps inevitably, both Richard and his former groom turn to horsemanship for a vocabulary with which to describe what has gone wrong:

> *Groom.* O how it ern'd my heart when I beheld
> In London streets, that coronation-day,
> When Bullingbrook rode on roan Barbary,
> That horse that thou so often hast bestrid,
> That horse that I so carefully have dress'd!
> *K. Richard.* Rode he on Barbary? Tell me, gentle friend,
> How went he under him?
> *Groom.* So proudly as if he disdain'd the ground.
> *K. Richard.* So proud that Bullingbrook was on his back!
> That jade hath eat bread from my royal hand,
> This hand hath made him proud with clapping him.
> Would he not stumble? Would he not fall down,
> Since pride must have a fall, and break the neck
> Of that proud man that did usurp his back?
>
> (5.5.76–89)

For Richard, the horse's behavior embodies a broader failure of relationship: a fracture of the bonds of gratitude and obedience that unite culture to nature and both to God. Thus the sin of pride binds Barbary and Bullingbrook together in Richard's imagination, and thus too Richard expresses particular surprise to find this sin disfiguring the singularly personal relationship he has shared with his horse. Barbary's willingness to bear Bullingbrook—his failure to refuse, in the manner of Baiardo, to turn against his true master—marks what one can only call a lapse of personal integrity. Indeed, if one views personal integrity as a function of personality in the modern, Cartesian sense of the term—that is, of personal agency grounded in introspective self-awareness—one must view the horse's lapse more broadly as the breakdown of a whole discourse of equine character, elaborated by the fabulous events of romance and subtended by the ethics of feudalism. When Richard finally absolves the horse of blame, he does so by depriving all horses, everywhere, of the capacity for personhood in this sense:

> Forgiveness, horse! Why do I rail on thee,
> Since thou, created to be aw'd by man,
> Wast born to bear? I was not made a horse,
> And yet I bear a burthen like an ass,
> Spurr'd, gall'd, and tir'd by jauncing Bullingbrook.
>
> (5.5.90–94)

Richard emerges from his play as one of Shakespeare's incredible shrinking men—a figure, like Antony, whose identity melts away inexorably over the course of five acts. If, at the end, this progressive loss of royal character is tied to the loss of animal character as well, it is because both of these exist in a world that has been revealed as a figment of Richard's imagination, a world governed by a divinely instituted system of degree and sustained by a universal harmony in the fabric of nonhuman nature.

Richard II derives its conflicted, mournful tone from this fact: not simply an enactment of the death of a great man or even of the untimely end of a monarchy and a dynasty, the play performs the loss of an entire world and the language that conjured it into being. It is interesting that Shakespeare returns to this world at the end of his career, in his collaborative work with John Fletcher, *The Two Noble Kinsmen* (c. 1613). Less openly political than *Richard II*, this late play situates itself more directly in the tradition of chivalric romance, drawing as it does on Chaucer's Knight's Tale for its main story line. The attribution of authorship in specific scenes remains uncertain, and to this extent it also remains tricky to fix upon specific passages as representative of one author's habits of thought or literary development. However, a broad if tentative scholarly consensus on the authorship question has developed, with general opinion crediting Shakespeare with most of acts 1 and 5, and Fletcher with most of acts 2–4.[8] While this broad hypothesis remains unconfirmed, it also seems reasonable to assume that the collaborating playwrights engaged in some fairly close coordination of plot lines and thematic issues. With these considerations in mind, we may read the play as a kind of farewell to romance that, especially in its final act, repudiates the practices of equine characterization typical of the romance tradition.

This repudiation occurs concurrently within the play's heroic main plot—which recounts the tragic sexual rivalry of the knights Palamon and Arcite—and in its comic subplot—which centers on the Athenian Jailer's Daughter's unrequited passion for her prisoner, Palamon, who enters her care after being taken captive in battle by Duke Theseus. In both plots the play reenacts chivalric conventions but in a queasy, discomforting, and in some cases openly parodic way, perhaps thus augmenting the gentler ironic distance imposed on the same subject matter by Chaucer's *Canterbury Tales*. The play's main plot centers at first on heroic friendship, the sort of loyalty foregrounded in much chivalric literature as, for instance, in cantos 18 and 19 of the *Furioso*. There the pagan warrior Medoro risks his life to retrieve the body of his slain lord Dardinello from a heavily guarded battlefield held by Charlemagne's army and is accompanied in the effort by his comrade Cloridano, who sacrifices his life to help Medoro escape with Dardinello's corpse. At the outset of Shakespeare and Fletcher's play, Palamon and Arcite depict their friendship in similarly extravagant terms: "dearer in love than blood" (1.2.1), the cousins claim that in war, "the blood we venture / Should be as for our health" (1.2.109–10); taken captive together, they imagine themselves as "one another's wife, ever begetting / New births of love" (2.2.80–81). Likewise, the play's comic subplot opens with a sudden infatuation that is similarly reminiscent of romance. Just as, in the *Furioso*, Angelica stumbles upon the wounded Medoro after his rescue of Dardinello's body and falls instantly in love with him, so the Jailer's Daughter exclaims of Palamon, "I love him beyond love and beyond reason, / Or wit, or safety" (2.6.11–12). However, in both plots of the play, the conventional romance pose malfunctions. Within a hundred lines of being "one another's wife," Palamon and Arcite have repudiated their friendship in the name of sexual rivalry: as Palamon declares, "Thou art a traitor, Arcite . . . / . . . Friendship, blood, / And all the ties between us, I disclaim" (2.2.171–73). Likewise, the Jailer's Daughter experiences a passion far less noble and enduring than its chivalric counterparts. Overlooked by an Emilia-besotted Palamon, she lapses into madness, but even this stance of heroic ardor dissolves in turn into self-parody when she is persuaded to accept an impersonator in Palamon's place.

As for Palamon and Arcite's courtship of Emilia, this too proceeds with the conventional trappings of chivalry, only to repudiate these, as it were, after the fact. Horses inevitably figure as part of the business. When first introduced to Emilia, for instance, Arcite declares, "I dare not praise / My feat in horsemanship, yet they that knew me / Would say it was my best piece" (2.5.12–14). Pirithous responds by promising, "because you say / You are a horseman, I must needs intreat you / This afternoon to ride" (2.3.45–46). As Arcite gains marks of favor from Emilia, his good fortune develops in equine terms:

> She takes strong note of me,
> Hath made me near her; and this beauteous morn
> (The prim'st of all the year) presents me with
> A brace of horses; two such steeds might well
> Be by a pair of kings back'd, in a field
> That their crowns' titles tried.
>
> (3.1.17–22)

Although Palamon and Arcite agree, prior to their first combat for Emilia, that they will "use no horses" (3.6.59), this decision is clearly made for practical theatrical purposes, so that the fight may be presented onstage, and Arcite at once recalls a previous battle in which Palamon "charg'd / Upon the left wing of the enemy, / I spurr'd hard to come up, and under me / I had a right good horse" (3.6.74–77). Likewise after their final duel, when Arcite has won and Palamon has lost, Theseus praises the latter in terms of his horsemanship: "He [Arcite] speaks now of as brave a knight as e'er / Did spur a noble steed" (5.3.115–16). The markers of sexual favor, heroism, and literary genre converge repeatedly on this form of cross-species troping.

That being the case, it comes as a particular irony that Arcite should meet his end in a riding accident—indeed, an accident that involves one of the horses Emilia presented to him as a mark of her favor. The passage describing this misfortune, a speech generally assigned to Shakespeare's authorship, comprises the play's greatest histrionic set piece:

> [Arcite,]
> Mounted upon a steed that Emily
> Did first bestow on him—a black one, owing
> Not a hair-worth of white, which some will say
> Weakens his price, and many will not buy
> His goodness with that note; which superstition

Here finds allowance—on this horse is Arcite
Trotting the stones of Athens. . . .
. . . .
. . . As he thus went counting
The flinty pavement, dancing as 'twere to th' music
His own hoofs made (for as they say from iron
Came music's origin), what envious flint,
Cold as old Saturn, and like him possess'd
With fire malevolent, darted a spark,
Or what fierce sulphur else, to this end made,
I comment not—the hot horse, hot as fire,
Took toy at this, and fell to what disorder
His power could give his will, bounds, comes on end,
Forgets school-doing, being therein train'd,
And of kind manage; pig-like he whines
At the sharp rowel, which he frets at rather
Than any jot obeys; seeks all foul means
Of boist'rous and rough jad'ry to disseat
His lord that kept it bravely. When nought serv'd,
When neither curb would crack, girth break, nor diff'ring plunges
Disroot his rider whence he grew, but that
He kept him 'tween his legs, on his hind hoofs
[. . .] on end he stands,
That Arcite's legs, being higher than his head,
Seem'd with strange art to hang. His victor's wreath
Even then fell off his head; and presently
Backward the jade comes o'er, and his full poise
Becomes the rider's load. Yet is he living,
Yet such a vessel 'tis that floats but for
The surge that next approaches.

(5.4.49–84)

As a virtuoso rhetorical performance, this speech proves almost impossible to abbreviate; its intricate syntax, like the tortuous action it describes, defies efforts at restraint or productive curtailment. At heart it rehearses a *mundus inversus* motif, a scene of catastrophic reversal that occurs not only on the level of plot—as Arcite's fortunes alter in a heartbeat—but on the level of personal status as well. Indeed, the horse's wild cavortings provide a spatial counterpart to the implied logic of degree that saturates the speech. Prancing on his hind legs so that Arcite's head hangs upside-down and his victor's wreath falls to the earth, the mount embodies a similar inversion. First introduced in act 3 as one of "A brace of horses [which] might well / Be by a pair of kings back'd" (3.1.20–21), the horse here "whines" in "pig-like" manner as he disobeys his master, his regression down the great chain of being providing both an occasion and a parallel for Arcite's similar dislocation. The whole set of reversals is introduced as an issue of character: the horse's black coat supposedly advertises his unreliability, so that "many will not buy / His goodness with this note" (5.4.52–53). And the character problem extends to Arcite as well insofar as the "brace of horses" Emilia has given him recalls the paired steeds of Plato's *Phaedrus*: allowing his passion for Emilia to ruin his friendship with Palamon, Arcite has arguably surrendered his reason to appetite, and thus he rightly meets his end in an accident involving an unruly horse—apparently the bad one of a pair.

The character-issue, in fact, remains annoyingly muddy. The horse, for one, is defined less by his possession than by his lack of specific personality traits; distrust of his all-black coat is dismissed as "superstition" (5.4.53), and his movement up and down the great chain of being suggests the absence of any specific nature as an individual. Likewise for Arcite, he may have succumbed ignobly to his passion for Emilia, but he is presented throughout this play in terms of heroic hyperbole. Even his death is recounted as a feat of horsemanship; Arcite so controls his unruly mount that no effort will "disroot" him (5.4.75), with the result that the horse collapses on himself out of sheer frustration. This is no picture of Phaeton, wanting the manage of unruly jades—at least not exactly. It *is*, however, another recollection of the old romance motif of equine civil disobedience, in this case presented without rational cause or moral application. In fact, Arcite's death functions as a parody of the topos whereby horse and master find themselves in such intimate agreement of character that the former refuses to harm the latter and, in fact, resists his enemies instead. Arcite's horse does to him what Richard wishes Barbary had done to Henry, only without motive. The unworthy acquiescence of one horse provides a counterpart to the unworthy resistance of the other, and both cases presuppose what one might call a post-Baiardan universe, marked by the absence of equine reason, equine agency, and a sympathetic concord between human and nonhuman animals.

That being the case, it should be no surprise that the equine conventions of chivalric romance also appear, once more in parodic form, within the comic subplot of Shakespeare and Fletcher's play. Here the pivotal moment again arrives in act 5, in the one scene of that act generally ascribed to Fletcher. There the Jailer and the doctor he has engaged to treat his daughter's madness conspire to restore the Jailer's Daughter to some semblance of mental health by supplying her with a nameless wooer, attired like Palamon, as a substitute object for her unrequited passion. Prior to the Wooer's appearance, the Jailer and his daughter exchange some words about Palamon, and these come to focus on a particular love token the Jailer's Daughter claims to have received from him:

> *Daugh.* He's a kind gentleman, and I am much bound to him.
>   Did you nev'r see the horse he gave me?
> *Jail.* Yes.
> *Daugh.* How do you like him?
> *Jail.* He's a very fair one.
> *Daugh.* You never saw him dance?
> *Jail.* No.
> *Daugh.* I have often.
>   . . . .
> *Jail.* Having these virtues,
>   I think he might be brought to play at tennis.
> *Daugh.* Alas, that's nothing!
> *Jail.* Can he write and read too?
> *Daugh.* A very fair hand, and casts himself th'accounts
>   Of all his hay and provender. That hostler
>   Must rise betime that cozens him.
>
> (5.2.44–60)

In a comic reversal of Emilia's equine gift to Arcite, the Jailer's Daughter imagines Palamon presenting her with a horse, one that is as special in its way as are the two that Arcite receives. If the latter two are distinguished by their nobility, the former is marked out by his intelligence, and the measure of both these qualities derives from the conventional gestures of medieval chivalric verse. However, in both cases an abyss separates the chivalric source motif from its parodic reenactment in Shakespeare and Fletcher's play. Arcite's steeds recall the courtly ideal of sympathetic loyalty between knight and steed as imaged in the topos of equine civil disobedience, only to empty that topos of its traditional courtly significance. Likewise, the Jailer's

Daughter imagines her horse within what we might call the equine wisdom tradition, which frames Baiardo's preternatural intelligence in terms of language skills and intellectual attainments. Thus the line of literary development that gives us a Baiardo with "intelletto umano" and "gesto umano," that provides us with a Bayard who understands Renaud "com mere son enfant" or "as thoughe he had been a man," and that depicts the exasperated Charlemagne as addressing a speech of triumphant mockery to the horse when he finally appears to have the animal in his power emerges in *The Two Noble Kinsmen* as lovesick nonsense, born of a mind enfeebled by unrequited passion. Here Baiardo's heirs seem to have less in common with the marvelous animal characters of medieval romance than with performing horses like the celebrated Morocco, who gained lasting fame in Elizabethan England "for dancing, (some say) singing, and discerning Maids from Maulkins" (*Dom Zara* 114).[9]

In this sense the Shakespearean plays surveyed here all seem to unfold in a disenchanted world—a world far different, let it be said, from that of Prospero's island or Macbeth's Scotland or the wood outside Athens in *A Midsummer Night's Dream*. The disenchantment in question may be partly understood from the standpoint of literary influence, as a repudiation of one established way of writing about heroic character in its relation to human society and to the natural environment. Plays like *Macbeth* and *The Tempest* may leave open the possibility for supernatural agency as this is figured in the activities of witches, the exercise of magic, and the appearance of species-bending anomalies like Caliban. However, the works we have surveyed here seem concerned with foreclosing that same possibility, at least in its knightly or chivalric dimension. They do so with a sense of regret, as if they were abandoning a long-cherished fantasy, but they do so nonetheless. One casualty of this abandonment is the romance tradition's privileged relation between horse and rider, a relation that provides space for the development of non-human character while also celebrating and exalting certain personal attachments that extend across the species barrier.

The Horses of Heaven

Half a century after Shakespeare, John Milton performs a similar act of repudiation, abandoning the romance tradition's cult of the horse and rider and the possibilities it creates for cross-species interaction. However, Milton dismisses this baggage more emphatically than does Shakespeare and with greater evident satisfaction. Indeed, for Milton this rejection forms part of an integrated program of political, spiritual, and literary reform. I have already made this basic case in an earlier publication that focuses primarily on equestrian representation in the classical epic (Boehrer, "The Horseless Epic"). However, as I point out in that earlier essay (1–2), there are good reasons to treat the epic and romance traditions as a cohesive whole from the standpoint of horse culture. The idea of Homer's *aristoi Achaioi*, like the Aristotelian perfectionist theory of justice it helped to inspire, is grounded in an elitist social vision similar in broad ways to the feudal hierarchical worldview. Classical models of heroic behavior provide the basis for much medieval romance material; in some cases (for example, Alexander and Bucephalus), this material incorporates character relations that cross the species divide. In addition, both the epic and romance traditions conceive of themselves as celebrating, in narrative verse, the heroic achievements of a warrior elite for whom the relationship between horse and rider held particular resonance.

In any case, Milton repeatedly elides the cultures of classical epic and medieval romance. In book 2 of *Paradise Lost* (1667), for instance, after Satan has embarked upon his solitary mission of discovering Eden and seducing Adam and Eve, his followers entertain themselves in Hell with a variety of leisure activities. As gradually becomes clear, these amusements include some of the greatest cultural achievements of Greco-Roman antiquity: for instance, "th'Olympian games" (2.530); "false Philosophie" (2.565); and heroic verse sung "[w]ith notes Angelicall to many a Harp" (2.548) and providing, in its infernal context, the historic original for Orpheus's mythic performance before Hades and Persephone. Also included within this catalog of pagan attainments is military exercise, but here, suddenly and to a modern ear incongruously, the description takes on very specific medieval tones:

> As when to warn proud Cities warr appears
> Wag'd in the troubl'd Skie, and Armies rush
> To Battel in the Clouds, before each van
> Prick forth the Aerie Knights, and couch their Spears
> Till thickest Legions close.
>
> (2.533–37)

Again in the autobiographical introduction to book 9, as Milton differentiates his epic project from its predecessors, he exalts his subject matter above

the wrauth
Of stern *Achilles* on his Foe pursu'd
Thrice Fugitive about Troy Wall
                    (9.14–16)

before similarly dismissing the stuff of romance:

[T]his subject for Heroic Song
Pleas'd me long choosing, and beginning late;
Not sedulous by Nature to indite
Warrs, hitherto the onely Argument
Heroic deem'd, chief maist'rie to dissect
With long and tedious havoc fabl'd Knights
In Battels feign'd.

                    (9.25–31)

In both these paradigmatic cases Milton's rejection of martial subject matter leads him to disparage classical epic and chivalric romance in practically the same breath, as subsets of a single larger category: the poetry of warfare. In an important sense here the differences between the two genres seem less important to Milton than their similarities.

From this standpoint, then, Milton's determination to supersede the poetry of warfare—to pioneer a superior model of verse grounded in "the better fortitude / Of Patience and Heroic Martyrdom" (9.31–32)—leads him to dismiss the martial furniture of both classical epic and medieval romance, and insofar as the horse-rider relationship comprises a prominent item of this furniture, it must go. As I have previously argued, raw word counts alone help to demonstrate the starkness of the contrast: as against *The Iliad*'s four hundred–odd mentions of horses and Ariosto's equally frequent references to equestrian subject matter, *Paradise Lost* uses the noun "horse" in any form only five times. It is almost as if, for Milton, this central accoutrement of knighthood did not exist at all.

If Milton's "dislike of war" (Freeman 6) thus translates into a dislike of horses—if his "rejection of the conventional heroic argument of warfare" (Steadman, *Paradoxes* 173) entails a comparable rejection of the animals most privileged by that argument—then the rare horses who actually remain in *Paradise Lost* should be something far different from those noble equine characters, such as Baiardo and Bucephalus, that populate chivalric narrative.

Even the few conventional chivalric steeds that do appear in *Paradise Lost* operate in a derogatory register of meaning, as when Adam's "compleat / Perfections" are contrasted with "the tedious pomp that waits / On princes, [with] thir rich Retinue long / Of Horses" (5.352–53, 354–56) or when the children of the sons of God and daughters of men from Genesis 6.2 join in "cruel Tournament" of "Horse and Foot" (11.652, 645) in *Paradise Lost* 11. Such references, brief and disparaging as they are, repudiate a prominent kind of cross-species relationship, and in doing so, they also repudiate the model of nonhuman character that makes this relationship possible. A poetry with no use for Rinaldo will likewise hold no place for Baiardo.

On the other hand, however, *Paradise Lost* does hold a privileged place for angelic transportation that, while not exactly equine, appears to be of a horselike nature. Milton's preferred word for the mounts of the angels is "steed"—more particularly "fiery steed"—rather than "horse," and these creatures clearly derive on some level from the "horses of fire" of 2 Kings 2.11 and the "white horses" of the angelic army at Revelation 19.14. While they are described performing activities similar to those of terrestrial warhorses (such as pulling chariots and conveying mounted warriors into battle) they are also endowed with certain anatomical peculiarities that distinguish them from their earthly counterparts. For instance, at *Paradise Lost* 11.706 they are described as "winged," and the adjective "fiery"—as in the phrases "fierie Steeds" and "fierie foaming Steeds" (6.17, 391)—deriving as it does from the descriptive vocabulary of 2 Kings, could refer equally to the creatures' temperament or to the material from which their bodies are fashioned. As chariot bearers, they seem ultimately connected to that mother of all Miltonic battle wagons, the "Chariot of Paternal Deitie," or *Merkabah,* which the Son mounts in order to confound the demonic host at *Paradise Lost* 6.750. This chariot, in turn, is "convoyd / By four Cherubic shapes" (6.752–53)—horse-angels, if you will—that seem irreducible to the earthly language of species difference.

This much I have already observed elsewhere. Here I want to return to the paradoxes that invest Milton's treatment of heavenly saddle stock and evaluate these paradoxes from the standpoint of Ariostan romance. To start, then, let us be aware of what we have in hand. Raphael's narrative of the heavenly war in *Paradise Lost* 6, and more generally Milton's description of heaven and its inhabitants throughout the poem, is self-consciously advanced under erasure, as an accommodational discourse that proceeds "By lik'ning spiritual to corporal forms, / As may express them best" (5.572–73). As an exercise in approximate rhetoric, this descriptive project lays no claim to literal accuracy.

Nor does it even offer an accurate account of its own inaccuracies, preferring instead to defer the issue via an unanswered question: "what if Earth / Be but the shaddow of Heav'n, and things therein / Each to other like, more then on earth is thought?" (5.575–77).

That being the case, one hardly has a right to be surprised when Milton's references to heavenly steeds prove inconsistent even on their own terms. Take, for instance, the "winged Steeds" that transport Enoch to heaven at *Paradise Lost* 11.706 or the "fiery Steeds" that convey Elijah to the same destination at 3.522. These creatures do not seem to differ in kind from the "fierie Steeds" that Satan's followers exercise in Hell at 2.531 or from the "fierie Steeds" that Abdiel encounters when returning to the heavenly host at 6.17, just prior to the war in heaven. However, while one may accept that human beings—even such gifted ones as Elijah and Enoch—might need special transportation to reach heaven, the angels and devils clearly require nothing of the sort. Satan brings no winged mount with him during his epic exploration of the passage from Hell to Earth in *Paradise Lost* 2–3; nor does Uriel when he comes "gliding through the Eeven / On a Sun beam" (4.556–57) to alert Gabriel and his armed guard that Satan approaches Eden; nor does Raphael when, obeying the Father's command in book 5, he travels from Heaven to Earth to converse with Adam and Eve. In fact, one of the most prominent features of angelic anatomy in *Paradise Lost* would seem to make winged steeds entirely superfluous; after all, Milton's angels have wings of their own. These are on prominent display when Satan disguises himself as a "stripling Cherube" to mislead Uriel in *Paradise Lost* 3: "wings he wore / Of many a colour'd plume sprinkl'd with Gold" (3.641–42). They are equally noteworthy on Uriel, whose "Locks behind / Illustrious on his Shoulders fledge with wings / Lay waving round" (3.626–28). And they are most sharply foregrounded at *Paradise Lost* 5.247 and following, as "the winged Saint" Raphael, "Vaild with his gorgeous wings," springs up from his place amid the heavenly host and swoops down to Earth below:

> Down thither prone in flight
> He speeds . . .
> . . . .
>   . . . till within soare
> Of Towring Eagles, to all the Fowles he seems
> A *Phoenix*, gaz'd by all, as that sole Bird
> When to enshrine his reliques in the Sun's
> Bright Temple, to *Aegyptian Theb's* he flies.

At once on th'Eastern cliff of Paradise
He lights, and to his proper shape returns,
A seraph wingd; six wings he wore, to shade
His lineaments divine.

(5.266–78)

"Symbolic" as these wings may be (Milton, *Riverside Edition* 484n86), Milton's angels (and devils) clearly have no need of fiery mounts to maneuver through their universe.

Then there is the *Merkabah*, the Father's "Chariot of Paternal Deitie" (6.750), which can best be described as a chariot in name only, driven by creatures that are draft animals in name only. Indeed, the chariot requires no external motive power, being "It self instinct"—that is, "'instigated' or 'impelled'" (Milton, *Riverside Edition* 341n752)—"with Spirit" (6.752). Likewise, the figures who convey it, "four Cherubic shapes" with "four faces each" (6.753), transcend any particular species identification and indeed seem to exceed even the distinction between subject and object: "With Starrs thir bodies all / And Wings were set with Eyes, with Eyes the wheels / Of Beril, and careering Fires between" (6.754–56). Extending an ancient mode of sacred representation centered on a "god-animal relationship in which the animal serves as a vehicle for the god" (Adamson 106), the *Merkabah* confounds the very idea of difference, figuring "a universal harmony of all being with the divine will" (Adamson 108). To this extent, any reference it makes to the world of species distinctions must function by default as a self-consuming artifact. Thus, as a whole, Milton's language of accommodation leaves us with a trail of equine references in heaven, none of which may be taken quite literally and all of which work against the logic of differential observation upon which biological taxonomy is grounded.

At the same time, Milton's fiery, winged steeds also work to appropriate the topoi and exemplary figures of chivalric romance. The Ariostan model here, itself "a descendant of the high-leaping Baiardo of the *Morgante*" (Rodriguez 23n18) with an additional source in Boiardo,[10] is the celebrated hippogriff of the sorcerer Atlante. This winged mount, "gotten of a Griffeth and a Mare" (4.13.2; ["ch'una giumenta generò d'un grifo" (4.18.2)]), itself a hybrid creature, passes from one rider to another over the course of the *Furioso*. Atlante trains the beast and rides it into battle against his enemies, who, limited to earth-bound transportation, naturally find themselves unable to defeat him; when finally bested in combat by Bradamante, Atlante arranges for the hippogriff to carry off his ward Ruggiero to the far ends of the earth; abandoning Ruggiero, the hippogriff returns to Atlante's care; after himself defeating Atlante, Astolfo, son of the King of England, claims the hippogriff for his own; and Astolfo eventually rides the beast partway on his journey to the moon, home to everything that is lost on earth, to reclaim the love-maddened Orlando's sanity. First appearing in the *Furioso* within the context of knightly combat, the hippogriff is specifically identified as a "destriero" (4.4.7), that is, a warhorse; however, Astolfo's trip to the moon also demonstrates the hippogriff's function as a means of moving between heaven (or at least the heavens) and earth. While Ariosto's winged horse anticipates the fiery steeds of *Paradise Lost* in these capacities, Ariosto is careful to insist that the hippogriff is an earthly creature of flesh and blood: "[n]on finzion d'incanto, come il resto, / ma vero e natural si vedea questo" (4.19.7–8).

Of course, Ariosto's hippogriff, like Milton's angelic steeds, locates itself within and modifies a long-standing tradition of winged warhorses, a tradition whose most immediate representative occurs in Boiardo but which originates in the classical figure of Pegasus. By admitting fiery steeds to heaven, Milton assimilates this entire tradition to his epic universe; yet, as so often with Milton, the assimilation is also a correction, a revision that supersedes—or, more correctly, *precedes*—the originals on which it is ostensibly based. In this case the supersession in question occurs by way of a refinement of substance, a displacement of the coarse material bodies of men and horses by the airy, diaphanous bodies of angels and angelic chargers. One consequence of this shift is to render the mechanics of warfare suspect or even ludicrous; after all, if angelic bodies cannot be wounded or destroyed as ours can, then how can angelic combat signify as heroic behavior? The answer is, only in what we traditionally call a spiritual sense: Milton translates heroism of the body into heroism of the mind. In the process he also realigns traditional models of equine heroism so that they come to represent not physical fortitude but rather sacred inspiration.

Ariostan chivalry falls victim to this realignment, and Milton's recorded references to Ariosto suggest the mixed but largely critical view the English poet took of his Italian predecessor.[11] In *Of Reformation* (1641) Milton translates with approval some verses from *Orlando furioso* denouncing the Donation of Constantine. However, in the very same passage, referring to Astolfo's flight to the moon on the hippogriff's back, Milton describes the episode as "a difficult knot" and adds that Ariosto "feignes" the English knight's meeting on the moon with Saint John: "*Ariosto* of *Ferrara* . . . following the scope of his poem in a difficult knot how to restore *Orlando* his chiefe Hero to his lost senses, brings *Astolfo* the English Knight up into the moone, where S. *John*, as he feignes, met him" (884). As Roy Flannagan observes of the "knot image" here, Milton "does not appear to use it in a complimentary way" (Flannagan 5), especially if we contrast it with his praise of the "sober, plaine, and unaffected stile" of scripture (Milton, *Of Reformation, Riverside Edition* 886). As for Ariosto's feigned meeting between Astolfo and Saint John, the solecism here may simply involve bringing Saint John to the moon. Yet in a broader sense, this error extends a centuries-long tradition of mythic embellishment that confuses the sacred with the profane. Thus the verb "feignes" in *Of Reformation* reemerges in *Paradise Lost* when Milton emphasizes Eve's beauty through a sneering reference to the judgment of Paris:

> *Eve*
> Undeckt, save with her self more lovely fair
> Then Wood-Nymph, or the fairest Goddess feign'd
> Of three that in Mount *Ida* naked strove,
> Stood to entertain her guest from Heav'n.
> (5.379–83)

Here as elsewhere, *Paradise Lost* asserts its unique status among cosmogonies as the sacred original from which other poetic narratives—whether mythic, epic, or chivalric—devolve into self-serving falsehood. The naked pseudo-goddesses of Mount Ida emerge from this comparison as diabolically inspired distortions of Eve's unfallen beauty.

Milton makes the single direct reference to Ariosto's hippogriff within his epic verse in much the same spirit. In book 4 of *Paradise Regain'd* (171), Milton's treatment of the temptation on the mount reaches its climax as Satan, increasingly impatient, seizes Jesus and conveys him by air to the temple of Jerusalem:

> [H]e caught him up, and without wing
> Of *Hippogrif* bore through the Air sublime
> Over the Wilderness and o're the Plain;
> Till underneath them fair *Jerusalem*,
> The holy City lifted high her Towers,
> And higher yet the glorious Temple rear'd
> Her pile.
> (4.541–47)

As in the "fairest goddess feigned" reference, the comparison here is again managed in negative form, once more revealing an elaborate poetic fiction to be a debased imitation of scriptural truth. Satan has no need of hippogriffs or fiery steeds for aerial transportation. Once more Milton's efforts "to spiritualize the heroic poem" (Steadman, *Renaissance Hero* 193) leave the culture of the warhorse in a space of redundancy and anachronism, relevant only in its irrelevance.

Yet, useless as they are for warfare and transportation, Milton's fiery steeds nonetheless abide, deriving a new and singular power from their status as animal figures of divine inspiration. This symbolism may receive its preeminent martial treatment in the chariot of paternal deity, but it also returns in the figures of Pegasean flight that Milton associates with his own poetic and prophetic vocation. Thus the single most famous Miltonic adaptation of Ariosto occurs at the outset of *Paradise Lost*, within just such a vocational context:

> Sing Heav'nly Muse, that on the secret top
> Of *Oreb*, or of *Sinai*, didst inspire
> That Shepherd, who first taught the Chosen Seed,
> . . . .
> . . . I thence
> Invoke thy aid to my adventurous Song,
> That with no middle flight intends to soar
> Above th'*Aonian* Mount, while it pursues
> Things unattempted yet in Prose or Rhime.
>
> (1.6–12)

James H. Sims has remarked that the "allusions [to Ariosto] at both the outset and the close of Milton's companion epics . . . strengthen . . . the impression that heroic flights in Milton's epic[s] resonate with Ariostan associations" (132). In fact, Milton's heroic flights allude to Ariosto while translating heroism into a category of interpretive rather than physical action. Here the figure of Ariosto's winged horse reemerges triumphantly, in places the Italian poet did not provide for it. *Paradise Lost* 1 may echo Ariosto's determination to pursue "cosa non detta in prosa mai né in rima" (1.2.2), but the original context of Ariosto's line includes no equestrian imagery at all, whereas this imagery proves central to Milton's poetic and vatic self-presentation. It appears at least briefly in all four of the invocations to *Paradise Lost*: where book 1 promises to soar "[a]bove th'*Aonian* Mount," book 9 frets over the "intended wing" of the poet's song (9.45), and book 3 describes the poem's opening depiction of Hell as a "flight / Through utter and through middle darkness borne / With other notes than to th'*Orphean* lyre" (3.15–17). However, book 7 renders this language most explicit. There, finished with his account of the war in heaven, Milton implores his muse to bring him back to earth safely, as if he were the mythic rider of a winged mount:

> Return me to my Native Element:
> Least from this flying Steed unrein'd, (as once
> *Bellerophon*, though from a lower Clime)
> Dismounted, on th'*Aleian* Field I fall
> Erroneous there to wander and forlorne.
>
> (7.16–20)

For Milton's heroic poet, as for Milton's heroic Son, the sublime transcendence of divine inspiration is figured in the relationship between horse and rider.

This relationship spells the death of equine character in its Ariostan sense, as exemplified by the ties that bind Rinaldo to Baiardo. If Baiardo is to be a fully fledged literary character, after all, he must demonstrate it most clearly by having a mind of his own, which he displays through calculated acts of disobedience that can be directed even at his own master. The transcendent interspecies harmony of the *Merkabah* offers no space for such discord, and while the Pegasean relation of Milton to his muse images such disagreement in Bellerophon's fall to the Aleian plain, this clearly represents a failure of the author-muse affinity. The Son on his chariot and the poet on his Pegasus are equally rapt in a sacred frenzy that exceeds the boundary of species just as it surpasses the limits of individuated personality. To this extent they mark the annihilation not just of *animal* character but of all character whatsoever. Yet by the same token, the divine transcendence in its generative aspect comprises the beginning of all life and hence the wellspring of all identity, both human and nonhuman. Likewise, as the originary source of all literary inspiration, the heavenly muse marks the point at which the *artificial* individuation of character emerges into possibility. The paradox of Miltonic transcendence, explored early in the poet's career through the swain's self-effacement in "Lycidas," is this: to become oneself one must lose oneself, and to create individual personalities in literature one must accept that the personalities thus created exist only in the realm of illusion.

If this paradox represents Milton's considered response to the problem of literary character for both human and nonhuman beings, it leaves open a secondary question: what of animals *outside* literature? How does the poet evaluate the inner lives of living, breathing nonhuman beings? To what extent does he consider them capable of self-awareness, reason, and experience? Does he regard them, in Tom Regan's phrase, as subjects of a life? Fortunately, Milton has left clear indications of his views on this score, and while they lead away from our chapter-long fixation on horses, they bear brief mention here nonetheless.

While still at Cambridge in his mid-twenties, Milton discussed the intelligence of animals as part of his final university prolusion, an oration titled "In Defense of Learning," which he delivered in the chapel of Christ's College during the summer of 1632. There, as he builds to his peroration, the young poet peremptorily dismisses the figure of Ignorance from the company of human beings, bidding her to "throw off her human shape, and walk no longer erect, and betake her to the beasts" (872). Indeed, he then notes in instant self-revision, even the beasts are too good for the company of such a figure:

> To the beasts, did I say? they will surely refuse to receive so infamous a guest, at any rate if they are either endowed with some kind of inferior reasoning power, as many maintain, or guided by some powerful instinct, enabling them to practice the Arts, or something resembling the Arts, among themselves. For Plutarch tells us that in the pursuit of game, dogs show some knowledge of dialectic, and if they chance to come to cross-roads, they obviously make use of a disjunctive syllogism. Aristotle points out that the nightingale in some sort instructs her offspring in the principles of music. Almost every animal is its own physician, and many of them have given valuable lessons in medicine to man; the Egyptian ibis teaches us the value of purgatives, the hippopotamus of blood-letting. . . . The beasts are too wise to admit Ignorance to their fellowship and society; they will force her to a lower station. (872)

The examples of animal intelligence Milton cites here are only part of a larger list; I have eliminated several more for brevity's sake. Still, the ones noted above, drawn from Plutarch, Aristotle, Cicero, and Pliny, respectively, reveal the young poet to be an intent student of natural history, particularly as it bears on the human-animal divide. Plutarch's argument about dogs and dialectic makes for an intriguing case in point. Derived originally from the *Moralia*, it enjoyed a revival of sorts in early modern England; indeed, seventeen years before Milton mentioned it in his prolusion, it had inspired a formal debate, conducted at Cambridge University before King James I, concerning "whether dogs could make syllogismes" (Ball 23).[12] As an avid hunter and dog fancier, James could hardly fail to enjoy the topic, and in the event he entered into the discussion on the side of the dogs, instancing behavior in his own hunting hounds that attested to their reasoning ability. Thus, Plutarch's argument marks a rare instance of philosophical agreement between Milton, the defender of regicide, and James I, the exponent of divine-right absolutism.

The older Milton did not abandon the view that animals could reason. It reappears prominently on two separate occasions in *Paradise Lost*. Eve, confronted by the anomaly of a talking serpent, raises the question of animal reason when she distinguishes between language and its "sense":

> What may this mean? Language of Man pronounc't
> By Tongue of Brute, and human sense exprest?
> The first at lest of these I thought deni'd
> To Beasts, whom God on their Creation-Day
> Created mute to all articulat sound;
> The latter I demurre, for in thir looks
> Much reason, and in thir actions oft appeers.
>
> (9.553–59)

For Eve, the question remains open: while she accepts that animals are unable to communicate their intelligence through language—at least not "Language of Man"—she nonetheless understands their behavior, as in the case of syllogistic hunting dogs, to provide evidence of the capacity for reason. And if Eve remains agnostic on the subject of animal intelligence, God is a firm believer. When the newly created Adam asks for a companion to enrich his solitude, the Son offers him company of a cross-species nature:

> What call'st thou solitude, is not the Earth
> With various living creatures, and the Aire
> Replenisht, and all these at thy command
> To come and play before thee, know'st thou not
> Thir language and thir wayes, they also know,
> And reason not contemptibly; with these
> Find pastime, and beare rule; thy Realm is large.
>
> (8.369–75)

Nonhuman animals may be deprived of "Language of Man," but according to the Son they exercise their own native linguistic skills, presumably of an inferior nature, which Adam shares. Adam goes on to argue, to the Son's satisfaction, that animal intelligence is insufficient for full human companionship, that he, Adam, needs "fellowship . . . / . . . fit to participate / *All* rational delight" (8.389–91; italics mine). However, this argument does nothing to contest the Son's initial claim that other animals "reason not contemptibly." Indeed, for both Adam and the Son, the species barrier remains a distinction of degree, not of kind, and to this extent Milton's thinking on the subject remains conservative throughout his career. The Cartesian cogito, with its absolute division between humanity and all other forms of earthly life, finds no place in the universe of *Paradise Lost*. Instead, Milton's paradise still bears the imprint of earlier notions of species difference, derived partly from skeptics such as Plutarch and partly from the Aristotelian taxonomic tradition, in which animals possess *ethos* [character], and in which this character enables them to reason, to communicate, and to conduct personal relationships not only with each other but also, in limited ways, with human beings.

To summarize, then, the Miltonic rejection of animal character, although more programmatic and consistent than Shakespeare's, draws its intellectual inspiration from the same lineage of skeptical philosophers (in Milton's case particularly Plutarch; in Shakespeare's, Montaigne) that looms large in the earlier poet. However, as with Shakespeare (who, of course, precedes Descartes by a couple of decades), so with Milton the denial of animal character does not mark an investment in the revised skepticism of the Cartesian moment, which posits an absolute distinction between human and nonhuman species that fails to leave its imprint on *Paradise Lost* or elsewhere in the Milton canon. Instead, Milton's problems with animal character derive not from new philosophical efforts to theorize the species boundary but from his dissatisfaction with the politics of feudal hierarchy and the aesthetics of courtly romance. These he regards as compromising the dignity of God's creation in the service of a literature distinguished by its intellectual poverty, preciosity, and self-serving dishonesty. As an antidote to this literary tradition, Milton conceives a model of epic that still leaves open the possibility for nonhuman life to retain personality and agency: both in a diminished way, within the realm of created things; and more important by far, within the transcendent and eternal space of divine inspiration, beyond and before difference, in which "God shall be All in All" (*Paradise Lost* 3.341). However, neither of these contexts proves congenial to animal characters such as Baiardo or their privileged human masters.

Tantum Pellis et Ossa

Of course, Baiardo's legacy does not end with Ariosto, nor are Shakespeare and Milton the only later writers to allude to it. Indeed, Milton derives his model of sacred poetry from an author who explicitly revisited the Rinaldo-Baiardo dyad within his own work. Torquato Tasso not only bequeathed to Milton a theory of heroic verse aimed at producing "a serious, dignified poem which would instruct and improve its readers, using an historical basis and a grand Christian theme" (Brand 251); he also began his career by returning to the subject matter of the *Quatre fils Aymon* in his own juvenile romance, the *Rinaldo* (1562). Here Tasso opens his poem by providing the backstory for the Rinaldo-Baiardo relationship. The young knight, eager for fame, learns of a mighty stallion, once belonging to Amadis of Gaul, which dwells in a secluded cave. There, gripped by a sorcerer's spell, the horse resists all efforts to tame him and indeed kills those unfortunate enough to try. Yet it is prophesied that he awaits the hand of one descended from his original master, a knight who will dispel the enchantment that controls him and for whom alone he will grow mild and obedient (*Rinaldo* 1.283–326). In the event, of course, Rinaldo proves to be the knight in question, and thus Tasso's early poem begins by nodding in the direction of the Alexander romances, in which Bucephalus typically eats human flesh and refuses to submit to any hand other than that of Alexander.[13]

Tasso's early work retains other motifs from the chivalric romances as well, albeit in a subdued way. For instance, when Rinaldo confronts another knight who has acquired Baiardo, the narrator observes that he, Rinaldo, "knew / No foreign hand could e'er, by force or slight, / Bayardo lead against his lord to fight" (10.480–81; ["colui non mai potrebbe / spingere il suo Baiardo a fargli oltraggio" (10.70.3–4)]), a reference to the topos of equine disobedience that falls short of actual demonstration. When reunited with his master, Tasso's Baiardo displays signs of greeting drawn straight from Ariosto but without the Ariostan "gesto umano":

His courser's back he [Rinaldo] press'd—the courser, proud
To bear his master, neigh'd with joy aloud,

And every sign of gratulation show'd.
Thus oft we see beside his patron stand
A trusty dog beneath the fondling hand.

(10.510–14)

[. . . [S]u 'l caro destrier d'un salto ascese.

Quello lieto il riceve, e del su' amore
mostra con l'annitrir segno evidente,
e con mille altri aperti indizii fuore
scopre il piacer che dentro 'l petto sente:
così fa can fidele al suo signore,
il qual di lusingarlo usi sovente,
ch'é d'intorno gli salta, e con la bocca
e con la coda dolce il bacia e tocca.]

(10.73.8–74.8)

John Hoole's eighteenth-century translation does no justice here to Tasso's original, which describes in detail how the trusty dog in question often flatters his master by dancing about him, kissing and brushing him with mouth and tail. Such language recalls Baiardo's greeting to Angelica in *Orlando furioso* I (75.2–4): "con umile sembiante e gesto umano, / come intorno al padrone il can saltella, / che sia duo giorni o tre stato lontano." However, Tasso's sense of decorum, like Sir John Harington's in his translation of Ariosto, leads him to erase the earlier poet's equation of horse behavior to human behavior while expanding on the subsequent comparison of horse to dog. The bond between rider and steed no longer challenges the barrier between human and nonhuman species.

In the *Gerusalemme liberata* (1581) the species barrier widens into a gaping gulf. Here, as Tasso sets himself the task of composing a new kind of heroic poem, he also creates a new kind of hero: a second Rinaldo, son of Bertoldo d'Este and descendant of the first Rinaldo's sister, Bradamante. This new Rinaldo not only forges a link between the chivalric lineage of earlier romances and Tasso's own historical moment; the son of Bertoldo also in effect supersedes the standards of heroism embodied in his earlier namesake. When it comes to equestrian relations, the difference could hardly be more pronounced. Arrived before the gates of Jerusalem in canto 3 of the *Liberata*, Tasso's new Rinaldo enters into battle with marvelous prowess, only to see his exploits frustrated by a horse malfunction:

Tancred and young *Rinaldo* breake the presse,
They bruise the helme, and pearse the seuenfold targe,
. . . .
Argantes selfe, feld at one single blow,
Inglorious, bleeding lay, on earth full low:
Nor had the boaster euer risen more,
But that *Rinaldoes* horse eu'n then downe fell,
And with the fall his leg opprest so sore,
That for a space there must he algates dwell.
                    (*Godfrey of Bulloigne* 3.41.3–42.4)

[Tancredi e Rinaldo il cerchio han rotto
benché d'uomini denso e d'armi fosse.
. . . .
Argante, Argante stesso, ad un grand'urto
di Rinaldo abbattuto, a pena è surto.

Né sorgea forse, ma in quel punto stesso
al figliuol di Bertoldo il destrier cade;
e restandogli sotto il piedo oppresso,
convien ch'indi a ritrarlo alquanto bade.]
                    (3.41.3–42.4)

Thus awkwardly immobilized, Rinaldo remains sidelined for seven long stanzas of mortal combat until, as the skirmish reaches its end, the narrator finally remembers him: "But now *Rinaldo* from the earth vp lept, / Where by the leg his steed had long him kept" ["Ma già Rinaldo, avendo il piè sottratto / al giacente destrier, s'era qui tratto" (3.49.7–8)].

It is a disconcerting image to attach to Tasso's hero and (for want of a better phrase) wholly out of character with the original dyad of Rinaldo and Baiardo. And while Tasso may not deploy it in an entirely comical or antiheroic vein, it certainly provides occasion for satirical laughter on its reappearance in 1605, in the first part of Miguel de Cervantes' *Don Quixote*. There, as Cervantes' narrative opens with an account of its romance-addled hero, we learn that Quixote is himself an avid admirer of the Rinaldo legends:

He used to say the Cid Ruy Diaz was a very good knight but that he was not to be compared with the Knight of the Burning

Sword. . . . He thought more of Bernardo del Carpio because at Roncesvalles he slew Roland in spite of enchantments. . . . He approved highly of the giant Morgante, because, although of the giant breed which is always arrogant and ill-mannered, he alone was affable and well-bred. But above all he admired Reinaldos of Montalbán, especially when he saw him sallying forth from his castle and robbing everyone he met, and when beyond the seas he stole that image of Mohammed which, as his history says, was entirely of gold. (1.1, 27)

Hence the irony grows all the greater when Quixote's own maiden efforts as a knight-errant recall not the original Rinaldo of Ariosto and the *Quatre fils* but rather Tasso's updated hero of the same name. Having just sat vigil over his armor and received the honor of knighthood, Don Quixote encounters a crew of silk merchants on the road from Toledo to Murcia. When he demands that they do homage to the beauty of his lady Dulcinea and one of the merchants responds with less than the requisite enthusiasm, Quixote prepares for battle:

[H]e charged with leveled lance against the one who had spoken, with such fury and fierceness that, if luck had not contrived that Rocinante should stumble midway and come down, it would have gone hard with the rash trader. Down went Rocinante, and over went his master, rolling along the ground for some distance. When he tried to rise he could not do so, being encumbered with lance, shield, spurs, helmet, and the weight of his old armor.

"Fly not, cowards and caitiffs!" he kept saying, all the while struggling to get up. "Stay, for not by my fault, but my horse's, am I stretched here." (1.4, 43)

Thus immobilized, Quixote receives a sound thrashing from the merchants, but he eventually collects himself and goes his way, believing "that this was a real knight-errant's mishap and . . . entirely the fault of his horse" (1.4, 44).

Both Rinaldo and Baiardo figure in *Don Quixote* as standards of comparison for the behavior of Cervantes' hero. As noted, Quixote is addicted to the romances of Rinaldo. As for Baiardo, his name comes up in part 2 of *Don Quixote* (1615) as Sancho Panza and his master await the arrival of an enchanted wooden horse endowed with the power of flight. When Sancho

asks the enchanted horse's name, he receives in response a recusatory catalog of the famous horseflesh of romance: "His name . . . is not the same as
Bellerophon's horse that was called Pegasus, or Alexander the Great's, called
Bucephalus, or Orlando the Mad's, the name of which was Brigliador, nor
Bayard, the horse of Reinaldos of Montalbán, nor Frontino like Ruggiero's,
nor Bootes or Peritoa, as they say the horses of the sun were called, nor is
he called Orelia, like the horse on which the unfortunate Rodrigo, the last
king of the Goths, rode to the battle where he lost his life and his kingdom"
(2.40, 643). Amid this negative inventory, Sancho has the temerity to include
his own master's horse: "I'll bet . . . that since they haven't given him [the
wooden horse] any of these famous names . . . , they haven't given him the
name of my master's Rocinante, which for being apt surpasses all that have
been mentioned" (2.40, 643). Of course, the aptness of Rocinante's name derives from its recollection of the noun *rocín* [workhorse], which in turn signals
the immense conceptual distance that separates Cervantes' parodic narrative
from the romances that inspired it and that likewise distinguishes Cervantes'
parodic figures from the earlier literary characters, both human and animal,
to which they respond. Rocinante, we have already been told, is a "nag,"
"*tantum pellis et ossa*," with "cracked hoofs and more blemishes than the steed
of Gonela," and yet in his master's eyes he "surpassed . . . the Bucephalus of
Alexander or the Babieca of the Cid" (1.1, 28). The gulf separating Quixote's
perception of Rocinante from the horse's actual condition is identical to the
space dividing Ariosto's romance from Cervantes' satire. Within this space
the idea of Baiardo—of the horse as a heroic and rational agent—vanishes
from the dominant European literary tradition.

Chapter 2

The Cardinal's Parrot

Michael Randall has recently remarked that symbolic animals, like real ones, "must adapt to their environment or die" (126). This melancholy principle is well illustrated by the history of the European Reformation, whose cultural climate changes proved sudden and drastic enough to endanger even the most resilient of symbolic species. Juliana Schiesari, for instance, has noted how Henri III's fetish for toy *chiens de Lyon,* lapdogs like those adored barely two centuries earlier by Chaucer's silly but benign Prioress,[1] could exemplify, for Agrippa D'Aubigné, the collective financial, spiritual, and erotic vices of the Catholic Valois court (Schiesari passim). *Sic transit gloria animalium mundi.*

My theme here is similar to Schiesari's, although I focus on the fate of a different symbolic species, one that has, perhaps surprisingly, received considerable attention of late. Since 1999 the representational history of parrots has inspired a monograph, an essay collection, various articles and book chapters, and at least one academic conference.[2] Here I want to revisit the subject briefly in order to place it in the context of Reformation polemic. It should be noted, first, that by the late fifteenth century parrots had been installed in various ways in the institutional culture of the papacy; second, that Reformation controversialists take advantage of this association to the disparagement of the pope and his followers; third, that this satirical move coincides with—and arguably helps inaugurate—a much broader shift in the dominant meaning of parrots within the contexts of European literary and visual representation; and fourth, that this shift entails various consequences for Renaissance theories of imitation, education, and the relation between humanity and the natural world. Among these consequences, the one of greatest moment for this present study is the parrot's own metamorphosis, both as a literary figure and as a cultural presence, into an entirely new species. By the time Renaissance polemicists and satirists are through with this bird, it has ceased to be the sentient, articulate, and miraculous figure of much medieval discourse and has become instead what it remains to the present: a conventional emblem of mindless iteration. In effect, the wondrous parrot-as-character of the Middle Ages is flattened into the mindless prattling bird of modern representation, and this latter figure, in turn, interferes even now with efforts to conduct serious research into the mental capacities of psittacine species.

Before pursuing this argument in detail, however, a note of caution. While I intend to trace the development of a particular network of negative and satirical parrot associations in early modern literature and art, it is not my aim to suggest that these represent western culture's first appropriation of parrots for either negative or satirical purposes. The record on this point is too lengthy and complex to rehearse in a single chapter, and it has already been dealt with elsewhere. Suffice it to say that parrots are objects of satirical denigration in western culture at least as early as Ovid's *Amores* 2.6, with its mock elegy on the death of Corinna's pet rose-ringed parakeet (c. 20 B.C.), and that from their earliest entry into western cultural awareness, these birds have been subject to conflicting representational impulses that seek to depict them as exotic and miraculous while simultaneously exposing them to various kinds of ridicule and contempt. The following will explore a specific historical manifestation of this duality through description of the emergence of parrots as an emblematic (and literal) appurtenance of medieval Catholicism and by accounting for their negative counterappropriation in the work of reform-minded writers of the sixteenth century. As limited in scope as this tale may be, it embraces a dauntingly interdisciplinary range of materials, and it helps to account for the special vigor with which parrots have been assimilated to the language of western satire and invective over the past five centuries. It is also, to my knowledge, a story never told before in continuous form.

Princely in a Cage

As has been shown elsewhere, the conceptual association between popes and parrots developed in the Middle Ages, apparently through transference from the conventions of Greco-Roman encomiastic verse.[3] Martial exemplifies those conventions in his epigram 14.73, a famous distich supposedly uttered by a parrot in praise of Emperor Domitian: "A parrot, I shall learn from you the names of others; this I have learned to say by myself: 'Caesar, hail!'"

["Psittacus a vobis aliorum nomina discam. / hoc didici per me dicere: 'Caesar have'"]. Juxtapositions of this sort, which connect parrots to royal patrons by virtue of the former's rarity and seemingly miraculous ability to speak, translate easily into the register of papal anecdote. Thus in the late twelfth century Alexander Neckam's *De Naturis Rerum* (c. 1180) can describe parrots as a particular object of papal admiration while relating pontiff to bird through a typically medieval false etymology: "The parrot is vulgarly called the popinjay, that is, noble or princely creature in a cage. . . . Alternatively this is understood as marvelous in a cage. For the parrot is a typical object of the Pope's admiration" ["Psittacus . . . vulgo dicitur papagabio, id est, principalis seu nobilis gabio. . . . Vel interpretatur mirabilis gabio. Papae enim admirantis est" (1.36)].[4] About fifty years later Thomas of Cantimpré's *De Rerum Natura* (c. 1240) revisits this association in ways that make clear the transference from emperor to pope:

> The parrot . . . has by nature a voice with which it greets emperors. It so happened that when Charlemagne was traveling through the wilderness of Greece he was met by some parrots, who greeted him, as it were, in the Greek language, saying: Hail, Emperor. Later events were to prove the truth of this expression, almost like a prophecy, because while at that time Charles was only king of France, in the subsequent period he became Emperor of the Holy Roman Empire. There is also a story in the life of Pope Leo, that a certain nobleman had a talking parrot, which he sent to Pope Leo as a present. When the parrot was on its way there and met passers-by, it cried out: I am going to the Pope, I am going to the Pope. And as soon as it reached the presence of the Pope, it cried out: Pope Leo, hail! At this the Pope was rightly delighted, and often afterwards, as a relaxation from the labors of the day, he would talk to the parrot.

> [Psitacus . . . habet quandam vocem naturaliter, qua salutare videtur cesares. Unde factum est, ut erranti Karolo Magno per deserta Grecie obvie essent aves psytaci et quasi Greca lingua salutaverunt eum clamantes: Imperator vale. Quarum verbum instar cuiusdam prophecie enuncciacione complevit eventus, quia cum tunc eo tempore tantam rex Gallie Karolus esset, sequenti tempore Romanorum factus est imperator. Sed et in vita papa Leonis legitur, cum enim quedam nobilem avem psytacum abilem ad loquendum, Leoni pape

eam pro exenium misit, que cum adhuc esset in via et homines ob-
vios haberet, clamabat avis: Ad papam vado, ad papam vado. Hec
mora cum introiret ad papam clamavit: Leo papa vale. Que iure
multum exhylaratus papa quasi pro recreaciones post labores cot-
tidianos confabulacione psytaci sepius utebatur.] (5.109)

In addition to such tales, parrots acquired further connections to medieval
Catholicism through a variety of incidental traditions. They were said to be
born in the earthly paradise, to inhabit the biblical Mount Gilboa, and to be
so pure and fastidious of behavior that they could not tolerate contact with
water.[5] They were affiliated, by virtue of this purity, with the Virgin Mary.[6]
In addition, they figured in manuscript illustrations of sacred subject matter,
while also providing a decorative motif for clerical garments such as the "ves-
timentum album, braudatum cum compass', et infra compass' papyngays"
that Henry Snayth dedicated to the high altar at York Minster in his will
dated February 5, 1380 (Surtees Society 111).

These symbolic associations have been established by previous scholarship. It remains here to document their amplification in the century leading
up to Luther's theses. During this period, parrots become, if anything, more
firmly entrenched in the papacy than ever, for during the Quattrocento the
relationship between popes and parrots, which was hitherto largely mythic
and anecdotal, acquires an increasingly important material dimension. This
development coincides with the heroic phase of European naval exploration;
with the conquest of the Canary Islands, begun in 1402 and completed some
fifty years later, Europeans encountered for the first time the most intelligent and articulate of psittaciformes, the African grey parrot (Juniper 40).
(Before that, only certain Indian species—in particular the Alexandrine and
rose-ringed parakeet—had been well known to Europeans.) As the 1400s
progressed and Portuguese explorers established direct trading ties with sub-
Saharan Africa, these birds became increasingly visible and popular among
European collectors. Reaching the Senegal River in 1455, Alvise da Cadamosto
devoted a chapter of his African travel narrative to the numerous parrots encountered there, including the Senegal and Cape species (47–48); arriving at
the Gambia River a year later, Diogo Gomes was likewise impressed by the
local parrots (Cadamosto 97). Within forty years the post-Columbian rush
of American exploration introduced the Old World to a wide range of additional psittacine species that also served as lucrative and fashionable imports.[7]
Specimens from South and East Asia grew more available as well.

The result was a rapid shift in Europe's cultural engagement with parrots. During the 1400s, as they became subject to increased study and importation, they assumed a correspondingly prominent place as objects of display in aristocratic households and menageries. Given the sacred associations that these birds had already acquired in the preceding centuries, it seems in retrospect inevitable that the papacy would have lent particular energy to such a trend; in any case, that is just what happened. Gustave Loisel, author of what remains the best available history of European menageries, declares that the popes of the Quattrocento "suivirent le mouvement general de grand luxe qui s'étendait peu à peu alors dans toute l'Italie," and that this inclination led early on to a fetish for "animaux d'appartement, des oiseaux, surtout des perroquets" (1:202). Pope Martin V (Oddone Colonna), for instance, licensed payment on March 15, 1418, of one florin to Peter Stoyss and Johann Holzengott for attending to "the parrot of His Holiness with its cage" while the pope traveled from place to place (Gebhart 178–79). Pope Pius II (Enea Silvio de Piccolomini), who taught his parrot to recite Latin verses, similarly authorized payment of five ducats on April 20, 1462, to "master Giachetto, keeper of the parrot" (Gebhart 179). On December 4 of the same year he paid a merchant named Gabazzo for fabric to be fashioned into a cover for the bird's cage, and two weeks later, on December 17, he disbursed three ecus to a master joiner named Domenico, from Florence, for boards and nails to be used in repairing the bird's cage (Gebhart 179). Pope Sixtus IV (Francesco della Rovere) maintained a papal parrot as well, and under Leo X (Giovanni de Medici) the Vatican menagerie achieved its most formidable development, including, among numerous other beasts, "molti papagalli di diversi colori" (Vasari 6:135).

Of course, the popes were not unique in their psittacophilia, although their unique position within Christendom, coupled with the old medieval associations, lent their mania a particular prominence. By 1511 Jakob Fugger of Augsburg was sending African grey parrots as gifts to the bishop of Breslau, while as early as 1458 the city council of Nuremberg could think it wise to present the archbishop of Mainz with a parrot as an official civic gift. The bird in question, purchased from one Anton Baumgartner, cost twenty-five florins, with another seven florins expended on the gilding of the birdcage and a further nine schillings, four hellers going for a cage cover; the total expense of the gift, including the costs of delivery, was fifty pfunds, one schilling, and eleven hellers (Loisel 1:232). Moreover, the Nuremberg magistrates were at it again two years later, this time presenting a parrot worth twenty-five florins to the queen of Bohemia (Loisel 1:232). And while magnificence may have been the duty of the prince, it did not always elicit universal admiration. An inventory of possessions and expenses drawn up on September 25, 1403, for Duke Louis of Orleans mentions a parrot, purchased at Avignon, which cost fifty ecus; parrot food for two ecus; two more ecus for transporting the bird from Avignon to Pont-Saint-Esprit; yet another six ecus for carrying the bird thence to Lyon; and finally two ecus more for a "drap vert gay pour couvrir la cage dudit papegault" (Champollion-Figeac 252). As one historian notes, "It is no wonder if such prodigality gave birth to rumors, spread among the public, that the tax of seventeen thousand [ecus] levied by the princes [of Charles V] had been entirely dissipated by the Duke of Orleans" ["Il n'y a donc pas de s'étonner si toutes ces prodigalités donnèrent lieu a bruit, alors répandu dans le public, que la taille des dix-sept millions (d'ecus) levée par les princes (de Charles V) avait été dissipée entierement par le duc d'Orleans" (Champollion-Figeac 253)].

In pursuing his passion for parrots, Louis d'Orleans set the trend for further members of the French nobility as well. In 1439 his royal nephew Charles VII, who already maintained an aviary at the Hotel des Tournelles, installed an octagonal cage at the Hotel Saint Pol to house his "papé-gaut," which facility came to be known as "la cage au pape-gaut du Roi" (Sauval 2:282). By the first decade of the sixteenth century Margaret of Austria, who had spent ten years at the court of Louis XI betrothed to the dauphin who would become Charles VIII, found herself acting as regent of the Netherlands and guardian of the future Emperor Charles V. In this capacity she established, in her palace at Malines, a menagerie that housed many animals, among them a parrot of which she was most fond. The bird in question fell prey to a palace dog while Margaret was away on a prolonged visit to Austria, and upon her return to the Low Countries she mourned it extravagantly. The most prominent consequence of her bereavement may be the two *Epîtres de L'Amant Vert* composed by Jean Lemaire de Belges in the persona of the unfortunate fowl, the former purporting to explain the parrot's demise as an act of despair prompted by Margaret's departure for Austria (besotted by grief, the bird precipitates itself into the dog's jaws), the latter recounting the bird's experiences in the afterlife. Lemaire's work has been characterized as "frivolous and decadent" (Hatton), and despite recent efforts to rehabilitate it, one may still feel that these elaborate verse epistles on the death of a noblewoman's pet parrot reveal a lot about the self-indulgence and silliness of the sixteenth-century courtly aesthetic. Among other classically inspired excesses, Lemaire makes serious use of Ovid's parrot elegy in the *Amores*, offering a detailed account of the "volucrum locus . . . piarum" (2.6.51) to which Ovid there consigns Corinna's pet bird. Moreover, Lemaire follows Dante in giving his Amant Vert a guide through this avian Elysium: a "cler esprit pourprin et rubicunde" (2.352) that had been, in life, the pet parrot of Margaret's mother, Marie de Bourgogne. Where a generous understanding can find Lemaire's verse "charming" (Sells 48), a more censorious—one might say, in the broad sense, a reformist—sensibility could just as easily discern preciosity and the waste of a good education.

Of course, Margaret of Austria was no pope, any more than was Louis d'Orleans. However, through her ward, the future Emperor Charles V, she arguably exerted indirect influence over the fate of the papacy during the early years of reformation, and her taste in companion animals bespeaks an ethos of conspicuous consumption common to both sacred and secular nobles of the early sixteenth century. In this respect, indeed, popes and princes seem to have egged each other on; the latter sought to compete with the papal menageries by constructing private zoos of their own, and at the same time, knowing that such gifts would find favor, they contributed choice animals to the papal collections. This pattern reached its apotheosis virtually on the eve of the Reformation, in the celebrated papal embassy of Tristão da Cunha, who arrived in Rome on March 20, 1514, to convey the respects of King Manuel I of Portugal to the newly elected Pope Leo X. Da Cunha's mission sought to boost his king's prestige by flaunting the wealth of the Portuguese East India trade, and Manuel had chosen exotic animals as the principal medium for doing so. The centerpiece of the embassy was, of course, the famed elephant Hanno, who—recalling Thomas of Cantimpré's tale of a parrot and an earlier Pope Leo—inspired amazement by kneeling before the pope and trumpeting "three great barks" of salutation (Bedini 52). However, Hanno was by no means the only exotic animal Manuel presented to the new pontiff. Accompanying the elephant were a cheetah, two leopards, a Persian horse, Indian dogs and fowl, and "numerous parrots," these last displayed in cages drawn by mules and bringing up the rear of da Cunha's formal entry procession into Rome (Bedini 28, 48).

If parrots had ceased by 1514 to be central to such a spectacle, that is because they had already proved sufficiently popular to be well assimilated into European courtly circles. Twelve years after da Cunha's mission, Gonzalo Fernández de Oviedo remarks in the *Sumario* of his *General and Natural History of the Indies* that "so many species [of parrot] have been carried to Spain, it is hardly worth while to take time to describe them here" (65). By the first quarter of the sixteenth century they had become a standard piece of the era's cultural furniture, and in the process they acquired specific associations: with wealth and luxury; with the secular nobility; with Catholic traditions and practices; and with the papal court. Inevitably these associations proved symbiotic; before he became Pope Leo X, Giovanni de Medici had been raised in Florence as the second son of Lorenzo the Magnificent, in surroundings that included the splendid Medici family menagerie. Toward the end of the sixteenth century another member of the same family, Catherine de Medici, assembled a menagerie at the Tuileries and Louvre before instigating that most traumatic event of the French Wars of Religion, the Saint Bartholomew's Day Massacre. Catherine kept monkeys and parrots at Saint-Germain, and as early as 1558 she is on record for paying six sols to a boy who had brought the parrot of a certain "dame de Beauvais" there (Cimber 9:116). By July 1576 her favorite son, Henri III, had supplemented her collection of exotic animals with a further large consignment of monkeys, toy dogs (presumably the *chiens de Lyon* that so exercised D'Aubigné), and parrots (L'Estoile 1:137).

The story does not end there, for on the night of January 20, 1583, the king dreamed that the beasts of his menagerie threw themselves upon him in order to devour him. The next morning, still trembling from his vision and "having attended holy service, very devoutly, at the monastery of the Bon-Hommes at Nigeon, . . . he returned to the Louvre and with an arquebus slew the lions, bears, bulls, and other such beasts that he raised to fight his dogs" ["après avoir fait ses Pasques et ses prières et dévotions, bien dévotement, au couvent des Bons-Hommes a Nigeon, . . . s'en revinst au Louvre, où arrivé il fist tuer à coups de harquebuzes les lions, ours, taureaux et autres semblables bestes qu'il souloit nourrir pour combattre avec les dogues" (L'Estoile, 2:99)]. One assumes that the royal parrots escaped this slaughter, but even so, the anecdote deserves mention here for its linkage of the king's exotic animals to his religious fervor and capacity for bloodshed. In effect, Henri's degenerate extravagance interacts with his paranoia to produce an animal massacre conducted, like the carnage of Saint Bartholomew's Day, under the auspices of Catholic ritual. Indeed, the bond between parrots and aggressive Catholicism extended even to early Stuart England, where another Medici princess, Henrietta Maria, kept parrots under the supervision of her groom of the chamber, Richard Scutt (Ravelhofer 236). Barbara Ravelhofer declares that "[t]hese rare birds would have been associated with her [that is, Henrietta Maria]" (236), which means that they would likely also have been associated

Figure 1. Jan van Eyck, *Virgin with Canon van der Paele*, 1436. Stedelijke Musea, Bruges. © Lukas–Art in Flanders VZW.

with the queen's notorious efforts to encourage a return to Catholicism in her adopted land.

Elsewhere the connection between parrots and papacy gained iconographic and architectural reinforcement. Leo X commissioned Giovanni da Udine to decorate certain of the Vatican apartments with figures, including parrots, drawn from his menagerie. (In a fit of reformist zeal, Pope Paul IV (Giovanni Carafa) caused these rooms to be painted over [Vasari 6:135–36].) A century earlier Pisanello had included parrots among the designs he executed while studying the papal menageries (Todorow 190). Moreover, the Cortile del Belvedere, which housed the papal zoo during the early 1500s, rapidly became one of Rome's landmarks; in 1510 Francesco Albertini remarked, "In the quarter called the Belvedere . . . are . . . groves containing beasts and birds, along with gardens and avenues, in which spots people may wander and disport themselves for refreshment" ["In loco, qui Belvedere dicitur, . . . [s]unt . . . nemora ferarum et avium cum viridiis et hortulis, quibus in locis homines solatii causa vagari debaccharique possunt" (38–39)]. In this context the infinitive "debacchari" makes for a revealing lexical choice. Albertini clearly means it as a playful bit of humanist erudition, but to later, Protestant ears it can only have been an ill phrase, a vile phrase, right in its very wrongness.

As these developments in design and construction helped to affiliate the papacy with exotic beasts, including parrots, a further bond of association evolved through the conventions of medieval Mariolatry as reflected by the visual arts. As already noted, parrots had achieved a symbolic identification with the Virgin Mary by the fifteenth century; thenceforward they began to figure in sacred iconography on a fairly regular basis. There appear to be two separate but interrelated regional traditions here, one located in northern Europe and the other in Italy. The former is well represented by a series of works that include Jan Van Eyck's *Virgin with Canon van der Paele* (1436; see Figure 1), Martin Schongauer's *Madonna with Parrot* (c. 1474; see Figure 2), and Hans Baldung Grien's *Madonna with Parrot* (c. 1528; see Figure 3). Of these, Van Eyck's painting offers a particularly rich scene of fifteenth-century splendor: Mary, clad in a blue tunic and scarlet cloak, each with embroidered hems, sits on an elaborately carved throne, her invisible feet resting on an intricately knotted carpet that resides, in turn, on a floor of patterned marble. She is surrounded by the figures of George van der Paele, secular canon of Saint Donatian's in Bruges, and his patron Saint George on the viewer's right, with Saint Donatian standing to the left. This last figure is

Figure 2. Martin Schongauer (1445–1491), *The Madonna with the Parrot*, c. 1474. Engraving, 15.5 x 10.7 cm. Fine Arts Museum of San Francisco, gift of Mrs. Philip N. Lilienthal, Hillsborough, California, A010020.

Figure 3. Hans Baldung Grien (1484–1545), *Madonna with Parrot*, c. 1528.
Germanisches Nationalmuseum, Nuremberg, Germany. Photograph: Scala/
Art Resource, NY.

rendered with great sumptuousness, "in full pontificals, a mitre with lappets, a cope, with matching vestments underneath," as well as "gloves with pontifical rings" and "a processional cross with its vexillum attached" (Monnas 149). The bishop's cope, done in "brilliant blue velvet, voided and brocaded with gold," is "a magnificent thing" (Monnas 149). In the event this rich clerical garb seems more than incidental to the painting's theme, for as a whole *Virgin with Canon van der Paele* reflects its patron's "corporate ecclesiastical orientation" (Harbison 59). When he commissioned this work, van der Paele was living in wealthy retirement in Bruges, but he had spent most of his career in Rome, as a scribe to the papal curia. While there, he had collected a series of lucrative benefices at the hands of a series of popes.

Canon van der Paele kneels, clutching a book of devotions and staring off demurely across the picture plane. Mary, on the other hand, sits in state, dandling the Christ child on her right knee. The infant extends both his hands into the very center of the composition, where Mary's left hand intersects them. In his left fist Christ clutches a nosegay; in his right, adopting a highly unnatural pose, is a rose-ringed parakeet. Both Jesus and Mary direct their gazes toward the kneeling canon, and the curvature of the parrot's entire body reflects this alignment. Taken together mother, child, and bird form a configuration with Trinitarian overtones, centered on the green form of the parakeet Paraclete.

Schongauer's and Baldung's images, on the other hand, offer less opulence and more intimacy, but in Baldung's case at least, the resulting shift arguably reflects tensions in the nature of post-Reformation iconography. Linda Hults's account of the painting makes this point most cogently:

> Here the parrot, an old symbol of virginity, indicates that the work should ostensibly express the purity of Mary. But the combined effect of certain details presents us not with a vision of innocence, but with a quasi-erotic situation. Mary, posed alluringly and glancing out at us from almond-shaped eyes, holds her hand to call attention to her bared breast. A parrot nibbles at her jeweled neck. . . . The child's puckered mouth rests against her nipple. We are struck simultaneously and equally with the remote ideality of the image, the sense of a refined, elegant, and distant world, and by the pointedness of the sensual details. (52)

Baldung's personal ties to the reformed community of Strasbourg offer one possible reason for this conflicted approach to sacred representation; still, "[i]t seems unlikely that we should interpret the image as a totally secularized version of the Madonna and Child, even though the worship of Mary in Catholic practice drew sharp criticism from Reformers. It is more likely a compromise between the old devotion to Mary and the new awareness of the autonomy of art" (Hults 52). One of the factors making this compromise possible, or necessary, is the parrot's growing cultural association with extravagance, conspicuous consumption, and sensuality—in a word, with *luxuria*.

However, if Baldung's painting suggests the future of parrot symbolism in the reformed idiom, certain Italian painters maintain the old sacred associations well into the seventeenth century. In Vittore Crivelli's *Enthroned Virgin and Child, with Angels* (c. 1481; see Figure 4), a profusion of rich brocade, musical instruments, and gold leaf—to say nothing of the rose-ringed parakeet perched by Mary's right knee—recalls the hieratic sumptuousness of Van Eyck. If anything, Andrea Mantegna's *Madonna della Vittoria* (1496; see Figure 5) expands upon such opulence, placing the Virgin and child on an elevated marble throne amid a throng of saints and patrons, their backs to an elaborate niche festooned with fruits, flowers, and a rare sulfur-crested cockatoo. A considerably later work such as Il Grechetto's *Holy Family and Saint John the Baptist* (c. 1650; see Figure 6) may offer a more restrained treatment of the same Virgin-child-parrot configuration, but it remains quietly lush and firmly within the conventions of Catholic iconography, as well as within the collections of the Vatican Pinacoteca.

In each of these works the parrot preserves a set of sacred associations that ally it with Catholic belief and papal culture. This is essentially the same set of associations one encounters, on the literary level, in Richard de Holland's Scottish beast fable, *The Buke of the Howlat* (c. 1450), which presents the "Pacocke of pryce" as the pope of birds and "the proper Pape Iaye, provde in his apparele," as the papal chamberlain (Amours 90, 125). In this semiotic realm parrots function as fully fledged persons: self-aware, rational, articulate, endowed with a status and dignity appropriate to their sacred connections. However, other sources, as we shall see, begin to offer a different view.

"Portingall Parrott"

In the first half of the sixteenth century one can detect the emerging traces of a parrot symbology that runs sharply contrary to the one described above.

Figure 4. Vittore Crivelli, *Enthroned Virgin and Child, with Angels*, c. 1481. Philadelphia Museum of Art, purchased with the W. P. Wilstach Fund, 1896.

Figure 5. Andrea Mantegna (1431–1506), *Madonna and Child,* called *Madonna della Vittoria (adored by Gian-Francesco II Gonzaga),* 1496. A sulfur-crested cockatoo perches in the third upper window from the viewer's left, directly above the crucifix to Mary's right. Commissioned for the Chapel of S. Maria della Vittoria in Mantua in commemoration of the Battle of Fornovo (1495). Louvre, Paris, France. Photograph: Réunion des Musées Nationaux/Art Resource, NY.

This emerging symbology takes satirical advantage of the association between parrots, luxury, and the Catholic culture of late fifteenth-century Europe by presenting the birds as a type of inane repetition and intellectual vacuousness. This new turn in parrot symbolism proves especially congenial to literary expression, and it adapts most easily to the environment of religious satire and polemic. Various impulses for ecclesiastical reform, both within and outside of the late medieval Catholic consensus, supply it with its original motive force. However, by the late 1500s this new pattern of symbolism has proved so popular that it develops into an all-purpose satirical tool: a convenient means of insulting almost any person or persons one might wish to depict as loud, repetitive, and mindless. To this extent, the Reformation produces a new and highly successful species of satirical language. In the process, it also produces a new species of bird.

The two most famous early exercises in this new idiom both arise from reformist impulses within the Catholic Church. The earlier of these, John Skelton's "Speke, Parrot" (c. 1521), places its psittacine narrator within a framework of conventional medieval associations that include miraculous Edenic origins ("In Paradyce, that place of pleasure perdurable, / The progeny of Parrottis were fayre and fauorable" [191–92]), connections to the aristocracy ("I am a mynyon to wayte vppon a quene" [21]), glossolalia ("Parrot can mute and cry / In Lattyn, in Ebrew, Araby, and Caldey" [26–27]), and extravagant luxury ("Parot must haue an almon or a date; / A cage curyously caruen, with syluer pyn, / Properly painted, to be my couertowre" [9–11]). Beyond all this, Parrot also proves himself familiar with scripture, and his conversation bristles with arcane biblical references whose immediate application remains often unclear: "Melchisedek mercyfull made Moloc mercyles" (62); "Iobab was brought up in the land of Hus" (67); and so forth. As the bird boasts, "Parrot pretendith to be a bybyll clarke" (121).

The most obvious effect of these associations is to render Parrot both eloquent and yet almost incomprehensible. His narrative never moves for long in a straight line, and it refuses to settle on a single subject or even on a single language in which to speak. C. S. Lewis memorably described "Speke, Parrot" as a "cryptogram of which we have lost the key" (141), but one might also wonder to what extent a key existed in the first place, for as a literary character, Parrot clearly functions in the capacity of an idiot savant, an allowed fool whose folly provides the vehicle for an unsettling wisdom. A certain amount of sheer nonsense is essential to this role, and thus Skelton's protagonist becomes a kind of literary parallel to the bird in Baldung's *Madonna of the Par-*

Figure 6. Giovanni Benedetto Castiglione, called Il Grechetto (1609–65), *The Holy Family and Saint John the Baptist*, c. 1650. A scarlet macaw appears in the upper right-hand corner of the painting, over the Virgin's left shoulder. Pinacoteca, Vatican Museums, Vatican State. Photograph: Scala/Art Resource, NY.

rots: a figure indebted to traditional modes of symbolic association but also reconfiguring those modes in response to the artist's changing circumstances. In effect, Skelton's Parrot preserves his late medieval cultural affiliations while also gesturing toward the bird's predominant future role as a "conventional image of [the] mimic-fool" (Fish 136).

As it happens, Parrot's folly offers a convenient screen for his poem's one indisputable purpose, which is to denounce the administration of England's archbishop of York, cardinal, and aspirant to the papacy, Thomas Wolsey. In an envoy that survives in manuscript but not in the earliest printed version of Skelton's poem, Parrot abandons his usual tomfoolery to offer a furious indictment of Wolsey's policies:

So many vacaboundes, so many beggers bolde;
So much decay of monesteries and of religious places;
So hote hatered agaynste the Chyrche, and cheryte so colde;
So myche of my lordes grace, and in hym no grace ys;
So many holow hartes, and so dowbyll faces;
So myche sayntuary brekynge, and preuylegidde barrydd;—
Syns Dewcalyons flodde was nevyr sene nor hyerd.

(491–97)

As Arthur Kinney has pointed out, this attack is prompted by Wolsey's recent assumption of far-reaching ecclesiastical authority and privilege: "On 1 April 1521 Wolsey was given papal powers to legitimize bastards, to reform secular clergy no matter how eminent, to dispense with canonical impediments to holy orders, to appoint to ecclesiastical benefices at will, and to absolve men from all ecclesiastical penalties including excommunication" (*Skelton* 28). Moreover, while Wolsey's support of the new learning might seem to mark Skelton's politics as the more conservative of the two, there was no question, in 1521, as to who represented the supreme majesty of the Catholic Church in England. Thus, "Speke, Parrot" must be read, in the narrow sense at least, as an attack on episcopal privilege and as a call for ecclesiastical reform. While Skelton's Parrot does not yet stand as an emblem of Catholic vacuousness and decadence, he has clearly begun to function as a vehicle for satire and also, to some extent, as an object of ridicule.

The second great sixteenth-century satirical narrative to make use of a psittacine persona appears in 1562, as chapters 1–8 of the dubiously ascribed *Cinquième livre* of Rabelais. If one accepts the attribution of these opening chapters to Rabelais, they extend the tone of anti-Tridentine Gallicanism that characterizes the *Quart livre* as well. If one rejects the attribution, then they may figure among the Protestant satires that Bakhtin derives from Rabelais's example (99–101, 183–84). (One author of these satires, Henri Estienne, has been proposed as a possible author of the *Cinquième livre* as well [Rabelais 2:271].) In any case, the opening episode of the fifth book places a parrot at the center of a fully developed lampoon of Catholic practice. As Pantagruel and Panurge arrive at the Isle Sonante, or Ringing Isle, they find it inhabited by a hierarchy of anthropomorphic birds—"Clercygaulx, Monesgaux, Prestregaulx, Abbegaulx, Evesquegaulx, Cardingaulx," with their female counterparts, "Clercigesses, Monegesses, Prestregesses, Evesgesses, Cardingesses, Papegesses" (2:290)—all governed by a single elusive Papegault, or popinjay.

These birds chant constantly to the accompaniment of the bells that lend the Ringing Isle its name, and they reproduce asexually, in an obvious parody of the rule of clerical celibacy, each superior species of bird drawing its numbers from the ranks of the species directly subordinate to it.

At heart, the episode of the Ringing Isle takes aim at the "idle gluttony" and "conspicuous consumption" that disfigure the land's ecclesiastical birds (Frame 90). The lowest order of these, the Clercygaulx, are drawn from the countries of "Jour-sans-pain" and "Trop-d'iceulx" [Breadless Days and Too Many Children], which periodically unload their unwanted offspring on the Ringing Isle. Once in their new home, these Clercygaulx—"a useless burden on the earth" and originally "as thin as magpies" ["poix inutile de la terre . . . maigres comme pies" (2:294, 295)]—"grow fat as dormice" ["demeurent gras commes glirons" (2:295)]. As for their diet, it comprises a litany of delicacies: "pheasants . . . , partridges, wood hens, turkeys, fat capons from Loudun, all kinds of venison, and all kinds of game" together with "myrobalans and confit of green ginger, abundant hippocras and delicious wine" ["faisans . . . , perdriaux, gelinottes, poulles d'Inde, gros chappons de Loudunois, venaisons de toutes sortes, et toutes sortes de gibier"; "mirabolins et gingembre verd confict, force hippocras et vin delicieux" (2:300, 302)]. Such dainties flow into the Ringing Isle "from all the rest of the world, . . . except for certain countries to the north" ["de toute l'autre monde, . . . exceptez moy quelque contrée des regions Aquilonaires" (2:300)], and they arrive in such profusion that "if heaven were bronze and earth were iron, we would still lack no provender, not even for seven or eight years" ["quand le ciel seroit d'airain et la terre de fer, encores vivres ne nous faudroyent, fussent par sept, voire par huit ans" (2:301)]. The birds' cages are "grand, rich, and sumptuous, and of marvelous design" ["grandes, riches, et somptueuses, et faictes par merveilleuse architecture" (2:289)], located in rooms "well furnished, well covered with tapestries, gilded throughout" ["bien garnye, bien tappissée, toute dorée" (2:302)], and the birds are adorned with precious insignia that recall the Orders of the Garter and of Saint-Michel (2:298). The overall impression is one of nauseating luxury.

Given its various medieval associations, the popinjay proves right at home in this environment. Indeed it seems only natural that a bird so connected to the magnificence of princes and prelates should eventually become connected to their decadence as well. That is exactly what happens in the opening chapters of the *Cinquième livre*; the Papegault, idle and elusive, emerges as the Ringing Isle's ultimate revelation, and he appears in a capacity at once

sinister and banal. When, after much hanging about, Pantagruel and Panurge are finally granted a view of him, they find him sitting in a cage "with
two little Cardingaulx and six large, fat Evesquaulx" ["accompagné de deux
petits Cardingaulx et six grands et gras Evesquaulx" (2:308)], doing nothing.
Panurge calls him a hoopoe ["une duppe" (2:308)]—a multilayered pun that
involves not only a differing species of bird but also a reference to the bird's
crest ("huppe"), which suggests the papal crown, together with a glance at the
noun "dupe"—to which his guide responds in horror, "Speak softly. . . . If he
once hears you blaspheming like that, you're lost, my good fellows. Do you
see that basin in his cage? Out of that will come thunder, lightning, devils,
and tempests which will bury you a hundred feet under the earth" ["Par-
lez bas. . . . Si une fois il vous entend ainsi blasphemant, vous estes perduz,
bonnes gens: voyez vous là dans sa cage un bassin? D'icelluy sortira fouldre,
esclers, diables et tempestes, par lequelz serez en un moment cent pieds soubz
terre abysmez" (2:308)]. When Panurge threatens to strike an old Evesquault,
or bishop bird, with a stone, the guide admonishes him again:

> Strike, slash, and murder all the kings and princes of the world, by
> treason, by poison, or otherwise, as you wish; expel the angels from
> heaven; for all this you will be pardoned by the Papegault. But do
> not touch these sacred birds, as you love life, prosperity, and well-
> being, both your own and that of your relatives and friends, both
> alive and dead; even those yet to be born would be blighted by it.

> [(Frappe, feris, tue et meurtris) tous Roys et princes du monde,
> en trahison, par venin ou autrement, quand tu vouldras; (denige)
> des cieulx les anges; de tout auras pardon du Papegault. A ces
> sacrez oyseaulx ne touche, d'autant qu'aymes la vie, le proffit et
> le bien, tant de toy que tes parents et amys, vifz et trespassez; en-
> cores ceulx qui d'après d'eulx naistroyent en sentiroyent infortune.]
> (2:309–10)

If the Papegault serves as a revelation, what he reveals is not the splendor and
sanctity of the church, but rather its self-indulgence, stupidity, and brutality.

Perhaps oddly, the *Cinquième livre* makes no use at all of the parrot's out-
standing feature as a satirical figure: its loud, repetitious mimicry. Likewise,
the chatter of Skelton's Parrot serves only ambiguously as an instrument of
satire, for it associates the bird with traditions both of folly and of prophetic

inspiration. Instead, the parrot seems to evolve as an emblem of mindless repetition at the hands of first-generation Protestant reformers, who use it to exemplify the alleged ignorance of Catholic priests and the alleged emptiness of Catholic rituals. In this respect, the early reformers play a major role in creating one of the most enduring clichés of modern western animal representation.

By 1520 talking birds already appear in Protestant polemic, although the birds in question are not yet parrots. In the epistle to Hermann Tulich that opens *The Babylonian Captivity of the Church*, Martin Luther turns a jaundiced eye on his critics Isidoro Isolani, Thomas Cajetán, and Augustinus Alveld, who have endeavored to refute his earlier reformist works in a sequence of multilingual tractates and debates. Mocking their erudition—and especially the bizarre title page of Alveld's *Tractatus de communione sub utraque specie*, which runs on for twenty-six polyglot lines—Luther sneers, "Here it seems three magpies are addressing me, the first in good Latin, the second in better Greek, the third in purest Hebrew. What do you think, my dear Hermann, I should do, but prick up my ears?" (1:365). By 1581 Luther is dead but still under attack, and Walter Haddon steps up to defend his reputation in a way that both echoes and alters this earlier talking-bird image. Replying to Jerónimo Osório's charge that Luther "doth subuerte and ouerthrowe all dueties of uertue and godlynesse," Haddon retorts, "Speake out Parrotte, in what place doth Luther subuerte the dueties of uertue? Where doth hee blotte out honesty and godly carefulnesse of good men? May this be tollerable in you, with slanders, and lyes, to deface the good name of a man, that neuer deserued it, who is also dead?" (Haddon 107). Haddon is clearly attached to this expression. He uses it again to contrast the "libertye" and "bou[n]tifull mercy of God" manifested in "the tongues and mouthes of godly preachers" with the "prat[ing]" of the "Portingall Parrot" Osório (480). Elsewhere still he derides Osório as a "Parrotte of Portingall" (41), as a "Parrotte" (278), and once more as a "Portingall Parrott" (476). Such insults arguably trade not just on the alliterative capacities of the words in question but also on the association of exotic parrot species with Portuguese exploration of West Africa and Brazil.

In fact, by 1581 such turns of phrase have already become standard usage in English religious polemic, and one author who pioneered their application was Luther's student William Tyndale. Tyndale's polemical works crackle with sardonic figures of speech, among which the association of parrots with Catholic mindlessness seems to have served as—for want of a better word—a pet expression. At the outset of his *Obedie[n]ce of a Christen Man* (1528), for instance, Tyndale assails the Catholic priesthood as follows: "[T]he curates them selves (for the most parte) wote no moare what the newe or olde testamente meaneth / then do the turkes. Nether know they of any moare then that they reade at masse / mate[n]s and evensonge which yet they understonde not. Nether care they but to mumble up so much every daye (as the pye & popyngay speake they wote not what) to fyll their belyes with all" (sig. B5v–B6r). Here, as in the later *Cinquième livre*, parrots exemplify Catholic practice in a context that also accommodates priestly gluttony. However, the particular innovation of passages such as this is to connect psittacine mimicry with the repetition of liturgical forms, a repetition that seems especially mindless when performed in a foreign tongue.

Thus when Tyndale discusses the sacrament of baptism in the *Obedie[n]ce*, he reverts to this same figure of speech to describe how the rite should *not* be performed: "Baptim [*sic*] hath also his worde and promise which the prest ought to teach the people a[n]d Chasten them in the english tonge / and not to play the popengay with Credo saye ye / volo saye ye a[n]d baptismum saye ye / for there ought to be no mummynge in soch a mater. . . . The washynge without the worde helpeth not: but thorow the worde it purifieth and clenseth us" (sig. M1v–M2r). The argument here conforms to Luther's view of baptism, in which "the first thing to be considered . . . is the divine promise," which regards "the immersion in water" as a "sign" of that promise, and which vigorously opposes the notion that "there is some hidden spiritual power in the word and water" capable of effecting grace (2:410, 416). In a theological universe that emphasizes the "worde and promise" of baptism, the relegation of these to a foreign and inaccessible tongue reduces the sacrament to an empty spectacle. It becomes a species of "mummynge" understood both as "the action of disguising oneself" so as to participate in "a mummers' play" ([*OED,* s.v. "mumming," vbl. sb. 2]; on this view, the sacrament is rendered ineffective by the act of concealing its "worde and promise" in an unknown language) and as the more straightforward act of "inarticulate murmuring" (*OED,* s.v. "mumming," vbl. sb. 1).

In his 1531 *Answere vnto Sir Thomas Mores Dialoge*, Tyndale reverts to the sacrament of baptism in order to tell a parable of its degeneration within the framework of Catholic practice. According to this tale, the primitive church maintained an active program of spiritual instruction such that worshipers "shuld not be all waye ignoraunt and faithlesse / but be taught the professyon of their baptim [*sic*]" (71). With the growth of episcopacy, however, individual priests and prelates found this labor "tediouse and paynfull" (72), with the result that they gradually abandoned serious spiritual discipline for the easier business of mummery and mumbled prayers:

> [T]he prestes no lenger taught them [that is, the recipients of bap-tism] / but committed the charge to their godfather and godmothers / and they to the father and mother / dischargynge them selues by their awne auctorite with in half an houre.
>
> And the father and mother taught them a monstrous laten pater noster and an Aue and a crede. Which gibbresh euery popiniaye speaketh with a sundrye pronunciation and facion / so that one pater noster semeth as many languages all most as there be tonges that speke it[.] (72)

In Tyndale particular words take on an elastic quality that admits of various interpretation. Thomas Wolsey becomes "Wolfsee," a prelatical jackal rav-ening on the sheep of the English church. "Puppetry" becomes "popetrie," a childish entertainment but also another example of papistical mumming. Alongside such wordplay, "popinjay" takes its place as yet another marker of popish practice, eliding the loud, repetitive quality of psittacine repetition to the body of Catholic worship. Tyndale's popinjays embody a fatuous, self-serving government of the papal, by the papal, and for the papal.

Such wordplay seems to have adapted well to the idiom of religious con-troversy. Thomas Cartwright's *Confutation of the Rhemists Translation, Glosses and Annotations on the New Testament* appeared in print in 1618, but En-glish reformers were calling for its allowed publication as early as 1588, in the first of the Marprelate tracts.[8] In the work's preface Cartwright attacks the Catholic practice of singing the Latin mass: "It is false also, that either they [the priests] sung in an *unknown language*, or *without knowledge of the sence* in some profitable measure: which had been liker vnto the prating, pratling, and parating of birds, tickling the eares of fond men; then to any Christian melodie, pleasant in the eares of the onely wise God" (sig. B3r). Indeed, parrot references become understandably common in Protestant discussions of the efficacy of prayer, both in Latin and in English set forms. Thus, John Norden, writing of the Lord's Prayer in 1614, complains that "this Prayer of Prayers is farre more common, then commonly rightly vnderstood. For euery word therein implieth matter of great importance: yet passeth the lips oftentimes, before it come at, much lesse before it bee truely digested in the heart, and therefore withereth without fruit" (258). So, Norden continues, "[o]thers in like sort, like Parrots, patter forth Pater noster, &c. & know no more what the words import the[n] the senselesse Parrot. And yet they think it a worke of great deuotion" (258). Likewise, William Vaughan, writing in *The Soules Exercise* (1641), touches on the proper form of prayer, describing Christ's precepts on the subject as follows:

> He God forbad with Babling to abuse,
> But when we pray, the briefest Termes to use,
> More tending to his *Praise*, then our supplies,
> Which last wee season must sometimes with sighes:
> Not *Parrot*-like by rote, but from the *Roote*,
> And *Bottome* of the Heart with *Abbaes* Note.
>
> (142)

A year later William Ames specifically denounces "that speech . . . which he that prayeth understandeth not . . . ; for such a repeating of unknowen words is not properly the speech of a man, because it is no more formed of the inward conceivings then those words which are sometimes uttered by a Parrot" (283).

Such cases bear witness to the development of what we might call a motif of liturgical psittacism in English Protestant polemical writing of the sixteenth and early seventeenth centuries. This motif is sufficiently common to give rise to at least one notable subvariant as well, one exemplified by Gervase Babington, the establishmentarian bishop of Exeter, in his 1588 *Profitable Exposition of the Lords Prayer*. For Babington, even the birds and beasts "wold not speake they know not what," and even if they did, "as Plinies raue[n] that could say *Aue Caesar Imperator*, Al haile Emperor Caesar, or the Cardinals Popiniay that could pronounce distinctly all the Articles of the Creed, & yet knew not what they said: shame we not to be like them?" (43). The tale of Caesar's raven derives from Macrobius (3.30), but that of the "Cardinals Popiniay"— necessarily more recent—deserves special attention here. This anecdote reappears variously in the nineteenth, twentieth, and twenty-first centuries, without attribution and with inconsistent detail; most recently Tony Juniper alludes to it in his history of Spix's Macaw. Writing of the African grey parrot, Juniper remarks, "It was believed by the Roman church that these birds' ability to speak elevated them in the hierarchy of creation. A parrot belonging to a Venetian cardinal no doubt reinforced this impression; his bird could faultlessly repeat the Lord's Prayer" (47). Juniper, like other recent purveyors of this story,[9] gives no source documentation. However, Babington was clearly familiar with the anecdote, and he just as clearly viewed it not as elevating parrots on the great chain of being but rather as demoting Catholics.

In fact, the tale in question originates in the *Antiquae Lectiones* of Caelius Rhodiginus (Lodovico Ricchieri), first published in Florence in 1516. Assigning the parrot to Cardinal Ascanio Sforza, scion of the Milanese ruling family, Rhodiginus mentions the bird amid a lengthy discussion of the anatomy of the tongue and its contributions to the act of speech:

> For the rest, I shall not omit with respect to this subject an extraordinary miracle seen in our times: there was a parrot in Rome belonging to Cardinal Ascanius, a bird for which he paid a hundred pieces of gold, who most distinctly and continuously recited the entire confession of Christian truth in unbroken words, just as a trained cleric would pronounce it. Because this was very famous, and said to be most rare, it would not be good to pass over this matter by negligence.

> [Caeterum nec silebo parte hac miraculum insigne nostris visum temporibus: Psittacus hic fuit Ascanii cardinalis Romae, aureis centum comparatus nummis, qui articulatissimè continuatis perpetuò verbis Christianae veritatis symbolum integrè pronuntiabat, perinde ac vir peritus enu[n]tiaret. Quod quia praeclarum est, ac dictus rarissimum, non fuit consilium, transilire per incuriam.] (Rhodiginus 134)

For Rhodiginus, the parrot's performance remains a marvel—"miraculum insigne," "praeclarum"—and he adduces the bird's extraordinary price not as evidence of self-indulgence or ostentation but as proof of its miraculous rarity. As the case of Babington suggests, others would not necessarily view the anecdote from this same perspective.

Indeed, this bit of pre-Reformation parrot culture seems to have fired the imaginations of English Protestants, many of whom saw it as exemplifying the Catholic faith's greedy materialism as well as its failures with respect to questions of prayer and spiritual understanding. Thus, Bishop Jewel refers to it in his controversy with John Harding. "Where you saie," Jewel charges Harding, "the whole people before these fewe late yeeres had one Faith, ye shoulde rather haue saide, they were al taught by you in a straunge vnknowen Tongue, to pronounce, as they could, a strange unknowe[n] Fourme of

Faith. . . . Cardinal Ascanius had a Popiniay, that was taught to say distinctly al the Articles of the Creede, from the beginning to the ende. Yet, I trowe, ye will not say, the same Popiniay Beleeued in God, or vnderstoode the Christian Faithe" (83–84). In 1606 William Attersoll returns to the tale while arguing that the words of the Eucharist "are to be published and pronounced openly, distinctly, plainely, not in a strange language, but in a knowne tongue. The people of God must not be like Parrots, or Pies, or Rauens, or such birds that chatter with voice, record mens words, and sounde a sentence, but vnderstande not the meaning thereof. As . . . *Celius Rhodiginus* writeth, that Cardinall *Ascanius* had a *Popiniay*, that coulde pronounce distinctly and orderly all the Articles of the Creede" (232). In 1631 Samuel Page mentions the story again when urging, "We must pray with vnderstanding, that is, wee must know what we aske of God in our petitions" (24). Citing Augustine's *Enarrationes in Psalmos* for support ["humana ratione, non quasi avium voci cantemus"], Page then goes on to offer the obvious negative example: "*Caelius Rhodiginus* writeth that Cardinall *Ascanius* had a Popiniay that could pronounce distinctly all the articles of the Creed" (24). In 1647 John Trapp could tell another version of the same tale, to very similar effect. Commenting on 1 Corinthians 14.15 ("*I will pray with understanding*"), Trapp observes, "To an effectual praier there must concur *intentio & affectus*, the intention of the mind, and the affection of the heart. Else it is not praying but parotting. I have read of a Parot in *Rome*, that could distinctly say over the whole Creed" (sig. I1v).

This chapter opened with Michael Randall's claim that even symbolic animals must adapt to changes in their environments, and now we are perhaps in a position to understand what such adaptation meant for the parrots of western Europe in the fifteenth, sixteenth, and early seventeenth centuries. First of all, it meant accommodating a new climate of sectarian controversy marked by increasing hostility between proreform and antireform movements, both within the Catholic consensus and later across the divide created by the Reformation. Second, this accommodation involved a reversal of the birds' dominant cultural affinities such that their prior status as an emblem of the wonder and majesty of the Catholic faith led to their later evolution into a symbol of the same faith's self-indulgent idiocy. Third, this evolution occurred largely in genre-specific terms, manifesting itself first within the very select literary forms associated with theological disputation and controversy and then migrating rapidly into broader forms of parody, burlesque, and satire. Against this background of events some final remarks are in order regarding the figure of the repetitive parrot and its future as a satirical trope.

What Subtlest Parrots Mean

So far I have argued that the cultural meaning of parrots underwent a major shift in mid-sixteenth-century Europe, a shift related to developments both in the European market for exotic animals and in the character of sixteenth-century religious controversy. However, it is perhaps also necessary to observe that I am *not* arguing in favor of certain related points. For instance, I do not mean to suggest that an early reformer such as Tyndale was directly influenced by—or even necessarily aware of—Skelton's "Speke, Parrot" or that the author of the *Cinquième livre* was influenced by—or even aware of—either Skelton or Tyndale. While such patterns of influence do, of course, occur (as, for instance, with the anecdote of the cardinal's parrot) and while they may sometimes be traced in linear fashion, it is at least as common for related patterns of cultural association to develop independently of one another, in response to similar circumstances. I also am not arguing that the cultural significance of parrots changes in the same way or at the same time throughout Renaissance Europe. On the contrary, Il Grechetto's *Holy Family and Saint John the Baptist* exemplifies the survival of an essentially medieval mode of figuration well into the seventeenth century, whereas the new way of understanding parrots seems to have received a peculiar impetus from literary developments in England, in the genre of religious polemic, during the first fifty years of the Reformation. Likewise, I do not mean to suggest that parrots were completely unavailable as satirical figures for empty repetition prior to the religious upheavals of the Reformation. They occasionally appear in this capacity in both classical and medieval writing, as, for instance, when Thomas Hoccleve's "Humorous Praise of his Lady" (c. 1430) declares back-handedly that the mistress in question "syngith / fol lyk a pape Jay" (20).

By contrast, I *do* claim that over the past five hundred years or so, the figure of the chattering, repetitive parrot has become the dominant form whereby western cultures have learned to think with these birds, and that this particular strain of parrot symbolism achieves such dominance as a result of its new associations with sectarian controversy and satire in the Reformation. On this view, the identification of parrots with religious polemic must be regarded as an early modern novelty with far-reaching implications. For instance, while it initially functions as an invidious metaphor for the Catholic Latin liturgy and later, by extension, for Anglican set forms, it eventually becomes available for conservative critique of the radical reformers too. As these reformers develop a theory of prayer that increasingly emphasizes spontaneity and enthusiasm, they come in the process to countenance devotional practices, such as glossolalia, that seem as devoid of meaning as any hocuspocus paternoster. Thus, Humphrey Crouch's broadsheet satire *A Whip for the Back of a Backsliding Brownist* (c. 1640) opens by announcing that "the *Lords Prayer* [is] almost out of date," discarded by "new *Disciples*" who "of set forme of Prayer would not allow." These "Brethren of the Seperation," according to Crouch, are functionally indistinguishable from Catholics:

> These with the Papists breed the mischeife here,
> Whilst Cockle Braines builds Castles in the aire,
> Who Parrot like they having learned to prate,
> Disturbe the Church the Common-wealth and State. (Crouch n.p.)

This mode of comparison survives into the Restoration, allowing Samuel Butler to extol the wisdom of Sir Hudibras's squire Ralph in the following mock-heroic terms:

> He understood the Speech of Birds
> As well as they themselves do Words:
> Cou'd tell what subtlest Parrots mean,
> That speak and think contrary clean:
> What Member 'tis of whom they talk,
> When they cry Rope, and Walk, Knave, walk.
> (1.1.547–52)

Likewise, a similar kind of antireformed parrot reference surfaces as early as 1590, when the author of the anti-Marprelate tract *An Almond for a Parrat*—sometimes ascribed to Thomas Nashe—belittles the "Parrats tonge" of the Puritan Dame Margaret Lawson (Nashe 3:344).

Likewise, this same insult rapidly detaches itself from the religious matrix, so that by the late 1500s one already encounters fully secular versions of it in sources ranging from drama to jest books and beyond. Having surveyed these elsewhere, I will not repeat the process here, but one particularly well-developed instance of the empty-headed parrot motif may deserve brief reappraisal in the sectarian context.[10] I refer to Jonson's *Volpone*, which memorably embodies the topos of mindless, psittacine repetition in the character of Sir Politic Would-Be.[11] As a satirical caricature, Sir Politic eschews religious themes in favor of social, political, and sexual ones, and this choice may seem strange, given the customary interrelation of religious with political matter in early modern discourse and also given the confrontation of English and Italian manners that *Volpone* explicitly stages. However, from start to finish Sir Politic will have nothing to do with questions of faith. Four lines into his opening speech he disclaims "any salt desire / Of . . . shifting a religion" (2.1.4–5); he develops various idiotic proposals—for regulating the possession and use of tinderboxes, for instance, and for determining whether a ship carries the plague before it is allowed to disembark—but none of these engage religious issues; and when Peregrine finally humiliates him, it is with the nonsectarian rumor that he has plotted "To sell the state of *Venice*, to the *Turke*" (5.4.38). Indeed, Sir Politic's head seems to be crammed chaotically full of everything in the world *except* religion, and this makes perfect sense, given that Sir Politic is the brainchild of a covert Catholic. Jonson, who converted to Catholicism while imprisoned in 1598 for the murder of Gabriel Spencer, is generally reckoned to have returned to the Anglican communion around 1610, some four years after the composition of *Volpone* (Riggs 176). In April 1606, much closer to the date of the play's original performance, he found himself summoned before the Consistory Court of London to answer allegations of being "a seducer of youthe to the Popish Religion" (Riggs 142). In short, Jonson would have had excellent motive to steer clear of sectarian issues in his writing. Likewise, while assessing the possible Catholic tendencies of Jonson's friend Shakespeare, Stephen Greenblatt has argued that the elder playwright "would have had particular reason to be cautious about disclosing any residual Catholic loyalties" to his professional colleagues (162). For writers in such a position, the secular turn becomes a natural adaptive mechanism, a means of deflecting attention from dangerous issues. In this context it is understandable that Sir Politic should operate as a secularized version of what was originally a sectarian insult; in any case, all of Shakespeare's dozen-odd parrot references assume an equally secular frame of reference.

Whether in their earlier sectarian or their later secular incarnations, the mindless parrots of early modern writing come to stand as never before for the failures of rote learning and indiscriminate repetition. In this respect Judith Dundas has observed that parrots provide an emblematic focus for the tensions associated with *imitatio* in the sixteenth-century rhetorical tradition. If "imitation and discipline are one and the same" from the standpoint of early modern pedagogy, "there is a negative aspect of imitation as well" (Dundas 293) that proved particularly troublesome to European intellectuals sorting out the legacy of first-generation humanism. To the extent that humanism drew its mandate as an intellectual movement from the impulse to restore scripture to its original form—a form rendered indistinct by centuries of faulty transcription and translation—a certain kind of imitation must actually be understood as the movement's natural enemy. As a result, the instability of *imitatio* as a trope helps to shape a series of ongoing Reformation quarrels over use of the Latin liturgy, set forms, spontaneous prayer, and speaking in tongues, thereby providing a new discursive habitat to which the parrots of the early modern period adapt with ease. Thus, by the late sixteenth century these birds have become firmly associated with the worst defects of imitative discipline.

In his work on early modern acoustic culture, Bruce Smith has drawn a sharp contrast between the sensory dimensions of Catholic worship and Protestant worship, which for him embody the opposition between visual and verbal modes of experience: "Where the elevation of the Eucharist, viewed from afar by the congregants, had been the highlight of the Latin liturgy, Protestant theologians of all persuasions designed worship services to lead up to the sermon" (261). However, the present context reminds us that Catholicism had its acoustic rituals as well; these, after all, are just what the satirical trope of the empty-headed, prattling parrot is best adapted to ridicule. Laura Feitzinger Brown has recently pointed out that because of "significant differences in the acoustic landscape . . . early modern writers experienced noise more acutely than most scholars do now" (961). One consequence of this experience was that for writers of both Catholic and Protestant convictions, "[n]oise could become synonymous with incorrect worship" (957). On this view, it makes perfect sense that during the same centuries in which parrots become associated with sectarian controversy and satire, their clamorous vocality also acquires proverbial status. John Clarke's *Paroemiologia Anglo-Latina* of 1639 lists the phrase "He prates like a parrot" among a series of similar expressions, such as "His mouth runs over" and "His tongue run's on wheeles" (76), and one encounters forms of the adage in numerous sixteenth- and seventeenth-century contexts.[12]

In addition, the association of parrots with satire participates in a broader reorientation of religious practice that seeks to dissociate it from wonders, charms, and miracles. For Keith Thomas, this transition, embodied in the shift from Catholic to Protestant devotional forms, is to be understood as a conflict between notions of religion as a "practice" and "religion as a belief" (*Religion* 76). On Thomas's view, the practice in question was specifically that of magic, with Protestant reformers rejecting "the magical powers and supernatural sanctions which had been so plentifully invoked by the medieval Church" (68). From this standpoint one should recall that the parrots of medieval Catholicism—the birds of Alexander Neckam and Thomas of Cantimpré—are at heart mythic and supernatural creatures, tied to the church through their miraculous associations with prophecy and purity and sacred geography. It makes sense that a reformed faith suspicious of such stuff should instinctively produce a demystified, disenchanted understanding of these same birds; indeed, to judge by changes in vocabulary usage, the parrots of Protestant England are literally a different kind of bird from their Catholic predecessors. On one hand, "the Middle English noun *popinjay* gradually loses its currency, to be replaced by the Modern English *parrot*," which "comes into usage in the early sixteenth century (c. 1525, according to the *OED*)," and "over the next century . . . steadily muscles the word 'popinjay' into archaism" (Boehrer, *Parrot Culture* 60). On the other hand, the word "popinjay" survives in modern English primarily in a derogatory, metaphorical sense, as "a type of vanity or empty conceit" (*OED*, s.v. "popinjay," sb. 4b.)—a figurative meaning that also attaches to the new noun "parrot" (*OED*, s.v. "parrot," sb. 2). This rapid lexical shift suggests a concomitant shift on the level of social signification, one that occurs contemporaneously with the English Reformation. It seems reasonable that England's repudiation of Rome, coupled with the gradual development of English maritime interests, might encourage a contemptuous reappraisal of the exotic birds associated with Catholic wealth and exploration in the early 1500s. This reappraisal makes still further sense when viewed as participating in a broader Protestant rejection of the miraculous.

In literary-historical terms, this rejection also entails a newly impoverished sense of the character potential of articulate birds. Where the linguistic ability of magpies, jays, and especially parrots might be viewed from an earlier perspective as evidence of these same animals' self-awareness, intelligence, and—for want of a better word—personhood, the polemical and satirical discourse of early modern Europe puts paid to this possibility. In its place, the Renaissance controversialists give us a new kind of talking bird, one that has been firmly divested of human personality and just as firmly excluded from human society. Thus, in brief, the history of parrot character in the west: what starts out as a miracle ends up as a joke.

Ironically, this new view of parrots remains as inaccurate, in its way, as the old one. Irene Pepperberg's well-publicized work on language acquisition among African grey parrots has revisited the related subjects of psittacine mimicry and intelligence, suggesting that the former is more meaningful, and the latter more advanced, than biologists have traditionally acknowledged.[13] From this standpoint the image of the mindless, chattering parrot seems as wrongheaded as do tales of miraculous, prophetic birds sharing after-hours small talk with popes. However, from another standpoint such inaccuracy is easy to understand; after all, the idiot-as-parrot is at heart a metaphorical figure, and as a figure of speech, metaphor tends to emphasize tenor over vehicle, idiots over parrots. The vehicle becomes infected, as it were, with the shortcomings of its associated tenor, and thus when parrots *do* engage in behavior that seems meaningful and miraculous, the inclination may be to view this as evidence not of intelligence but of something far darker. Consider, for instance, Increase Mather's *Essay for the Recording of Illustrious Providences* (1684), which revises the old tale of the cardinal's parrot to particularly lurid effect: "It is reported that one of the Popes, in way of pleasancy, saying to a parrat, 'What art thou thinking of?' the parrat immediately replied, 'I have considered the dayes of old, the years of antient times'; at the which, consternation fell upon the Pope and others that heard the words, concluding that the devil spake in the parrat, abusing Scripture expressions; whereupon they caused it to be killed" (Mather, *Remarkable Providences* 141). Ironically, this instance of papal behavior elicits no criticism from Mather. On the contrary, Mather assumes, as does his nameless pope, that a parrot speaking meaningfully can only be a product of demonic inspiration and that, as such, it must be destroyed.

Chapter 3

Ecce Feles

Sometime between 1553 and 1563 the students of Christ's College, Cambridge, entertained themselves with the comedy now called *Gammer Gurton's Needle*, *"Made by Mr. S. Mr. of Art"* (title page). The author's M.A., like the play's university setting, now seems in some ways incongruous. *Gammer Gurton* is a work of the broadest slapstick humor, a kind of Tudor *Three Stooges*. It famously begins with the loss of a needle, moves through various resulting confusions, and concludes with the needle's rediscovery. For hilarity, it relies on pratfalls, insults, penis envy, and anal matters, but for all its crudeness, *Gammer Gurton* achieves a number of literary firsts. It has been called "the earliest regular English play" (Schelling 1.92) and "the earliest surviving comedy in English to use Roman comic form" (Duncan 177). It appears to be the first published English play "to announce on its title page that it was performed at a university, played on a stage, and defined as a 'comedy' rather than an interlude" (Wall, *Staging Domesticity* 85). In addition, it is the earliest surviving English play to bring a cat onstage (Cartwright 136; Robinson 63).

This last feat was clearly meant to elicit laughter from the comedy's earliest audience. However, it could have done so only by terrorizing "poor Gib, the cat" (Robinson 63), who is held aloft—no doubt squirming—for a full scene while the bumpkin Hodge, convinced that Gib has swallowed the play's lost needle, first threatens to kill him and then prepares to probe the animal's rectum. Like the play's first human actors, the original Gib—"presumably the college cat" (Duncan 177)—would have been a recognizable member of the immediate academic household, but this in itself need not have preserved the creature from maltreatment. Some forty years later Shakespeare's Shylock could still describe cats as "harmless *necessary*" animals (4.1.55; my italics), and the one in *Gammer Gurton* would have earned his keep by hunting vermin. He would not have served as a pet, at least not primarily, so there would have been little reason not to treat the beast as an object of mildly sadistic fun. In the event that is just the treatment Gib receives.

The present study seeks to account for this treatment by reading it against particular historical traditions involving the festive and ritual abuse of cats. In doing so, I argue that Gib embodies a range of social and spiritual associations that mark cats out for regular persecution in Renaissance society; that these associations undergo a shift in meaning as a consequence of Reformation doctrinal controversy; and that this shift, too, may be discerned in the general treatment of cats in *Gammer Gurton*. As a consequence, Mr. S.'s play operates not just as a landmark of English literary and dramatic history but also as a noteworthy document for the study of early modern English household animals and their relation to contemporary domestic and symbolic economies.

This is so despite the fact that Mr. S. seems to have paid little attention to Gib—so little, indeed, that he does not even get the cat's gender right. At certain moments Gib is apparently female: on one occasion a character claims that the cat "shut her two eyes" (1.5.195); and later, as Hodge prepares his anal exploration, he declares, "[C]hil take the pains to rake her" (3.4.704). However, earlier, as he approaches a house in commotion over the loss of Gammer's needle, Hodge worries that someone might have "stolne her ducks or henes, or gelded Gyb her cat" (1.2.82). Recent critics have seen this instability as a glance at the transvestism whereby college students played the women in *Gammer Gurton* (Grant ms. 148–51), but this strikes me as overartful. A simpler explanation for the inconsistency is that Mr. S. just did not care much about the cat's sex and assumed—insofar as he thought about it at all—that nobody else would either.

What he *did* care about was the cat's ability to make trouble. Gammer Gurton misplaces her needle when she spies Gib lapping up a pan of milk intended for the household's supper (1.3.117–22); setting aside her needle to save the meal, she ends up losing both. Later, as Hodge tries to raise a fire to aid in his search for the needle, he mistakes the cat's eyes for coals. Gib then bounds upstairs, "among the old postes and pinnes" (1.5.203), where Hodge breaks both his shins in vain pursuit. So when Gib's choking raises suspicion that he has swallowed the needle, and Hodge responds by threatening to kill and then to rake him, the scene feels both like an extension of prior antics and like a kind of poetic justice.

In short, Gib figures as a major source of disorder in Mr. S.'s play. However, since a cat—even a clever one—can raise only so much trouble, Mr. S. provides Gib with a human accomplice. Diccon the Bedlam, a sturdy, semilunatic beggar who apparently lent his name to the play when it was first entered in the Stationers' Register,[1] improves upon Gib's mischief by falsely accusing Gammer's neighbors of stealing her needle. With this and similar rumors he sets the villagers at odds, and his motive for doing so places him firmly in league with the cat: like Gib, he wants a meal. He steals a slip of bacon that Gammer has set aside for supper and that survived Gib's earlier ravages (1.1.41–42). He manages the villagers' business so that, in the end, Gammer buys him a pot of ale as well (5.2.1268–71). And when Hodge misses the bacon, he assumes, with Diccon's tacit encouragement, that it was pilfered by Gib (2.1.306–9). Between them Gib and Diccon consume all of the play's edibles while causing all of the play's trouble. In this sense, Diccon serves as an articulate extension of the cat.

While Diccon and Gib thus function as a single dramatic character, they play a highly conventional role in the process. Diccon has long been identified as "Vice-like" (Wilson 111), as a rendition of "the native English Vice, who first appears in English drama in John Heywood's plays in the 1530s and appears frequently in plays throughout the remainder of the century" (Robinson 52).[2] Incorporating elements of classical dramatic roles as well (particularly the tricky servant of Plautus and Terence), Diccon displays the Vice's signature delight in disorder for its own sake. In the process he also acquires certain ominous metaphysical associations, which are best illustrated when he terrifies Hodge by pretending to conjure a devil to determine the whereabouts of Gammer's needle (2.1). When the gullible Hodge beshits himself with fear, Diccon raises a laugh by exclaiming, "The devill—I smell hym—wyll be here anone!" (2.1.389). However, Hodge has already picked up the scent himself, as it were; hence his "shameful uncontrol" (Paster 121).

In one way, it hardly matters whose sense of smell is better. *Gammer Gurton*'s villagers, uniformly credulous, ascribe instant validity to their most whimsical fears and suspicions, with the result that these come to define the play's sense of reality. Hodge, in particular, "lives by omens, premonitions, and luck, which he discovers everywhere" (Cartwright 130). In the resulting mental environment Diccon acquires a sort of preternatural stature, enhanced by his apparent summoning of devils, by the play's diabolical darkness and scatology,[3] and by his insistence that Hodge kiss his breeches as a sign of submission before he conjures his devil (2.2.356 s.d.). It has been suggested that this act alludes to the 1560 Geneva—or Breeches—Bible (Kozikowski 12–14), but in its necromantic context it seems more naturally to suggest the ritual kiss of the devil's anus whereby witches were understood to pledge their obedience (de Givry 87; Kittredge 241). To this extent Diccon comes to occupy the place not only of Gib but of Satan as well.

The result is a conventional sequence of association—a signifying chain that links Gib the cat to Diccon the Bedlam to necromancy to the devil—that Mr. S. apparently uses to foreground the superstition and credulity of the villagers in his play. The play's vocabulary of insult draws on this same nexus of language: Hodge wishes that "a foul fiend" might "light" on Gib the cat (2.1.304), while Gammer is reviled as an "old gyb" and an "arrant witch" in the space of six lines (3.3.619–25). Within this framework of meaning, cat abuse acquires a venial, indeed a natural, character, and while *Gammer Gurton* as a whole seems gleefully invested in deriding its villagers' ignorance, it displays no comparable interest in satirizing their treatment of animals. Gib is left to fend for himself in a world that regards him as at best a nuisance and at worst a portent. In this regard he may be viewed as a fairly typical early modern English cat.

The Finest Pastime Under the Sun

Scholars like to ponder the "ambiguous ontological position" of "certain animals," which "straddl[es] . . . conceptual categories" (Darnton 89) and unsettles our sense of order and identity in the process. As it happens, any number of beasts—from the dog and the pig to the parrot and the monkey—can occupy a liminal position of this sort, forcing us to revise our notions of who we are and how we relate to the world around us. As a result of this inconvenient discursive placement, most such animals have come in for a fair amount of literal and symbolic violence during the course of their history with human beings. Yet even among these animals, cats elicit an unusual amount of hostility, a hostility that seems all the more notable for the cheerful mode of its expression. "So many cats," a contemporary bumper sticker declares, "so few recipes." The sentiment here is so jocular that one has trouble taking it seriously as a statement of violent intent, but then, the violent treatment of cats has often assumed a festive character.

The most famous modern historian of cat torture, Robert Darnton, has connected the physical abuse of cats to cycles of seasonal festivity in early modern Europe, particularly "the cycle of carnival and Lent" and "the cycle of Saint John the Baptist, which took place on June 24, at the time of the summer solstice" (83). In fact, this oversimplifies the history of cat abuse, even in the case with which Darnton is most concerned, that of early modern France. (As we will see, England presents a still more complicated picture.) Even so, despite the fact that cats were tortured throughout early modern Europe on numerous occasions that do not bear any clear relation to seasonal holidays, Mardi Gras and Saint John's Eve did prove conducive to their maltreatment, at least on the Continent. This seems to have been so because these holidays roughly coincided with—and coopted—two of the year's four great pagan witch festivals, Candlemas and Beltane. In Poitou and Limousin, thus, the evening of Mardi Gras was held to be a particularly important time for the staging of witches' conventicles (Sebillot 3:122); there and elsewhere the witches "invited to Sabat" were rumored to appear as "nothing but a troop of cats, of which Marcou (a gib-cat) is prince" (Brand 3:313). As a result, various customs developed on or around carnival to ward off sorcery, and these sometimes entailed cat abuse. In the Vosges cats were burned on Mardi Gras (Frazer 11:40). In the area around Semur the following Sunday marked the beginning of the ancient Celtic holiday of Candlemas (in that area called Brandons), a fertility festival that involved the construction of a large community bonfire. The children who traditionally built this fire would place a live cat in it on a pole, where it would be burnt to death (Sebillot 3:112). Midsummer Eve witnessed similar diversions, these developing largely around the holiday's traditional bonfires. In various parts of France, including Paris, it was the practice to place cats in a bag or barrel and burn them alive; at Metz, where the custom persisted until 1765, "midsummer fires were lighted with great pomp on the esplanade, and a dozen cats, enclosed in wicker cages, were burned alive in them, to the amusement of the people" (Sebillot 3:112; Frazer 11:39). As late as the turn of the twentieth century, such customs persisted in parts of Alsace-Lorraine (Sebillot 3:112). In 1572 the teenaged (and not-yet-knighted) Sir Philip Sidney found himself in Paris, on an early version of the Grand Tour, when a huge midsummer bonfire was constructed at the Place de Grèves for the entertainment of King Charles IX. After the animal baitings and fireworks that served as prelude to this event, a bag containing live cats and a fox was lowered into the flames (Osborn 43). Indeed, conflagrations at the Place de Grèves provided regular seasonal fare for French royalty until 1648, when Louis XIV, "crowned with a wreath of roses and carrying a bunch of roses in his hand, kindled the fire, danced at it, and partook of the banquet afterwards in the town hall" (Frazer 11:39).

Beyond the annual church festivals, cat torture also comprised a traditional element of other, less officially sanctioned activities. These did not always carry the same overtones of witchcraft and spirituality, but on some occasions, at least, they did. Continental witch lore is full of tales such as that from the *Malleus Maleficarum* in which a man chopping wood near Strasbourg found himself suddenly attacked by three cats; fighting them off with difficulty, he returned home to find the blows he had given them transferred to the bodies of local women, witches to whom the cats acted as familiar spirits (Krämer and Sprenger 126–27). More rooted in actual social practice were the charivari and its regional variants, which often employed cat abuse to help create the rough music that provided the soundtrack for such humiliating processions. Local names for these spectacles—which include *faire le chat* and *Katzenmusik*—speak to the connection here, as does Cervantes' famous, albeit fictive, description of a similar event in *Don Quixote*. There, as the hero sings a ridiculous antilove song to the lady Altisidora, who has feigned passion for him, Quixote's hosts enrich the jest with live animals:

> [A]ll of a sudden from a gallery above, that was exactly over his [Quixote's] window, they let down a cord with more than a hundred bells attached to it and immediately after that dumped out a great sack full of cats, which also had bells of smaller size tied to their tails. Such was the din of the bells and the squawling of the cats . . . that . . . the contrivers of the joke . . . were startled by it, while Don Quixote stood paralyzed with fear. And as luck would have it, two or three of the cats made their way in through the grating of his chamber, and flying from one side to the other, made it seem as if there was a legion of devils at large in it. They extinguished the candles that were burning in the room and rushed about seeking some way of escape. . . . Don Quixote sprang to his feet and, drawing his sword, began making passes at the grating, shouting out, "Avaunt, malignant enchanters! Avaunt, ye witchcraft-working rabble!" . . . And turning upon the cats that were running about the room, he slashed away at them. They dashed at the grating and escaped by it, except one that . . . leapt at his face and held on to his nose with tooth and nail. (2.46, 677)

In its occasion this joke recalls the traditional charivari, which typically sought to correct perceived violations of normative gender roles: wifely infidelity, husband beating, or—as in the present case—May-December courtships. For present purposes, though, the passage's infernal overtones seem equally interesting. Evoking the cat's folkloric association with witchcraft, they also appear in a context reminiscent of the scene from *Gammer Gurton's Needle* (1.5) in which Gib leads Hodge on a humiliating comic chase through a darkened room.

In England such impromptu divertissements seem to have been the rule. The nonseasonal practice of whipping a cat to death, for instance, proved lastingly popular in some parts of the realm. In 1615 Richard Braithwaite could ask rhetorically, "Set out a Pageant, whoo'l not thither runne, / As twere to whip the cat at Abington" (M1v). Over two centuries later a village inn at Albrighton in Shropshire still retained an inscription reading, "The finest pastime, that is under the sun, / Is whipping the cat at Albrighton" (Moesen n.p.). In a related vein, Benedick's famous remark in *Much Ado about Nothing*, "If I do [marry], hang me in a bottle like a cat, and shoot at me" (1.1.256–57), alludes to a form of early English archery drill in which a live cat was placed in a bag or basket and used as a target. Shakespeareans have unearthed a range of other references to this and similar sports,[4] the most detailed of which relates to a Scottish custom that was still alive in 1789:

> There is a society or brotherhood in the town of Kelso, which consists of farmers' servants, ploughmen, husbandmen, or whip-men, who hold a meeting once a year for the purpose of . . . viewing the merriment of *a cat in a barrel*, which is highly esteemed by many for excellent sport. The generalissimo of this regiment of whip-men, who has the honourable style and title of *my lord*, being arrived with the brotherhood at the place of rendezvous, the music playing, the drum beating, and their flag waving in the air, the poor timorous cat is put into a barrel partly stuffed with soot, and then hung up between two high poles, upon a cross-beam, below which they ride in succession, one after another, besieging poor puss with their large clubs and wooden hammers. The barrel, after many a frantic blow, being broken, the wretched animal makes her reluctant appearance amidst a great concourse of spectators, who seem to enjoy much pleasure at the animal's shocking figure, and terminate her life and misery by barbarous cruelty. (quoted in Brand 3:39)

The author of this description, a certain Ebenezer Lazarus, makes no effort to hide his disgust at the practice he relates; nor does he offer any account of its origin. Yet here at least, in Scotland, we have a seasonal event, perhaps corresponding to ancient fertility traditions such as the one occurring in Semur.

In any case, although the English followed the continental custom of building Midsummer's Eve bonfires, they do not seem to have shared the French predilection for roasting cats in them. Indeed, with the Reformation even the bonfires proved controversial since Protestant reformers concluded early on that the coincidence of Catholic feast days and ancient pagan festivals attested to the corruption of both. Joseph Justus Scaliger complained of the Irish, *"ils sont quasi tous papistes, mais c'est Papauté meslée de Paganisme, comme partout"* (quoted in Campbell 232), and this view could produce a smug pseudoethnographic view of bonfire building and related customs. Thus William Prynne could remark in his inimitable style that

> such was the puritanicall rigidnesse of the primitive Christians on the solemne birth-dayes and *Inaugurations of the Roman Emperors, when as other men kept revel-rout, feasting and drinking from parish to parish, making the whole Cittie to smell like a taverne, kindling bonefires in every street, . . . accounting their licentious deboistness at such seasons their chiefest piety and devotion,* (as our Grand Christmas keepers now doe:) *that they would neither shadow nor adorne their doors with laurell; nor diminish the day-light with bonefires and torches, . . . but kept themselves temperate, sober, chast, and pious.* (770)

As a contributor to *Gentleman's Magazine* observed in 1795 (once again skewering Ireland), "The Irish have ever been worshipers of fire, and of Baal, and are so to this day. This is owing to the Roman Catholicks, who have artfully yielded to the superstitions of the natives, in order to gain and keep up an establishment, grafting Christianity upon Pagan rites. The chief festival, in honour of the sun and fire is upon the 21st of June" (M'Queen 124), or Bealtine, two days before Saint John's Eve.

As fortune would have it, the English practice of bonfire building survived such criticism by migrating, after 1605, from the old holiday of Midsummer's Eve to the new festival of Guy Fawkes Day, which provided a rare opportunity for Puritans and Anglicans to celebrate together (albeit for different reasons). In this case, as in those of other, similar holidays, traditional wisdom has regarded the practice of building bonfires as a holdover from pagan festivals. However, David Cressy and Ronald Hutton have more recently demonstrated that the celebrations of Guy Fawkes Day had no direct calendrical precursor; instead, they appear to have sprung up spontaneously following the Gunpowder Plot, in ways that involved the transference of customs from other festivals such as Shrovetide and Saint John's Eve.[5] In the early Stuart period November 5 became host to a range of pastimes that included the building and leaping over of bonfires, the detonation of squibs and firecrackers, and the incineration of effigies. As to the bonfires, they sprang up "during the period 1625–40," with "fires and burning tar barrels being paid for by parishes in London, Cambridge, and Durham" (Hutton, *Stations* 395). These celebrations quickly escalated, with "the custom of burning effigies of the pope, the devil, or his agents" also introduced "in the reign of Charles I" (Cressy 147). Bonfire Night enjoyed steady growth through the seventeenth century thanks to its convenient political lability; Royalists could use it to mark their support of the monarchy, while Puritans could treat it as an occasion for disparaging the pope. As a result, the festival remained robust during the Interregnum and became, ironically, a site for the kinds of revelry that the Puritan Prynne had found so distasteful just a few years earlier. By 1652 John Evelyn could complain that Bonfire Night "insolensies" had rendered the streets of London impassable (3:77).

The story of these revels is further complicated by the revival, during the 1620s, of celebrations on Queen Elizabeth's accession day, November 17. This revival was clearly meant as an anti-Catholic gesture (Hutton, *England* 186), and it gained strength as hostilities grew between the Crown and Parliament under Charles I. Given that Guy Fawkes Day fell just two weeks before Elizabeth Day, and given the ideological similarity of the two festivals, it was perhaps inevitable that the latter should participate in the customs of the former. Thus, by the late seventeenth century Guy Fawkes Day had become a vehicle for "mass propaganda" (Harris 93), and Elizabeth Day "was already regarded as a Protestant carnival" (Williams 105). The stage was set for the notorious pope-burning processions of the Exclusion Crisis, which were typically organized on these two holidays.

Here, in the lead-up to the huge anti-Catholic processions of 1679–81, we are afforded a nearly unique glimpse of cat burning in the context of English calendar festivals. The place is London, the occasion is Elizabeth Day 1677, and the celebration includes "mighty bonefires and ye burning of a most costly pope, caryed by four persons in divers habits, and ye effigies of 2 divells whispering in his eares, his belly filled full of live catts who squawled most hideously as soone as they felt the fire; the common saying all ye while, it wase ye language of ye Pope and ye Divel in a dialogue betwixt them"[6]

(*Correspondence of Hatton Family* 1:157). Keith Thomas has been so bold as to declare that "during the Pope-burning processions of Charles II it was the practice to stuff the burning effigies with live cats so that their screams might add dramatic effect" (*Man* 109–10); however, one should at once concede that other accounts of pope-burning processions make no mention of roasted cats. In the absence of further such evidence, Ronald Hutton concludes that cat burning was "simply not a component part of British seasonal festivity,"[7] and under the circumstances this is surely the correct view. Still, Christina Hole, writing in 1949, remarked, "It is not so very long since cats were burnt alive in baskets at Lewes on Guy Fawkes' [*sic*] Day, their agonized shrieks drowned by the delighted shouts of the onlookers" (5). If her remark is anything more than lurid fantasy (which it might be), one must at least entertain the possibility that this practice did survive, without documentation and perhaps without much vigor, on the anti-Catholic holidays of November 5 and November 17, in a setting originally influenced by festival practices like those of Catholic Europe.

In any case, references to English cat burning survive in certain other contexts, none of them involving seasonal festivity but all immersed in what might broadly be called questions of spiritual exercise. The most recent of these appears late in Elizabeth Gaskell's 1855 novel *North and South*, when Gaskell's protagonist—the genteel clergyman's daughter Margaret—returns to her old haunts in the rural village of Helstone. There she discovers in conversation that one villager has stolen another's cat and roasted it alive:

> By dint of questioning, Margaret extracted . . . the horrible fact that Betty Barnes, having been induced by a gypsy fortune-teller to lend the latter her husband's Sunday clothes, on promise of having them faithfully returned on the Saturday night before Goodman Barnes should have missed them, became alarmed by their non-appearance, and her consequent dread of her husband's anger, and as, according to one of the savage country superstitions, the cries of a cat, in the agonies of being boiled or roasted alive, compelled (as it were) the powers of darkness to fulfil the wishes of the executioner, resort had been had to the charm. (2:288)

For her part, the cat's owner "evidently believed in [the charm's] efficacy; her only feeling was indignation that her cat had been chosen out from all others to sacrifice" (2:288). Gaskell employs this attitude to suggest the cultural abyss that separates Margaret from her former village companions, a gulf still further emphasized by the "Sunday clothes" whose loss triggers the "practical paganism" of the torture (2:289).

If this episode from Gaskell's novel seems immaterial to a study of cat abuse in sixteenth-century English writing, I would respond that it speaks to a pattern of such behavior, played out over the historical *longue durée* in both documentary records and literary representation. This pattern, in turn, helps define the semiotic potential of cat torture as much for Tudor playwrights as for Victorian novelists. In fact, one encounters a historical anticipation of Gaskell's cat roasting not only in the pope burning of 1677 but also in the earlier activity of parliamentary zealots before and during the civil wars. On New Year's Day 1638 a certain William Smyth caused "a great noise and disturbance neere the quire" of Ely Cathedral "by ye roasting of a catt tied to a spitt . . . whereby much people were gathered together and a great prophanacion made" (Gibbons 88). Similarly, in 1643 the parliamentary troopers who overran Lichfield Close used hounds to hunt cats through the cathedral on successive days (Guttery 38). As Katharine Rogers has observed, these incidents "were officially recorded as examples of vandalism and profanation rather than cruelty" (39); they were meant, that is, to register Puritan contempt for the spiritual practices associated with high-church Anglicanism.

If, in turn, these demonstrations still seem too chronologically remote from mid-sixteenth-century London to bear on our understanding of Tudor literary works, one might consider a similar incident, of great notoriety, whose date corresponds closely to the traditional *terminus a quo* for *Gammer Gurton's Needle*. In April 1554 London was afflicted by an unusually heavy atmosphere of political unease. Queen Mary had been crowned six months earlier, on October 1, 1553, after suppressing the duke of Northumberland's effort to install Lady Jane Grey on the throne. Northumberland was beheaded on Tower Hill in late August, and together with her young husband Guildford Dudley, Lady Jane was detained in the Tower. In January, Mary announced her intention to wed Philip II of Spain; in addition to causing widespread dismay, this declaration inspired the Wyatt Rebellion, which sputtered out on February 4. Lady Jane was beheaded eight days later, and Sir Thomas Wyatt, in turn, was condemned to lose his head on April 11.

In this poisonous atmosphere some unknown Reformer decided to make a statement. Different chroniclers offer different details of the event. According to Charles Wriothesley,

> Sunday the 8 of Aprill was a villanouse fact done in Cheape earlie
> or daye. A dead catt having a clothe lyke a vestment of the priest at
> masse with a crosse on it afore, and another behinde put on it; the
> crowne of the catt shorne, a peece of paper lyke a singinge cake putt
> betwene the forefeete of the said catt bownd together, which catt
> was hanged on the post of the gallows in Cheape beyond the Crosse
> in the parishe of St. Mathewe, and a bottle hanged by it; which catt
> was taken downe at vi of the clock in the morninge and caried to
> the Bishop of London, and he caussed it to be shewed openlye in the
> sermon tyme at Paules Crosse in the sight of all the audience there
> present. (114)

John Stow adds that the preacher at Paul's Cross on that Sunday was one "D. Pendleton" (623), that is, Henry Pendleton, Bishop Bonner's chaplain, who was advanced three days after this sermon to the prebend of Reculverland, Saint Paul's (Pollard 737). Wriothesley goes on to declare, "The Lord Mayre, with his brethren the alldermen of the Cittie of London, caused a proclamation to be made that afternoone that whosoever could utter or shewe the auctor of the sayde fact should haue vi l. xiii s. iv d. for his paynes, and a better rewarde, with hartie thancks" (114). John Foxe claims that the incident aroused "great evil-will against the city of London; for the queen and the bishops were very angry withal," and he adds that the initial reward of twenty nobles "was afterwards increased to twenty marks; but none could or would earn it" (6:548). Wriothesley agrees that "at that tyme, after much enquirie and searche made, it [the culprit] could not be knowne, but diverse persons were had to prison for suspicions of it" (114–15).

So, to summarize, we may trace a broad pattern of cat torture whereby the abuse originates within pagan rituals of both a seasonal and an impromptu nature, and in which these rituals are assimilated to—and hence associated with—the practices both of medieval witchcraft lore and of traditional Catholic worship, with the latter ostensibly functioning as a sanctified reversal of the earlier pagan charms. Then, with the advent of the English Reformation, this same abusive behavior is further assimilated to anti-Catholic protest in such a way that it emerges as a countersignifying practice, to be applied against the very rituals that had earlier employed it as a charm against black magic. This reformed, countersignifying cat torture eventually characterizes acts of resistance both to Catholic institutions and to high-church Anglican institutions. The hanged cat of 1554 and the burnt pope of 1677 provide instances of the former, and the roasted and hunted cats of 1638 and 1642, respectively, offer examples of the latter. Even late in this process of transference, the identification of cats with paganism (and hence witchcraft and devil worship) persists, as the example of Gaskell's novel suggests. As cat torture is integrated into Catholic festivals such as those of Mardi Gras and Saint John's Eve, it seems to function as a prophylactic charm, averting evil and assuring fertility, and to this extent it remains of a piece with the various other kinds of "supernatural intervention" that, according to Keith Thomas, had accrued to the Catholic church by the Reformation (*Religion* 41; see especially 25–50). However, as it migrates from Catholic to Protestant hands, this same abuse metamorphoses, predictably, from a charm into a sign. By Sunday, April 8, 1554, it has—for some people, at least—ceased to be a talisman and has become, instead, a brutal and scandalous insult.

"Alured by the Foxe"

The cat in *Gammer Gurton's Needle* pursues a similar symbolic trajectory. On one hand, Mr. S. ties Gib to events that strike the play's villagers as malign and inscrutable, the subject of prophecy and divination; yet on the other hand, the play's audience is encouraged to view these same events as comical and mundane, evidence of the villagers' own credulity and superstition. The result is a kind of demystification or disenchantment, as the audience sees the villagers' illusions reduced to the stuff of slapstick comedy. Of course, *Gammer Gurton's Needle* was obviously not composed as religious polemic, but just as obviously, it may still participate in the symbolic tensions accruing to the occult as a result of Reformation controversy. In fact, given what we know of the play's composition, it is hard to read the work in any other way.

For many years the prevailing view has been that *Gammer Gurton's Needle* was written by one William Stevenson, who appears in bursars' records as a Fellow of Christ's College, Cambridge, from 1559 to 1561 and also, earlier, from 1551 to 1554.[8] This Stevenson is the only fellow of the college whose surname begins with *S* and who is expressly connected with college theatricals between the years 1553 and 1563, during which time he is listed as composing plays for performance at the college in both 1559–60 and 1553–54. It has been speculated that the later play might, in fact, have been a revival of the earlier one, in which case *Gammer Gurton* would have seen two separate performances at Christ's College over the course of a decade. At any rate, when the curate of *Gammer Gurton* demands that the play's bailiff arrest Diccon "in the King's name" (5.2.1181), the play seemingly gestures toward an Edwardian—rather than a Marian or an Elizabethan—historical context. Stevenson was a churchman, ordained deacon in 1552 under King Edward and appointed prebendary of Durham in 1560–61 under Queen Elizabeth (Bradley 199). As for the curious gap in his association with Christ's College, "it may be presumed that he was deprived of his fellowship under Queen Mary, and was reinstated under Elizabeth" (Bradley 198).

This is the simplest available explanation for the circumstances of *Gammer Gurton*'s composition, and it points toward authorship by a man of Reformed sympathies in the broad sense of the phrase, who would have reason to look askance at Catholic practices and their reinforcement of rustic superstition. As for the play itself, while it seems unconcerned about the sex of Gib the cat, it takes pains to lend itself a pre-Reformation setting, and it does so in a notably contemptuous way. Describing the confusion Diccon intends to sow through false accusations, the prologue insists on the villagers' ignorance, declaring that they know "no more of this matter (alas) / Then knoeth Tom our clarke what the Priest saith at Masse" (prologue.9–10). This jab at congregational ignorance leads to a general depiction of the "villagers' religious customs" as "carryovers, exaggerated for comic effect, from pre-Elizabethan Catholicism" (Kozikowski 8).[9] And this pattern of religious representation reaches its climax late in the play when the village curate appears onstage, summoned by Gammer Gurton, who suspects her neighbor, Dame Chat, of having stolen her needle. The preposterously named Doctor Rat enters complaining about the villagers' impositions on his time and confesses that he only lends them aid in expectation of material rewards such as "a tythe pig or a goose" (4.1.732). Like everyone else, he accepts Diccon's story that Dame Chat has stolen the needle, and then, in a further twist of the knife, Diccon persuades Rat to seek its recovery by wriggling into Dame Chat's house through a privy hole. Of course, Diccon has also warned Dame Chat that a thief plans to pillage her henhouse, so when Doctor Rat makes his appearance in her home, predictable mayhem ensues, with the curate earning a broken skull for his pains.

This episode comprises Diccon's last, most elaborate practical joke, and the fact that it is carried out at the expense of the local cleric, a figure already drawn in unsympathetic terms, in a play that ridicules the superstitions of rustic spiritual life says a good deal about *Gammer Gurton*'s religio-political orientation. In the mid-sixteenth century Christ's College was not yet the "seed plot of Puritanism" it would become in the days of William Perkins and John Milton (Porter 236). Even so, scholars have recognized that the college's declared mission "'to produce an improved clergy' . . . privileges the satire on Dr. Rat" (Cartwright 119), who "is criticized throughout for his self-esteem" (Duncan 187). Yet beyond all this, Mr. S. points toward his nondramatic source for Doctor Rat's discomfiture, and it proves most revealing. As Rat nurses his broken skull and calls for justice from the town bailiff, Diccon mocks his stupidity with the following lines:

> God's bread, hath not such an olde fool wit to save his eares?
> He showeth himselfe herein, ye see, so very a coxe;
> The cat was not so madly alured by the foxe,
> To run into the snares was set for him doubtlesse,
> For he leapt in for myce, and this Sir John for madnes.
>
> (5.2.1173–78)

This speech caps an unusual series of references to foxes in the play's final scenes,[10] and it compares Doctor Rat directly with Tibert the Cat as this latter worthy appears in chapter 10 of William Caxton's *History of Reynard the Fox*. There, Tibert seeks to bring his kinsman Reynard to answer complaints at a court of law, but Reynard distracts the cat by declaring that he knows where Tibert may find an abundant supply of mice for supper. These mice, as it happens, reside in the barn of the local parish priest, whose henhouse Reynard has recently plundered and who is therefore alert for further trespasses.

Aware of this fact, Reynard conducts Tibert to the barn in question and urges him to enter it through a privy hole. Once the cat has done so, his head is caught in a snare laid by the priest and his household, who hurl themselves on the interloper:

> They lept and ran, all that there was. The priest himself ran all mothernaked. . . . The priest took to Locken, his wife, an offering candle and bade her light it at the fire and he smote Tibert with a great staff. There received Tibert many a great stroke over all his body. Martinet was so angry that he smote the cat an eye out. The naked priest lifted up and should have given a great stroke to Tibert, but Tibert, that saw that he must die, sprang between the priest's legs with his claws and with his teeth that he wrought out the right cullion or ballock stone. (68)

The priest's testicle falls to the floor, and in the resulting confusion Tibert makes his escape.

Even without Diccon's direct mention of this tale (and the string of fox references that precedes it in *Gammer Gurton*), Tibert's struggle with the priest can easily be recognized as the model for Doctor Rat's encounter with Dame Chat. The priest in *Reynard* has already lost one or more hens to the fox, whereas Dame Chat fears a similar loss; Reynard, knowing what will ensue, nonetheless urges Tibert to enter the priest's barn, just as Diccon encourages Rat to enter Dame Chat's house; both cat and curate make their undignified entries through holes in walls; and so forth. Moreover, one can easily see why the story of Tibert and the priest might appeal to a Tudor playwright with broadly Reformist sympathies. *Reynard*'s priest is a standard late medieval anticlerical caricature; with his staff, his "wife," and his testicles, he would be perfectly at home in the *Decameron* or any number of comparable works. Indeed, his story appeals directly to the reader's sense of irony, as one knave (Reynard) employs a fool (Tibert) to abuse another knave (the priest). Nor was this anticlerical vein lost on the tale's early readers. A Dutch version of the *Roman de Renart* with added commentary was published in the late fifteenth century and rapidly translated into German; in it the commentator—apparently in orders himself—declares "that the priest must have been a priest of a different religion" (Goossens 116).

In selecting this material as the basis for the last scenes of his play, Mr. S. deliberately nudged his work in the direction of anticlerical satire. In the process he also reengaged with the subject of cat abuse, played out this time in something like the religious context surveyed above. However, in adapting the *History of Reynard*, Mr. S. also alters his model in basic ways, most particularly through the elimination of Tibert the cat. This adjustment becomes necessary because Mr. S. is not writing beast epic, but he also simplifies the situation from *Reynard* so that only one individual, rather than two, sustains physical harm, while he retains the figure of the priest, now superimposed on that of the intruding cat. On one hand, the overall effect of these changes is to focus attention on the cleric's humiliation, which no longer has to compete with the spectacle of Tibert's beating. On the other hand, this focus is achieved by assimilating the role of the priest to that of the cat. In effect, if Diccon serves as an articulate extension of Gib, Doctor Rat functions as a body double for Tibert.

In the particular tradition of cat torture surveyed above, the abuse proceeds by a logic of substitution. Sir James Frazer voiced traditional wisdom when he declared that pagan rites of animal sacrifice served as a figural replacement for human sacrifice (11:25, 44). In witch lore cats double and supplement the bodies of the witches whom they serve. The persistence of animal sacrifice in Catholic calendar festivals suggests another kind of supplementary effect, whereby "the Christian church in its dealing with the black art merely carried out the traditional policy of Druidism" (Frazer 11:42), in effect reduplicating the very pagan observances that it stigmatized and sought to replace. In Protestant cat torture, on the other hand, the cat as sign stands in for the cat as efficacious charm, while on a more mundane level, a dead cat takes the place of a mass priest and live cats fill up the belly of a papal effigy, functioning as the proxy recipients of sectarian violence.

As it happens, *Gammer Gurton*'s cats make multiple kinds of meaning by the same process of assimilation and substitution. Diccon may double Gib, but by commutative reasoning, Gib also doubles Diccon, serving as his accomplice, in which capacity he also shadows the common witch-familiar relation of early modern occult lore. However, Gib also functions as a sacrificial stand-in, a scapegoat (scapecat?) for Diccon, a role most clearly illustrated by Hodge's willingness to blame the cat for Diccon's theft of bacon (2.1.306–9). In this respect, of course, Gib doubles a more resonant spiritual relation: that of the Atonement. By taking on the sins of his dramatic world, Gib is reborn as the Cat of Sorrows.

In this respect, Gib too generates his own double in the form of Doctor Rat. If Gib embodies the mode of symbolic relation whereby a cat stands in for a man, Rat embodies the complementary mode of relation whereby a man stands in for a cat. In the process, too, Rat performs his own unwitting expiatory function, satisfying the transgressions of others (both real and imagined) by enduring blows to his body. For both Gib and Rat, of course, the redemptive function resonates at the level of parody, particularly so for Doctor Rat, the defective man of God who, despite (indeed, because of) his own folly, ends up repeating Christ's sacrifice in a comic register. However, in the case of Doctor Rat, a further irony evolves from the cleric's substitution for the figure of Tibert, which reverses the standard animal-for-man troping of popular cat torture. In a sense, Rat does not simply take blows intended for Hodge (the intruder Dame Chat actually expects); the manner of his doing so inverts an entire tradition of interspecies violence.

Not, of course, that any of this is demonstrably on Rat's mind (to the extent that he has one) or even on the mind of Mr. S. Such inversions are best understood as products of the play's textual subconscious, the realm of implied relations arising from its socioliterary context. Five hundred years on, it may seem natural (for want of a better word) to view Gib and Tibert as exemplars of a cultural tradition that marks out animals as victims of human cruelty; this cruelty may seem suspiciously like a synecdoche of human relations with the natural world in general; and these relations may seem to demand their own karmic comeuppance, perhaps in the form of a natural environment so degraded by human abuse that it no longer sustains humanity. However, in *Gammer Gurton's Needle* such ideas remain half a millennium distant, present only by implication in the way the play treats its comic victims. It would be a mistake to read these ideas anachronistically as one of the comedy's overt concerns, but it would be equally a mistake not to recognize the comedy's historical implication in the development of such concerns.

"I Hate Cattis"

As luck would have it, at least two more roasted cats abide in the records of English literary history, both of them roughly contemporary with *Gammer Gurton's* Gib and both of them appearing in the same source. For scholars of Renaissance literature, that source could hardly be more appropriate: William Baldwin's *Beware the Cat*, published posthumously in 1570 and written in 1553, about a decade before its author's death. Where *Gammer Gurton* has been described as the earliest regular English play, *Beware the Cat* has earned recognition as "the first original work of longer prose fiction in English" (Ringler and Flachmann xiv)—in effect "the first English novel" (Ringler 113). Its "onionlike" story line is as tricky as *Gammer Gurton's* is simple:[11] the author claims to repeat a tale told by a friend named Gregory Streamer, in which Streamer in turn relates his own experiences along with four other stories told to him by human companions and one further narrative originally recounted by a cat. On the surface, these tales serve a united purpose: they argue that cats think as we do, speak to one another, and adhere to complex social groups with well-established legal and political hegemonies grounded, like ours, on established custom and consensually recognized authority.

Amid this discourse one of Streamer's fellows tells a brief personal anecdote to prove that "love and fellowship and a desire to save their kind is among cats" as among us:

[T]here was one that hired a friend of mine, in pastime, to roast a cat alive, and promised him for his labor twenty shillings. My friend, to be sure, caused a cooper to fasten him into a hogshead, in which he turned a spit, whereupon was a quick cat. But ere he had turned a while, whether it was the smell of the cat's wool that singed, or else her cry that called them, I cannot tell, but there came such a sort of cats that if I and other hardy men (which were well scrat for our labor) had not behaved us the better, the hogshead, as fast as it was hooped, could not have kept my cousin from them. (16)

The tale's casual asides deserve note: the reference to cat roasting as "pastime"—like playing the piano or a game of cards—can be chilling to twenty-first-century ears, and the sum of twenty shillings paid for the entertainment—four crowns or two angels or a pound sterling—can seem alarmingly steep. However, the main thrust of the anecdote, like many others in *Beware the Cat*, is to depict feline society as a sinister image of its human counterpart: a fellowship united by common interests, ties of loyalty, and self-preservation, keeping its own counsel, acknowledging no debt or kinship to human communities. Like people, cats may experience "love and fellowship and a desire to save their kind," but the similarity produces no amity or mutual understanding, only antagonism.

Again and again *Beware the Cat* urges us to fear and distrust cat society: "*Cats are malicious*" (45, marginal note); "*Cats are admitted to all secrets*" (38, marginal note); "*A cat eat a sheep*" (13, marginal note); "*Cats did kill and eat a man*" (14, marginal note). In one tale an Irish kern is confronted by Grimalkin, queen of the cats, and slays her with a dart; at once a huge band of other cats sets upon him, killing and eating his travel companion. Barely escaping them, the kern arrives at home and relates his adventure to his wife: "which, when a kitling which his wife kept, scarce half a year old, had heard, up she started and said, 'Hast thou killed Grimalkin!' And therewith she plunged in his face, and with her teeth took him by the throat, and ere she could be plucked away, she had strangled him" (14). In another story a cat named Mouse-slayer, the pet of a London bawd, aids her mistress in corrupting the virtue of a merchant's beautiful wife (41–46). In yet another tale Mouse-slayer resides with a knight so fond of books that he neglects the attentions of his fair wife. Moved with anger at the knight and pity for his lady, Mouse-slayer visits the former as he sleeps alone, where she sits on his face and "dr[a]w[s] so his breath that she almost stifle[s] him" (52).

In the broad sense, this sinister picture of feline behavior is not unusual. William Horman's *Vulgaria* of 1519 contains the exemplary sentence "I hate cattis," translated, more copiously than strictly necessary, as "Horreo/aluros/ siue feles/siue cattos" (16r). Mouse-slayer's attempt to smother her studious knight merely lends malicious intent to the long-standing belief (apparently inspired by common allergies) that cats sucked the breath out of human beings. Edward Topsell was repeating established wisdom when he declared in 1607, "It is most certaine that the breath and sauour of cats consume the radicall humour and destroy the lungs, and therefore they which keepe their cats with them in their beds haue the aire corrupted and fall into feuer hectickes and consumptions" (106). The proverbial bond between cats and witches only made matters worse; Streamer's companions speculate enthusiastically on whether "a witch should take on her a cat's body" (16). Yet Baldwin's anecdotes also seem to register—indeed, to react against—a less traditional development: the emerging popularity of cats as companion animals. Pace the advice of Topsell and his ilk, Mouse-slayer's knight sleeps with his cat rather than his wife. When in London with her bawd, Mouse-slayer "was alway much cherished and made of" (41). The kern is strangled by "his wife's pet kitten" (King 398). According to Keith Thomas, cats began to gain acceptance as pets in England only during the late sixteenth and early seventeenth centuries (*Man* 109). Baldwin's novel provides early evidence of this trend; indeed, the tales told by Streamer and his companions may be read as a disapproving conservative response to the emerging fashion for feline pet keeping.

However, as every scholar to study *Beware the Cat* has noted, Streamer is an unreliable narrator, his conservative impulses subject to severe implicit critique. He and his companions embody "the superstitious accretions imposed by the Church of Rome" on primitive Christianity (Ringler 117); *Beware the Cat* is "anti-Catholic satire" that assails "Catholic modes of knowledge acquisition and their rootedness in oral culture" (Gresham 114; Bowers 17). Indeed, the satirical trajectory of Baldwin's novel eerily repeats that of *Gammer Gurton's Needle*, with Gregory Streamer serving as Baldwin's version of Mr. S.'s gullible, superstitious villagers. Granted, Streamer is more urbane and better read than any of *Gammer Gurton*'s characters. His inflated self-regard finds an echo in *Gammer Gurton* only in the figure of Doctor Rat, and his penchant for the occult meets a parallel only in Diccon's conjuring of the devil. However, if we allow for certain differences in background, Streamer emerges as the same kind of half-wit that populates the village of Girton in

Cambridgeshire. *Beware the Cat* and *Gammer Gurton's Needle* are virtually contemporary, and their satirical purpose seems virtually of a piece.

So where *Gammer Gurton* connects Gib the cat to Diccon and the devil and the occult, only to expose the connection as risible and bogus, one should expect Baldwin's lurid view of cat society to elicit a similar kind of disenchanted amusement. Baldwin does not disappoint: Mouse-slayer's story of her "picaresque wanderings furnishes the narrative core" of his satire (King 401), presenting English Catholics as venal, superstitious adulterers. In one household "an ungracious fellow" places the cat's paws for sport in "four walnut shells . . . filled . . . full of soft pitch" until the pitch hardens (47). As the walnut-shod Mouse-slayer rattles around in the garret of the house, her owners assume she is the devil and fall into a panic. Summoning a priest to perform an exorcism, they reenter the house, but Mouse-slayer so unnerves them that they fall into a heap, with the priest's face upon the "bare arse" of a boy "which for fear had beshit himself" (49). The resulting configuration of cat, devil, conjuring, and scatology nicely recalls that moment in *Gammer Gurton* when Diccon summons the devil and Hodge fouls himself for fear. Continuing, Mouse-slayer's story next segues into a racy anecdote rather like that of Tybert and the priest from *The History of Reynard the Fox*. The cat's mistress entertains a lover in her husband's absence; the husband returns unexpectedly, forcing the lover to hide behind an arras; and the cat, wishing to expose him, scratches his legs, but to no avail until, as Mouse-slayer puts it, "seeing that scratching could not move him, suddenly I leaped up and caught him by the genitals with my teeth, and bote so hard that, when he had restrained more than I thought any man could, at last he cried out, and caught me by the neck thinking to strangle me" (50–51). The husband then raises the hanging to discover "this bare-arst gentleman strangling me who had his stones in my mouth" (51). Stories like these employ much the same associational vocabulary as that of Mr. S.'s play, and to much the same effect.

In the process they also seem, by negative inference, to acquit cats of the various outrages imputed to them by Baldwin's gullible characters. Indeed, the novel's second roasted cat appears in Streamer's narrative as a clear parody of transubstantiation, marking Streamer himself as a credulous simpleton. Deciding to attempt a charm that will allow him to understand the language of cats, Streamer visits Saint John's Wood and collects a skinned fox, a hare, a kite, and a hedgehog. Back in London at his lodgings above Aldersgate, he next procures a cat, "which for evil turns they had that morning caught in a snare set for her two days before" (27). Streamer takes "some of the [cat's] grease, the inwards, and the head," leaving the remainder with his housemates, who "parboiled the rest, and at night, roasted and farced with good herbs, did eat it up every morsel, and was as good meat as was or could be eaten" (27). For his part, Streamer then makes a cake out of the cat's liver, kidney, spleen, and heart, together with pieces of the other animals, and consumes this along with various other concoctions. His senses purged with this preparation, he discovers that he can miraculously hear cats speak, which skill in turn allows him to transcribe the autobiographical narrative of Mouse-slayer.

I give just the barest account of Streamer's magical preparations for the simple reason that his own report of them is so extravagant, involuted, and ridiculous as to comprise a minor masterpiece of satirical twaddle. More-over, its nonsense looms still larger against the background of Streamer's own prefatory remarks. As he looks for his animals in Saint John's Wood, he meets some hunters, who lash him with a slip when he asks them if they have seen that beast of ill omen, the hedgehog. Waxing indignant at this, Streamer complains, "And here, save that my tale is otherwise long, I would show you my mind of these wicked superstitious observations of foolish hunters, for they be like (as me seemeth) to the papists, which for speaking of good and true words punish good and honest men. Are not apes, owls, cuckoos, bears, and urchins God's good creatures? Why, then, is it not lawful to name them? If they say it bringeth ill luck in the game, then are they unlucky, idolatrical, miscreant infidels and have no true belief in God's providence. I beshrew their superstitious hearts" (26). The reference to "God's good creatures" an-ticipates later Puritan rhetoric, as when Philip Stubbes protests of animal baiting, "what christe[n] heart ca[n] take pleasure to see one poore beast to rent, teare and kill another[?] . . . For notwithstanding that they be euill to us, & thirst after our blood, yet are thei good creatures in their own nature & kind. . . . [S]hall we abuse ye creatures of God, yea take pleasure in abus-ing the[m], & yet think y^t the contumely don to the[m], redou[n]deth not to him who made them?" (P2r).[12] As a result, Streamer ends up in a badly compromised position, at one moment praising "God's good creatures" and inveighing against the "idolatrical," papistical miscreants who abuse them, yet in the next breath plumping for his own outlandish superstitions, which involve a Eucharistic butchering and consumption of cats, foxes, hares, kites, and hedgehogs.

In other words, while Gregory Streamer serves as an unreliable narra-tor and an object of satirical derision, that does not prevent him from also adding a voice to his novel's anti-Catholic chorus. He functions variously as a mixed satirical figure, the recipient of "idolatrical" lashes as well as the purveyor of idolatrical nonsense. In addition, in doing so he provides a kind of counterpoint to the cats of his narrative, who may claim their place among "God's good creatures," wrongfully maligned by the superstitious fools of Baldwin's novel, and yet nonetheless serve as a steady object of the novel's anti-Catholic invective. After describing how the cat Grimalkin consumed a whole cow, one of Streamer's companions imagines that she might have "the same dignity among cats . . . as the Pope hath had ere this over all Christendom . . . which Pope, all things considered, devoureth more at every meal than Grimalkin did at her last supper" (15). "*The Pope's clergy are crueller than cats*," declares the marginal note alongside this passage, and later another such note assures us that "*Cats hear mo masses than all men hear of*" (48). Again, Streamer's companions speculate that Grimalkin was "a witch in a cat's likeness" who convinced other cats to serve her "like as we silly fools long time, for his sly and crafty juggling, reverenced the Pope, thinking him to have been but a man (though much holier than we ourselves were), whereas indeed he was a very incarnated devil, like as this Grimalkin was an incarnate witch" (20). Among the magic preparations he assembles to help him understand feline conversation, Streamer compounds lozenges out of cat's, fox's, and kite's tongues soaked in wine and macerated with cat's dung, mustard seed, garlic, and pepper; in a parody of the Mass, he gives one of these to a saucy servant, who chews on it, "by means whereof when the fume ascended he began to spattle and spit, saying, 'By God's bones, it is a cat's turd'" (30). At such moments Baldwin's cats remain associated with the superstitious knaveries they exist to debunk. It is not enough that they should expose the mendacity and ignorance of Catholic traditions; they must also partake of the resulting abuse.

Baldwin's novel offers no better emblem of that abuse than the cake and lozenges Streamer concocts out of his roasted cat. In their Eucharistic parody, these edibles not only lend expression to early modern practices of animal torture; in doing so they also proceed by the symbolic elision of cat and savior. The satirical point of this elision, of course, is to contrast the divine humanity of the true Christ with the profane felinity of the mock Host. However, the violence of Baldwin's parody generates at least as much similarity as it does contrast. Christ's suffering ennobles him—even when, as in the crown of thorns, that suffering assumes a parodic dimension. If the reduction of cats to cakes and lozenges serves to recall Christ's sacrifice, it also recalls the sacrifice of those who followed in Christ's footsteps. Mouse-slayer offers her autobiographical narrative to a high commission of cats who have summoned her to answer charges of violating the laws of catdom, and under the circumstances, this court takes on the character of an inquisition for heresy. The court's setting, moreover, makes this similarity explicit. Streamer is drawn to the clamor of it, which disturbs his rest; "every night many cats assembled" in the leads of Aldersgate, "and there made such a noise that I could not sleep for them" (10). Indeed, it is through their place of assemblage that Streamer introduces them: "At the other end of the Printing House [at Aldersgate], as you enter in, is a side-door and three or four steps which go up to the leads of the Gate, whereas sometime quarters of men, which is a loathely and abhominable sight, do stand up upon poles. . . . And I marvel where men have learned [this practice] or for what cause they do it, except it be to feed and please the devils" (10).

Streamer's full adventure unfolds against this mise-en-scène. The leads "where the dead men's quarters were set up" provide a backdrop against which "one [cat] sang in one tune, another in another, even such another service as my Lord's chapel upon the scaffold sang before the King" (23). Likewise, the feeding of "ravens or rather devils" upon the quartered bodies (10) anticipates the tale of Grimalkin's companions killing and eating a man, which in turn prefigures, in inverted form, Streamer's Eucharistic consumption of roast cat. The entire satire is framed against this grisly setting of inquisitorial procedure, death, and dismemberment, which figures the coercive power of the state in both civil and ecclesiastical matters. To this extent, Baldwin's cats function both as objects of representational violence and as emblems of redemptive suffering.

The Brutes, the Brutes

I have argued that we need to understand *Gammer Gurton's Needle* and *Beware the Cat* across the divide of genre, as parallel expressions of a satirical impulse endemic to early modern religious controversy, and that in this light their common recourse to cat abuse seems especially revealing. In one sense this behavior participates in long-standing traditions of interspecies cruelty whereby cats serve as a convenient outlet for violent human impulses. Yet at the same time the maltreatment of Baldwin's and Mr. S.'s cats generates a pattern of redemptive figuration suggestive of the Atonement, with the tortured animals serving as the instrument of deliverance.

One might view it as more than coincidence that this same pattern of abuse resurfaces in the twentieth century, in the work of a writer exceptionally conversant with early modern English religious symbology. In his Christian allegory for children, *The Lion, the Witch, and the Wardrobe*, C. S. Lewis delivers his Christ figure, the lion Aslan, up to a humiliating death that emphasizes his character as a mere cat. As the children Lucy and Susan watch helplessly, Aslan surrenders himself to the White Witch, whose attendants bind him and drag him forth to undergo his version of the Passion:

> "Stop!" said the Witch. "Let him first be shaved."
>
> Another roar of mean laughter went up from her followers as an ogre with a pair of shears came forward and squatted down by Aslan's head. Snip-snip-snip went the shears and masses of curling gold began to fall to the ground. Then the ogre stood back and the children, watching from their hiding-place, could see the face of Aslan looking all small and different without its mane. The enemies also saw the difference.
>
> "Why, he's only a great cat after all!" cried one.
>
> "Is *that* what we were afraid of?" said another.
>
> And they surged around Aslan, jeering at him, saying things like "Puss, Puss! Poor Pussy," and "How many mice have you caught today, Cat?" and "Would you like a saucer of milk, Pussums?" (159)

In light of the precedent set by Streamer's cats, by Gib in *Gammer Gurton's Needle,* and by the various nameless historical cats whose tortures are described above, one is tempted to regard this scene as exemplifying the return of the repressed. A cat/god takes the place of a man/god whose crucifixion has been traditionally parodied by the ritual abuse of cats. Observing the spectacle, one of Lewis's child heroes, Lucy, draws the appropriate conclusion: "'Oh, how *can* they?' said Lucy, tears streaming down her cheeks. 'The brutes, the brutes!'" (159), but, of course, she is not referring to the cat.

Perhaps this should conclude our discussion, but one feels obliged to add a word more. One implication of Lewis's allegory—easily lost in the allegory's character as such—is that human salvation depends not on men and women but on animals: that the animal Aslan somehow helps us understand and indeed redeems the human in all of us. Conversely, to harm the animal in Aslan is to brutalize what is human in ourselves. While the popular American evangelical opposition to the theory of evolution insists, in the name of scriptural purity, on the difference between human beings and other animals, Lewis's allegory implies their connectedness. In the face of American evangelical bigotry, it is worth remembering that this latter remains a viable Christian position.

Chapter 4

The People's Peacock

Rounding the coast of Tierra del Fuego in late 1520, Ferdinand Magellan's sailors encountered a new kind of bird, the penguin. In his account of Magellan's voyage, Antonio Pigafetta identifies these new creatures as "geese" and goes on to describe the crew's predictable treatment of them: "Truly, the great number of those geese cannot be reckoned; in one hour we loaded the five ships [with them]. Those geese are black and have all their feathers alike on both body and wings. They do not fly, and live on fish. They were so fat that it was not necessary to pluck them but to skin them" (101). Pigafetta was trained as a navigator, not as a natural philosopher; if he refers to penguins as geese, it is possibly because that is what Magellan's sailors called them, and if the sailors called them geese, it is possibly because they became a bit easier to eat once their strangeness had been domesticated by this act of naming. For his part, Pigafetta seems a little unsure of the penguins' anserine character, noting that "[t]heir beak is like that of a crow" (101).

Elsewhere, of course, European explorers had encountered a wide range of other new birds, parrots being prominent among them. Unlike penguins, the Psittacidae presented no immediate problem to late medieval avian taxonomy; explorers from Columbus forward, already familiar with South Asian and West African specimens of the family, readily recognized New World parrots for what they were.[1] However, for this very reason they encouraged another kind of confusion altogether. Noting that such birds were well known from contacts with the East, and observing that Columbus's original plan was simply to go east by sailing west, Peter Martyr adduces the existence of parrots in the New World as tentative proof that Columbus had indeed reached his intended destination; as Martyr's first English translator, Richard Eden, put it in 1555, "Albeit the opinion of Christophorus Colonus (who affirmeth these islandes [the West Indies]) to be parte of *India*) dothe not in all poyntes agree with the iudgement of auncient wryters . . . , yet the Popingiaies and many other thynges brought from thence, doo declare that these Ilandes sauoure somwhat of *India*, eyther beynge nere unto it, or elles of the same nature" (Martyr, *Decades* A3v).

In slightly different ways these two moments illustrate a common impulse in European encounters with New World fauna: the tendency to understand the new as a recurrence of the old. Apart from the practical utility of this instinct, which offers explorers a convenient if arbitrary point of reference for their discoveries, Christian cosmology seems to demand it. As José de Acosta observes, almost a century after Columbus's arrival in America, "It is . . . difficult to establish the beginnings of different animals that are found in the Indies and not in our world here in Europe. For if the Creator produced them there, we need not have recourse to Noah's Ark. . . . But if we say that all these species of animal were preserved in Noah's Ark, it follows that these, like the other animals, went to the Indies from this continent. . . . And this being so, I must ask why their species did not remain in Europe" (235). Acosta concludes that "even though all the animals came out of the Ark, by natural instinct and the providence of Heaven, different kinds went to different regions and in some of those regions were so contented that they did not want to leave them" (236), an inference that strains credulity even as it reveals the mental gymnastics that New World exploration required of conventional natural history. For Christian travelers of the generation before Acosta, regarding New World beasts as unusual variants of those already familiar from the Old World seems like a perfectly reasonable reflex: a way to make sense of American biodiversity while still adhering to the Bible's account of the origin of species. However, by Acosta's day the profusion of newly discovered life forms has rendered this procedure impossible; as he puts it, "if we are to judge the species of animals by their characteristics those of the Indies are so diverse that to try to reduce them to species known in Europe would be like calling an egg a chestnut" (236).

Such warnings notwithstanding, the retrograde vision proved key to European cultural assimilation of certain New World species. Its representational consequences were seldom more complex than in the case of the wild and domesticated turkeys first discovered by Spanish explorers of the Caribbean basin during the 1490s and early 1500s. Here the impulse to understand a new species through the perceptual grid afforded by an old one asserted itself first as a well-documented crisis of nomenclature. Early forms of the tur-key's name—"turkey-cock" in English, *coq d'Inde* in French, *Kalecuter* and *türkische Henne* in German—attest to early modern associations of the bird not with the Americas but with the Middle East.[2] This prejudice is nowhere more clearly illustrated than by the Spanish *pavo*. Derived from the Latin for "peacock" (*pavo*) and cognate to the Italian *pavone*, Spanish *pavo* was ap-plied by extension to the turkeys of the New World on the assumption that peacocks and turkeys were different regional varieties of the same creature. By the late 1700s this original confusion, long since dispelled, led to "distin-guishing the peacock as *pavo real*" (Chiappelli, Allen, and Benson 2:598).

In the meantime, turkeys entered the Old World imagination with a prefabricated lineage and a preestablished set of cultural associations. In this sense the European discovery of the genus *Meleagris* may, in fact, be under-stood as a nonencounter, a moment of failed recognition. In an anecdote that became paradigmatic for the New Historicism of the 1980s, Clifford Geertz employed the phrase "turtles all the way down" to describe the kinds of in-finitely regressive formulation through which cultures generate themselves,[3] and scholars in the New Historicist tradition have sometimes employed this phrase to suggest the abiding emptiness at the heart of social signification, which in their view becomes "another instance of the onion peeling down to nothing" (Watson, *Back to Nature* 10). As should already be clear, the cultural history of turkeys, as I propose to tell it here, nicely illustrates the regressive character of such cultural constructions. In the process, it con-forms to Donna Haraway's recent assertion that human-animal relations are "co-constitutive," with "none of the partners pre-existing the relating" and "the relating . . . never done once and for all"; on this view she says, "There is no foundation [to human-animal interaction]; there are only elephants sup-porting elephants all the way down" (Haraway 12). Like other popular New Historicist formulations, this one says as much about the historian as it does about history; its wistful *mise-en-abîme* speaks volumes about the literary profession's frustrated yearning for meaning, both in what it studies and as a body of professional practice. In truth, the history of turkey cultivation *is* important; indeed (to modify another wistful New Historicist pronounce-ment) it holds no end of importance, only not for literary historians; for insofar as this history has biological, environmental, and moral implications concomitant with the domestication of a wild species and, eventually, the intensive cultivation of that species under factory-farm conditions for the satisfaction of another species' appetites, we might wish to resist the New Historicist tendency to view it as essentially empty. It is certainly not empty of consequences.

The Turkey Problem

What we might call the "turkey problem"—that is, the problem that the discovery of the turkey posed to early modern European models of zoological and geographical knowledge—is more complex than the foregoing overview of nomenclature suggests. Here are some of the associated issues:

1. It remains unclear when and where the New World turkey was first encountered.
2. It is nonetheless clear that this encounter led to confusion between the New World species and certain Old World species.
3. While one of the Old World species thus confused with the turkey was the peacock, it was clearly not the only one.
4. These confusions, in turn, were in part encouraged by and in part contributed to broader cultural confusions of which Acosta's dilemma over the origin of species may be taken as a prime example.

These individual issues impinge upon one another in ways that compound the overall problem. For instance, if early explorers do not recognize turkeys for what they are, it becomes commensurately more difficult for readers to know exactly what species of birds are being described or mentioned at different moments in the surviving accounts of these explorers' travels, and this uncertainty is further exacerbated if the explorers and/or their chroniclers cannot even agree on the kind of bird they *think* they have encountered. Likewise, to perceive one kind of bird as another, more familiar kind is arguably to influence one's understanding of the new species in ways that discourage one from recognizing or properly describing its distinctive attributes.

Thus even early scientific (or prescientific) descriptions of the turkey omit significant details. In his 1533 Latin edition of Aelian's *Characteristics of Animals*, for instance, Pierre Gilles introduces an account of the bird that recognizes it as a New World species but nonetheless fails to mention that the male has a beard; instead, Gilles remarks that "its feathers at first display the form and appearance of a hawk's, then appear white on their outer edge"

["Huius plumae tum Acciptris speciem similitudinemq(ue) gerunt, tum extremae albae visuntur" (Aelian 449)]. Commenting on Gilles's description some sixty-odd years later, Ulisse Aldrovandi takes him to task for his omission of the beard, as well as for a second apparent oversight:

> So Gyllius says these things, in which two points of no small moment are to be added: namely that the legs lack spurs, and the male is distinguished from the female, when they reach maturity, by a movable beard before the throat and by the caruncle, [which] is small in the female.

> [Haec itaq(ue) Gyllius, in quibus binae eaeq(ue) non parvi momenti notae desideratur; crura scilicet calcaribus carere, & marem à femina, cum iam ad maturem aetatem pervenerint, seracea barba ante gulam distingui carunculamq[ue] illam in faemina admodum exiguam esse.] (2:41)

Aldrovandi, in turn, will come under correction for suggesting that the turkey has no spurs at all (in fact, it has vestigial ones [Willughby 160]), but the point is not that natural historians only gradually recognized the species' distinctive physical traits. It is rather that the difficulty in doing so went hand in hand with a tendency to view the bird as a variant of something more familiar.

This same tendency is clearly on display in the very earliest accounts of the turkey to appear in Europe. Gonzalo Fernández de Oviedo, for instance, includes an entry on turkeys in the *Sumario* of his *Historia General y Natural de las Indias* (1526), where he opens his discussion by declaring that in the Indies "[t]here are both light and dark turkeys with tails like those of Spanish turkeys. . . . They are better to eat than Spanish turkeys" (63). Oviedo's English translator glosses this passage by noting, "The Spanish 'turkey' is really the peacock" (63n49), and this association, repeated elsewhere, carries with it very specific culinary overtones. Hernán Córtes, for instance, declares that the inhabitants of Yucatán "roast many chickens, like those of the Tierra Firma, which are as large as peacocks" (1.162), while Peter Martyr, synthesizing the earliest accounts of the conquest of Mexico, writes of "chickens, larger than our peacocks and of as delicate a flavour" (*De Orbe* 2:102). For others, the American turkey could be confused with a different Old World species entirely: the guinea fowl. Here the misrecognition extends into both ancient languages and modern biological taxonomy; as the *OED* observes, the guinea fowl was already "known to the ancients (the *meleagris* of Aristotle, . . . Varro and Pliny), the American bird being at first identified with or treated as a species of this" (s.v. "turkey-cock," sb.).[4] When, at length, "the two birds were distinguished and the names differentiated, *turkey* was erroneously retained for the American bird, instead of the African." As if this were not sufficient confusion, "[f]rom the same imperfect knowledge . . . , the ancient name of the African fowl, was unfortunately adopted by Linnaeus as the generic name of the American bird."

Thus one of the interlocutors in Conrad von Heresbach's *Rei rusticae libri quatuor* (1570; translated by Barnabe Googe in 1577) asks his companion to speak of the "outlandish Birds, called Ginny Cocks, & Turky Cocks," to which he receives the reply that "some haue supposed them [that is, American turkeys] to be a kind of the Birdes called in the olde times *Meleagrides*, because of their blewishe Coames, but these kind haue no Coames, but only Wattles. Others agayne reckon them for a kind of Peacockes, because they doo in treading time after the same sort, spread and sette up theyr tayles, bragging and vaunting them selues: howbeit, they neyther resemble these in all poyntes" (166–67). Beyond these primary confusions, the words "turkey" and *pavo* (or *gallina*) were also applied respectively to the capercaillie and to "the currasow (*Crax rubra*), crested guan (*Penelope purpurascens*), horned guan (*Oreophasis derbianus*), chachalacas (*Ortalis* and *Penelopina*) and the ocellated turkey (*Agriocharis ocellata*) of the Yucatán peninsula" (Schorger 3–4). Still further, the English noun "turkey-cock," like the Spanish *pavo*, was already in currency well before the European discovery of the genus *Meleagris*, as when, during the fourteenth century, the Devon county sheriff William Yoo displayed "three Turky-cocks in their Pride proper" (that is, peacocks) on his coat of arms (Izacke n.p.). Here, as elsewhere, the early cultural history of the turkey in Europe is complicated by a variety of biological, chronological, and geographical conflations.

Yet for all these complexities, the turkey's inherited capacities for meaning remain surprisingly coherent and straightforward, operating primarily on two levels: the gastronomic and the moral. In the former capacity not only does it become—in the *OED*'s words—"valued as a table fowl in all civilized lands" ("turkey,"[2] sb. 2), but in the process it also acquires associations with spectacular banqueting, culinary excess, and gourmandise. These associations, in turn, carry over into the moral register, where they reinforce the bird's proverbial affiliation with pride and vanity. Yet in the process one also witnesses a progressive devaluation of the turkey's moral significance, such that it gradually translates from an emblem of pride into the sign of a more contemptible, potentially more comical sin: gluttony. In this transformation the turkey inherits a body of symbolic values from the Old World birds with which it is initially identified, especially the peacock; these values, then, are reconfigured by the turkey's own contact with European culture.

On the culinary side of things, the peacock was already identified with elaborate and costly dining in the Roman period. There are no recipes for it in Apicius's *De re coquinaria*, but Martial's epigrams contain a notable sympotic reference to peacocks in his thirteenth book, called the *Xenia*. There the poet draws a contrast between the peacock's beauty and its edibility, exclaiming, "Do you marvel whenever this bird spreads its glittering feathers, and are you still able, oh hard-hearted man, to hand it over to the savage cook?" ["Miraris, quotiens gemmantis explicat alas, / et potes hunc saevo tradere, dure, coco?" (13.70)]. The *Xenia* are designed as wittily descriptive inscriptions to accompany gifts of food, these latter ranging in character from the humble to the extravagant, with the peacock occurring amid a run of grand banquet birds. (It is followed by the flamingo, the pheasant, the crane, and the swan, among others.) This context makes Martial's satirical point clear: the peacock is on the table less for its flavor than for its luxury value. The sentiment reappears elsewhere in Roman verse,[5] but Martial's epigram, in particular, becomes a standard feature of medieval bestiary entries on the peacock. There it is strangely assimilated to a second Latin tradition, this one stemming from Augustine's *City of God*, which holds that the peacock's "flesh is so hard that it scarcely putrefies, and it is very difficult to cook" (Barber 170).[6]

Yet for all this disapproval, peacock remained popular on the tables of privileged medieval and Renaissance diners, who regarded it as "'noble' game" and "fit only for the wealthy" (Toussaint-Samat 83–84; Albala 188). In Nicolas de La Chesnaye's morality play against gluttony entitled *La condamnacian de Bancquet* (c. 1506), the character Soupper invites his companions to dine on an array of fowl that anticipates similar catalogs in Rabelais, and that includes peacock:

> Ho there! barbarian servants,
> bring us broiler cocks,
> pullets and capons,
> swans, peacocks, and partridges,
> shoulders, legs of kid,

woodcocks, bitterns, hazel-hens
hares, conies, and baby rabbits,
herons, plovers, and blackbirds!

[Sus, ho! serviteurs barbarins,
Apportez-nous ces hustaudeaux,
Poullez et chappons pelerins,
Cignes, paons, et perdriaux,
Epaulles, gigotz de chevreaux,
Becquasses, butors, gelinettes,
Lievres, connins, et lappereaux,
Herons, pluviers, et alouettes?]
(228)

The play's overall tone of moral censure harmonizes with Martial's earlier epigram, but like Martial's lines, these attest to the peacock's continued popularity among gourmands. Taillevent describes the standard mode of its preparation, in which the bird was "blown up and inflated as are swans" ["les convient souffler et enfler comme les cignes"], roasted and gilded about the legs and beak, and served in its skin, with wooden skewers holding the tail-feathers in place "as if the peacock were displaying them" ["comme se le paon faisoit le roe" (Taillevent 130)]. This would have been the technique employed in Rome on Monday, June 7, 1473, when the wedding of Ercole d'Este, Duke of Ferrara, and Eleanora of Aragon, daughter of King Ferrante of Naples, was enlivened by a lavish banquet including "a peacock dressed in its feathers, then . . . Orpheus with his zither followed by four peacocks dressed in their feathers with the tail-feathers opened and a peahen and her young all dressed in their feathers" (Licht 25). Alternatively, Montaigne refers to an exotic mode of preparation whereby "the king of Tunis . . . stuffed his foods with aromatic substances, so sumptuously that one peacock and two pheasants came to a hundred ducats to dress them in that manner" (229). Here, as elsewhere, the peacock remained synonymous with "gastronomic pretension" (Toussaint-Samat 338).

Thus when European explorers reached Central America and encountered domesticated table fowl with iridescent neck feathers and elaborate tail displays, it seemed natural to assume that they were a kind of peacock, all the more so since they figured regularly in Aztec royal dining. Montezuma received tribute in the form of turkeys, and these were used for such purposes as religious sacrifice and feeding the carnivores and raptors in the royal menagerie, as well as for the king's own consumption (Schorger 10). Likewise, when Montezuma provided Córtes with a residence, he included within it accommodations for "fifteen hundred chickens . . . , not to speak of other farm stock, which the Spaniards judged to be worth twenty thousand dollars of gold" (Córtes 1:244). These "chickens"—or *gallinas*—were, in fact, a breeding stock of turkeys. Bernal Díaz marveled at the "birds with great dewlaps," which he encountered in the central market of Tenochtitlán (232), and in general Córtes and his followers identified them with the splendor and prosperity of the Aztec realm.

That being the case, it stands to reason that turkeys should become objects of royal interest and propagation in Europe too. This is so from the very beginning. For instance, the earliest Spanish documents relating to their importation date from 1511–12 and comprise a series of commands, issued to Miguel de Passamonte by King Charles V and signed by the bishop of Valencia, that "in each of those ships that come here from the above mentioned islands [that is, the West Indies], you bring us well guarded ten turkeys, half males and the other half females," for breeding at the Casa de la Contrataçion de las Indias in Seville, under the bishop's supervision (quoted in Schorger 464). Presumably the guard placed on the turkeys was designed to protect them from the surrounding Spaniards, rather than vice versa. In any event, by 1556 turkeys were well established in France, where the city council of Amiens presented King Charles IX with twelve of the birds as an official gift during a royal visit (Aussy 270). As for England, in 1550 King Edward VI granted Sir William Strickland of Boynton a coat of arms including a "turkey cock in his pride proper" (Mosley 2:2739), purportedly in celebration of the fact that Strickland had accompanied Sebastian Cabot to the New World and introduced the bird to England upon his return. Here, as elsewhere, the aristocratic associations may be understood to extend naturally from the character of the turkey as it was encountered in the New World and as it was conceptually assimilated to the peacock of classical and medieval elite culture.

That these associations took on a primarily gastronomic form is only to be expected; after all, the turkey was understood largely as a new and improved peacock, and the peacock, in turn, had been understood largely as a grand banqueting bird. Thus when Charles IX received his twelve turkeys from the city fathers of Amiens, they were only part of a larger package of related fowl, including twelve herons, twelve egrets, six cranes, and six swans

(Aussy 270). In fact, on this score the turkey rapidly outstripped its predecessors; in place of the "tough, insipid flesh" (Toussaint-Samat 338) of the
peacock and other magnificent birds, the turkey offered succulent, delectable
dining. In this respect, it really *was* a new and improved version of its medieval culinary forebears. In 1606 Joseph Duchesne could declare it "one of the
best, healthiest, and most delicious meats available" ["une viande des meil-
lure, plus saines et delicieuses qui se trouvent" (423)], a verdict that anticipates
by over two centuries Brillat-Savarin's description of it as "if not the most
delicate, at least the most flavorful of our domestic birds" (72). As early as 1541
it had established itself as a major banqueting bird even in distant, provincial
England, where Thomas Cranmer required his clergy, when dining on "the
greatest fyshes or fowles," to limit themselves to "but one in a dish, as Crane,
Swan, Turkeycocke," and so forth (Leland 6:38). Likewise, in 1557 the ruling
council of Venice issued an antiluxury ordinance prohibiting the consumption of turkey alongside a second gourmet fowl such as the partridge (Zanon
3:32–33). In effect, the turkey solved a long-standing problem in the theory of
medieval banqueting: how to produce a fowl that was both imposing enough
to serve as the centerpiece of a spectacular dining course and also sufficiently
flavorful to be worth eating for its palate appeal alone. As Heresbach declares,
"in dayntinesse and goodnesse of meate, [turkey] Hennes may compare with
either the Goose, or the Pehenne, and the Cocke farre excell them" (167).

Added to all this, the bird's initial association with exotic locales made
it an ideal object of high-end gastronomic desire in early sixteenth-century
Europe. Early modern celebrity chefs used the new fowl as a proving ground
for their culinary ingenuity. Pope Pius V's personal chef, Bartolomeo Scappi,
includes instructions for preparing "il gallo, & la gallina d'India" in book 2,
chapter 141 of his 1570 *Opera*—probably the most influential cookbook to
emerge from sixteenth-century Europe. The placement here can hardly be
accidental; the preceding chapter provides detailed instructions on how to
serve peacock ["il Pavone nostrale"], which Scappi recommends be presented
in the manner of Taillevent, "so that the neck, tail, and feet are attached . . . ,
and in all it has the same appearance as if it were alive ["in modo che il
collo, la coda, & li piedi stiano fissi . . . , & in tutto abbia la forma, come se
fosse vivo" (F2v)]. Whereas "magnificent fowl such as peacocks . . . were increasingly condemned by dieticians as tough and difficult to digest" (Albala
205–6), Scappi adopts a moderate stance on the subject, declaring that peacock flesh is "dark, but more savory than that of any other bird" ["la carne
è negra, ma piu saporita di tutti gli altri volatile" (F2r)]. Yet even so, Scappi

recognizes the turkey as an improvement: "it has flesh much whiter and softer than that of our peacock, and it grows tender faster than the capon or other such birds" ["ha la carne molto più bianca, & più molle del pavone nostrale, & si frolla più presto che il cappone, et altri simili volatili" (F3r)]. Likewise, "the cock and hen of India are much larger in body than our peacock" ["il gallo, & la gallina d'India son molto piu grossi di corpo che non è il pavone nostrale" (F3r)]—although "the gizzard of our peacock and that of the cock of India are more flavorful than those of all other birds" ["il magone del pavone nostrale, & del gallo d'India sono i più saporiti di quelli di tutti gli altri volatili" (F5r)]. The turkey cock "displays its tail as does our peacock" ["il gallo fa la ruota ancor agli come il pavone nostrale" (F3r)], but its feathers are not sufficiently spectacular to warrant the kind of table presentation customary for the peacock. All in all, Scappi clearly regards the turkey as a special kind of grand banquet bird, closely akin to the peacock and more distantly related to such fowl as the swan, the crane, and the goose.

As the sixteenth century gives way to the seventeenth, this initial perception tends to change, largely because the turkey adapts so well to European domestic breeding. The ready assimilation of turkeys to European animal husbandry quickly divests them of their exoticism and specifically aristocratic associations, and in place of these the bird develops a reputation for stupidity and an identification with gluttony. The latter of these, of course, is already implicit in the culture of aristocratic feasting, as witness the occasional regulations limiting the number and kinds of luxury fowl to be consumed in a single course or at a single meal. However, once the turkey ceases to be recognized as a food of privilege, it loses the redeeming cachet of the upper social ranks and is left, instead, as an emblem of silliness and overindulgence. Even the bird itself is reputed to be a glutton; Charles Estienne, writing as early as 1564, describes turkeys as "cofers to cast oates into, a deuouring gulfe of meate" (116) and declares of them, "the farmer may well say, that looke how many turkeies he hath in his yard, euen so many mule coltes he hath in respect of their feeding" (117). In 1581 Leonard Mascall repeats Estienne's strictures word for word and then adds that while the "training [of turkeys] is more easyer than of other Peacockes, . . . their feeding is a more greater destruction in Gardens, of leekes, onions, & al other kinds of other good herbs" (*Poultrie* G3v). Gervase Markham begs to differ, insisting that turkeys "are kept with more ease and lesse cost . . . then any other Bird"; yet even so, Markham acknowledges that "by some writers they are held deuourers of Corne, strayers abroad, euer puling for meate, and many such like fained troubles" (135). (Estienne, like Scappi, introduces his discussion of the turkey immediately after a chapter devoted to the peacock and compares the birds directly more than once; for both the chef and the husbandryman, these fowl remain intimately related.)

Elsewhere the turkey fits uneasily into the aristocratic order of dining. John Murrell's *Two Books of Cookerie and Carving* (1638, first part appearing in 1615), for instance, rehearses in detail the special terminology that evolved around the practice of carving before "your Soveraignes trencher" (161), and that, in its turn, extended the highly codified and rank-specific rituals involved in dividing the carcasses of animals killed in the hunt.[7] The resulting catalog of terms of art, ranging from the obvious to the bizarre, makes for amusing reading: "unlace that Cony, dismember that Herne, display that Crane, disfigure that Peacock, unjoynt that Bitterne," and so forth (151); but latecomer as it is to the culture of grand European feasting, the turkey gets no such specialized nomenclature. Murrell's ensuing "generall Table of directions for the order of Carving up of Fowle" does include two paragraphs describing how "To cut up a Turkie or Bustard" (168), sandwiched between the sections entitled "Reare the Goose" and "Dismember that Herne." However, this passage has the feel of an afterthought, not least of all because it concludes by noting, "You may cut up a Capon or Pheasant the same way" (169). Murrell's sample menu for "an extraordinary Feast for Summer season" consists of fifty dishes divided into three courses and includes grand banqueting fowl in the form of "A Swan," "A Bustard," and "A Heron or Bitter"; the turkey appears only as part of "A dish of boyld Pea-chickens, or Partridges, or young Turkey-chicks" (3–4). On the other hand, Murrell makes room for "A Swan, Goose, or Turkey" in his exemplary "small common Service of Meat" (7). Robert Appelbaum points out that Murrell sought to market his work by "[o]penly appealing to fashion and cosmopolitanism" (108) as these qualities were associated with the urban lifestyle of seventeenth-century London. Here, in a newly developing gastronomic sensibility, one encounters little of the old medieval bravado that dressed peacocks up in their own feathers and sauced dishes with heavy combinations of sugar, ginger, cinnamon, saffron, and so forth. Instead, Murrell's work anticipates a more relaxed and unaffected style of dining in which "good cooking gives 'each Meat his right' and 'each Dish his due'" (Appelbaum 109), and which would find its definitive expression in Pierre de la Varenne's *Cuisinier françois* of 1652.

The peacock is one casualty of this broad shift in culinary fashion— understandably so given that its primary appeal lay in the grandiose specta-

Figure 7. Marmaduke Craddock, English painted metal tea canister, decorated with turkey and peacock, 1685–1717. © V&A Images. Courtesy the Victoria and Albert Museum.

cle of its presentation. Despite the extensive character of La Varenne's work, peacocks receive no mention at all in *Le cuisinier françois*. Turkey, on the other hand, survives and grows in popularity as a table fowl no longer connected to the old order of courtly feasting. Its attraction resides in its tender and flavorful flesh as well as in the substantial but decidedly understated visual impression it creates at table. As for the standard mode of its preparation, this is already set in A. W.'s *Book of Cookrye* in 1591: "Season it with Pepper groce beaten and salt, and put into it good store of Butter, he must haue fiue houres baking" (18). By the late 1600s peacocks and turkeys consort with one another only in the field of visual representation: for instance, on a painted metal tea canister decorated between 1685 and 1717 by Marmaduke Craddock (see Figure 7), where the birds rest side by side in a scene that arguably speaks to the shared Middle Eastern associations of turkeys and peacocks and tea; or on the painted cover of a virginal produced in 1653 by John Loosemore (see Figure 8). Elsewhere by the mid-seventeenth century the turkey has shed its associations with the grand banqueting birds and

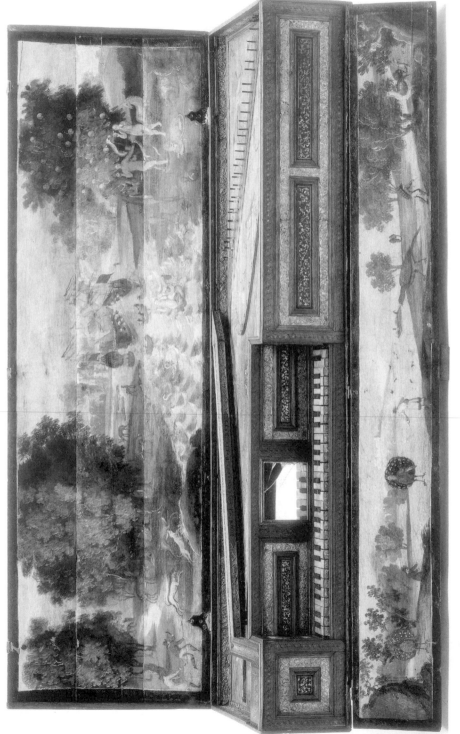

Figure 8. John Loosemore, painted virginal cover depicting the Garden of Eden with turkeys, 1653. © V&A Images. Courtesy the Victoria and Albert Museum.

culinary style of a previous era and has acquired a less exclusive, less aggressively elitist, less overtly ritualistic set of identifications in their place. Rather than being a sign of the exotic or the grandiose, it may be adopted instead as an emblem of gluttony and empty pretension.

Bills of Fare

Predictably, this shift in symbolic associations proves more far-reaching for the literary and visual arts than for the specialized vocabularies of animal husbandry and cookery. For satirical writers, in particular, the turkey displayed great potential early on.

Toward the end of Rabelais's *Quart livre* (1552), for instance, Pantagruel and his companions, who are sailing to the oracle of the Holy Bottle of Bacbuc for advice on whether Panurge should marry, land "on an island admirable above all others, both for its situation and for its governor" ["une isle admirable entre toutes aultres, tant à cause de l'assiete que du gouverneur d'icelle" (2:208)]. There, atop a steep mountain, Rabelais's narrator discovers a landscape "so pleasant, so fertile, so wholesome and delightful, that I thought it to be the true Garden and Earthly Paradise, whose location our good theologians so debate and belabor" ("tant plaisant, tant fertile, tant salubre et delicieux, que je pensoys estre le vray Jardin et Paradis terrestre: de la situation duquel tant disputent et labourent les bons Theologiens" (2:209)]. The land's ruler is "Master Gaster, this world's foremost master of arts" ["messere Gaster, premier maistre es ars de ce monde" (2:209)], a personification of the belly whose "imperious, rigorous, blunt, harsh, difficult, and inflexible" commands permit no disobedience ["imperieux, rigoureux, rond, dur, difficile, inflectible" (2:209)].

Assembled in Master Gaster's court are two sorts of irksome and officious men whom Pantagruel immediately despises, known respectively as Engastrimythes and Gastrolaters. Their names—Speakers from the Belly and Idolaters of the Belly—point clearly enough to their base and dishonorable character, and Rabelais's early allusion to scholastic debates about the location of the earthly paradise signals that the ensuing episode will function as "satire of monks and theologians" (Frame 76). By the end of his career Rabelais's difficulties with church authority were well attested. In 1523, a good decade prior to the composition of *Pantagruel*, his Greek books had been confiscated on orders from the Sorbonne; his dissection of a human body in 1537 ran afoul of university policies; and from 1533 forward the various installments of *Gargantua* and *Pantagruel* were regularly denounced and condemned by the doctors of the university. Thus the *Quart livre*'s Engastrimythes and Gastrolaters provide a late bit of satirical payback for a lifetime's worth of obstruction and hostility on the part of France's principal academic institution.

As for the Engastrimythes, Rabelais famously dismisses them (in a passage translated from Caelius Rhodiginus's *Antiquae lectiones* [1517]) as "diviners, enchanters, and abusers of the common people, appearing to reply to those who ask them questions by speaking not from the mouth but from the belly" ["divinateurs, enchanteurs et abuseurs du simple peuple, semblans, non de la bouche, mais du ventre parler et respondre à ceulx qui les interrogeoient" (2:212)]. Then proceeding to the Gastrolaters, Rabelais subjects them to extended anticlerical invective of a sort already applied elsewhere in his works to the various monastic orders: while differing in appearance, with separate groups distinguished by their diverse habits, "all [are] idle, doing nothing, performing no work, and [are] indeed a useless load on the earth, . . . fearing (as best one may judge) to offend and reduce the Belly" ["tous (sont) ocieux, rien ne faisans, poinct ne travaillans, poys et charge inutile de la Terre, . . . craignans (selon qu'on pouvoit juger) le Ventre offenser et emmaigrir" (2:213)]. Illustrating Saint Paul's warning from Philippians 3:18–19—"For many walke, of whom I haue told you often, and now tell you weeping, that they are the enemies of the crosse of Christe: Whose end is damnation, whose God is their bellie, and whose glory is to their shame"—they "all held Gaster for their great god, they adored him like a god, they sacrificed to him as to their omnipotent lord, they recognized no other god but him" ["Ilz tous tenoient Gaster pour leur grand Dieu, le adoroient comme Dieu, luy sacrifioyent comme a leur Dieu omnipotens, ne recongnoissoient aultre Dieu que luy" (2:214)].

This rather general anticlerical invective is given a specific twist toward the Sorbonne through an allusion to the Gastrolaters' "coquillons"— shell-shaped cowls distinctive of the university's doctors (2:214; Marichal 199)—and the entire episode culminates in one of Rabelais's patented catalogs, as the Gastrolaters range themselves into ranks as if for battle and then make sacrifice to Master Gaster with a bewildering array of foodstuffs:

> Leg of lamb with garlic sauce,
> Paté with hot sauce,
> Pork cutlets with onion sauce,
> Capons roasted in their juices,

Broilers,
Kids,
Fawns,
Hares and leverets,
Partridges and partridge-chicks,
Pheasants and pheasant-chicks,
Peacocks and pea-chicks,
Storks and stork-chicks,
Woodcocks, snipes,
Ortolans,
Cocks, hens, and chicks of India,
Wood pigeons and their chicks,
Pigs in must,
Ducks in onion sauce,
Blackbirds, rails,
Water hens,

[Eschanches à l'aillade,
Patés à la saulse chaulde,
Coustelettes de porc à l'oignonnade,
Chappons roustiz avec leur degout,
Hutaudeaux,
Becars, Cabirotz,
Bischars, Dains,
Lievres, Levreaux,
Perdris, Perdriaux,
Faisans, Faisandeaux,
Pans, Panneaux,
Ciguoignes, Ciguoineaux,
Becasses, Becassins,
Hostolans,
Cocqs, poulles, et poullez d'Inde,
Ramiers, Ramerotz,
Cochons au moust,
Canars à la dodine,
Merles, rasles,
Poulles d'eau,]

(2:217)

and so forth, ad nauseam, ad infinitum, ad fatigationem.

Rabelais's lists may be the most distinctive stylistic feature of his work. Embodying a "cornucopian movement" that "depends primarily on lexical productivity, that is to say, on the list of epithets" (Cave 184), each one represents a virtuoso exercise in *enumeratio* that delights and confounds in equal measure. To begin with, they elaborate on the giantism of Rabelais's first two books; *Pantagruel* opens, for instance, with a chapter-long catalog of the hero's ancestors (book 2, chapter 1), while *Gargantua* gives us a chapter listing the elder giant's childhood games (book 1, chapter 22). However, Rabelais's third book is "[c]ompletely devoid of giantism" (Frame 17), and the *Quart livre* likewise devotes most of its attention to the bizarre people and creatures that inhabit the lands visited by Pantagruel and Panurge on their way to the oracle of the Holy Bottle. As a result, where the lists function at first as folkloric burlesque, comically exaggerating the qualities of the protagonists, in the later books they translate increasingly—albeit not entirely—into an instrument of satirical abuse. The two monumental catalogs of the *Tiers livre* present the following: a humorous blazon of Panurge's testicles offered by Frère Jean as the latter urges him, through an exercise in "Topicques monachales" (1:439), to embrace cuckoldry (book 3, chapter 28); and a grand *récit* of the court jester Triboulet's attributes, serving him as a kind of curriculum vitae of folly (book 3, chapter 38). Prior to the episode of the Gastrolaters and the Engastrimythes, the *Quart livre* has already produced a three-chapter anatomy of Quaresmeprenant (Lent Observance), "a good Catholic of great devotion" who "weeps three quarters of the day" ["bon catholic et de grande devotion. Il pleure les troys pars du jour" (2:126)], as well as a heroic record of the cooks who join Frère Jean in making war upon those inveterate enemies of Quaresmeprenant, the Andouilles (book 3, chapter 40). This last episode involves a swipe at the Swiss, perhaps especially Geneva's Calvinists; as Rabelais's narrator remarks, "The Swiss are now a tough and warlike people, but who knows if they were not once sausages?" ["Les Souisses, peuples maintenant hardy et belliqueux, que sçavons nous si jadis estoient saulcisses?" (2:153)].

Against this developing background, the list of Master Gaster's food offerings gains a decided satirical edge, with the gargantuan menu marking not the comic-heroic physical scale of the Gastrolaters but rather the extent of their gluttony. The gigantic catalog becomes, ironically, a way of belittling them, a satirical technique of diminution by extension which associates them with the notion of "anticaritas" while developing into a "parody of the Eucharist" in the process (Duval 74–77; Alice Berry 106). Yet at the same time the menu proves to be "extraordinarily exuberant" (Alice Berry 106), as-similating the "verbal fecundity of the symposiac tradition" (Jeanneret 207) not to the Gastrolaters but rather to Rabelais's own satirical voice. As for the principle of extension itself, it may at first seem haphazard: the bit cited above moves from domesticated meats (lamb, pork), to domesticated fowl (capons), back to domesticated meat (kids), then to game (fawns, hares), thence to a combination of wild and domesticated fowl (partridges, pheasants, peacocks, storks, turkeys), then back briefly to domesticated flesh (pig) before plung-ing into a sequence of waterbirds. Taken as a whole, however, the catalog displays a clear sense of sequencing. For one thing, it is divided into eight sec-tions distinguished from one another by narrative interpolations of varying length, which range from the terse "Reinforcements of wine with this. Then huge . . ." ["Ranffort de vinaigre parmy. Puys grands . . ." (2:218)] to a chapter break followed by several lines of dialogue. For another thing, these divisions, as confusing as they may seem when examined item by item, display a broad sense of structural integrity. Section one consists of seventeen items, of which six are breads or couscous, five are soups or stews, and five of the remainder are grilled meats; this is followed by fourteen dishes, of which five are sau-sages and most of the rest are cold cuts. Section three then proceeds to list sixty-six foodstuffs, of which the vast majority—fifty-one—consist of fowl (the others are red meat, either wild or domesticated). Next comes a series of thirty-six plates, whereof nine are savory pies and most of the remainder sweets. The final four sections, distinguished from the main list as an alter-native for fish days, include a mammoth catalog of seafood divided into an introductory series of appetizers such as caviar, botargo, anchovies, sardines, and oysters; followed by a huge second course of whole fish—sturgeon, trout, salmon, turbot, and so forth; which is in turn succeeded by a shorter series of dried fish—stockfish, dried haddock—with shellfish and eggs. All of this is then concluded by a final, restrained series of eighteen items, most of which are fruits and nuts.

In short, and despite Rabelais's marvelous, chaotic logorrhea, the final product here involves a deliberate sense of gastronomic progression, a clas-sic order of courses: soup and bread, sausage and cold cuts, flesh and fowl, pasties and sweets. Surveying the culinary literature contemporary to Rabe-lais, Timothy J. Tomasik has recently traced this progression to the series of cookbooks published from 1536 onward by Pierre Sergent and his associates (ms. 30). These works, of which twenty-seven editions appeared between 1536 and 1620, prescribe a structure of banquet courses "virtually identical" to that observed by Rabelais's Gastrolaters (Tomasik, ms. 34). One cannot help wondering whether to attribute this arrangement to Rabelais's sensitivities as a physician; as Ken Albala has noted, early modern writers on diet and nutrition "complained" at length "about [the] lack of structure" of late medieval banqueting, which typically lacked any sense of course progression, and thus medical concerns can arguably have exerted some influence on the emergence, in the 1600s, of "a more rigid order of courses" (Albala 108). As for Rabelais's Gastrolaters, one would expect their gluttony to find its proper structural expression in a complete lack of arrangement—a promiscuous outpouring of undifferentiated foodstuffs. Instead, though, we are given the appearance of disorder imposed upon a broad but very clear sense of sequence. In some cases this sequence follows the broad advice of early modern dieticians, as when Rabelais includes "olives colymbades"—olives in brine—near the beginning of things, in the second section of his catalog (olives were considered stimulants to appetite and therefore good as hors d'oeuvres).[8] Elsewhere the order ignores basic dietary advice, as when figs and grapes appear near the list's end (the nutritionists consider fruits such as "peaches, sweet grapes, and melons" to be corruptible foods that should appear at the start of a meal and "must never be eaten as a dessert" [Albala 109]). However, in both cases the sense of sequencing remains, perhaps reflecting the habits of mind of an author conditioned to think systematically about food as a result of his medical training.

Rabelais's turkeys attest both to the generally systematic character of the catalog in which they appear and to the more erratic nature of the catalog's details. In the former respect, they appear in the lengthiest of the four lists devoted to sacrifice on flesh days, in a place of honor at the center of the meal, and they appear surrounded by other sorts of fowl. As "cocqs, poulles, et poulletz d'Inde," they retain their early Asiatic associations, and they also remain in fairly close proximity to their cultural antecedents, the peacocks, which appear in the list only four items ahead of them. Also in general proximity are other large banqueting birds; the stork makes its appearance three lines ahead of the turkey, and elsewhere in the same sequence one encounters flamingos, swans, herons, bustards, and geese, as well as equally prestigious if less spectacular fowl such as partridges and pheasants. Moreover, as Tomasik has shown, Rabelais's list of birds "begins to take on the character of a taxonomy, much like that in Pierre Belon's *Histoire de la nature des oyseaux,*" and in similar fashion his later catalog of fish seems drawn largely from the natural histories of Belon and Rondelet (Tomasik mss. 36, 38). Rabelais's catalog thus traces unmistakable patterns of culinary meaning, despite the fact that these must compete with a certain amount of random interference. This element of interference, in turn, is perhaps best represented by the various smaller wildfowl—ortolans, snipes, and so forth—that pepper the inventory, as well as occasional irruptions of red meat.

Noteworthy—and again perhaps in keeping with Rabelais's medical training—is the list's general lack of attention to methods of food preparation. Apart from an occasional specification of sauce, as in "eschanches à l'aillade" or "coustelettes de porc à l'oignonnade," there is almost no notice paid to how individual foodstuffs have been cooked or served. The emphasis lies squarely on the length of the catalog and the diversity of the edibles— particularly animal proteins—rather than on matters of culinary technique, with the result that substantial parts of the list, if taken out of context, could describe the animals entering Noah's ark as easily as those entering Master Gaster's gullet. From this standpoint Rabelais's turkeys provide a touch of exoticism, foregrounding the catalog's extremity and outlandishness. However, in the absence of serious attention to matters of culinary artistry, the result can hardly be called a menu or bill of fare. It reads more like an exercise in accounting: a ridiculously inflated restaurant check or a monstrous victualer's invoice. In this respect it invites comparison to the real thing: the records of accounts payable that survive from sixteenth-century banquets. Possibly the most famous of these to occur on French soil within Rabelais's lifetime would have been the feasting at the Field of Cloth of Gold in 1520, a "gastronomic marathon" (Russell 142) for which partial records of expenditure survive. In addition to "373 oxen at 29s. 10 ½ d. each, 2,014 muttons at 3s. 7d., 852 veals (from 2s. 4d. to 3s. 8d. each), 18 'hogs of grease' (specially fattened), 51 pigs, 16 lambs, [and] 101 flitches of bacon," English accounts for the meeting list the following purchases of poultry: "360 capons of grease (fat capons) at 2s. 4d., 901 less succulent ones at 12d., 82 pheasants at 2s., 2,445 quail at 4s. a dozen and 558 at 2s. 2d. a dozen, 506 geese at 7d. . . . , 2 peacocks at 5s. 4d., 199 gulls at 16d., 91 cygnets at 5s., 381 pigeons at 10d. a dozen and a further 252 at about the same price, 140 mews (gulls) at 10d., 32 heron at 2s., 65 shovellers at 2s., 78 storks at 3s., 86 bitterns at 2s., 113 'brewes' at 20d. and less . . . , [and] 11 egrets . . . at 21d." (Russell 151).

In such accounts, if anywhere, one may find a true literary antecedent for the offerings of Rabelais's Gastrolaters. These particular records from the Field of Cloth of Gold give us some sense of the prestige of individual food items; peacocks are the priciest bird on the menu, followed closely by the cygnets, with all the other fowl trailing at a respectful distance. These records also suggest Rabelais's attentiveness to avicultural novelty; there are no turkeys at the Field of Cloth of Gold, but in the thirty-two years separating that diplomatic event from the publication of the *Quart livre*, they come into their own as a new and trendy variety of banqueting fowl, to be associated with aristocratic foodways in all their splendor and excess. By 1559 a minor Norman nobleman such as Gilles Picot, Sieur de Gouberville, could receive a pair of turkeys as a Christmas gift from a neighbor (Fedden 63); to the servant who delivered the birds, Gouberville gave a tip of four sols, a substantial sum that reveals the value he placed on the gift. As for the more substantial feasting associated with courts and cities, it continues the tradition of the Field of Cloth of Gold, mutatis mutandis. A notorious example from across the English Channel involves the weekly dinners provided to the justices of Star Chamber at public expense whenever that court was in session. These meals, instituted early in the reign of Henry VIII, served Lawrence Stone as a prominent instance of the "culinary extravagance" (256) to which he partly attributed the decline of the Tudor and Stuart aristocracy, and they provide another bit of literary counterpoint to the offerings of Rabelais's Gastrolaters. Here, for instance, is the account for Wednesday, January 30, 1593, a flesh day:

> Item in Oysters—IIII^s in XVI^{tene} stone of beefe at XX^s the stone—XXVI^s VIII^d in Bacon—IIII^s in Neats toungs—VI^s in Joynts of Mutton to boyle and to rost—XII^s in Joynts of Veale to rost and for Pyes—XII^s in Suett—II^s VIII^d in Marrowebones—II^s in Lambe—X^s in zeame for Fritters—IIII^s in Capons—XVIII^s VIII^d in Turkeys—XX^s in Pullets—XIIII^s IIII^d in Partridge—XVI^s VIII^d in XII Mallards—XII^s in Teales—X^s in Woodcocks—X^s in Plovers—XII^s in Snyts—X^s in larks—V^s in Rabbetts—VI^s VIII^d in hearbes—III^s IIII^d in Eggs—VI^s in pounded butter—X^s in Creame—II^s IIII^d in Apples for tarts—II^s in Orringes and lemans—XII^d in Rose Water—XII^d in Barberryes—XII^d[.] (Scofield 86)

The Rabelaisian quality of the list remains, but now the peacocks are gone and the turkeys have replaced them as the most expensive bird at table. Apart from the beef and the mallards, we have no way of tracking the quantities of particular foodstuffs, but surely it must say something that the only expenditure to exceed that for turkeys is the twenty-six shillings and two groats disbursed for 224 pounds of beef. As for the Gastrolaters' offerings, they occupy a cultural space in between the Field of Cloth of Gold and the Star

Chamber dinners, a limited historical ambit in which peacocks and turkeys hold equivalent value as articles of conspicuous consumption and markers of gastronomic magnificence.

"Nothing distinguishes the Commons so much as their Eating"

The turkey's association with grand dining continues for some years, even as it is gradually undercut by more déclassé connections. In 1605 Sancho Panza can still declare, "what I eat in my corner without refinements or fuss tastes better to me, even though it's bread and onions, than turkey at those other tables where I am forced to chew slowly, drink little, wipe my mouth every minute, and cannot sneeze or cough if I want or do other things that liberty and privacy allow" (Cervantes 1.11, 74). Writing in 1598, Nathaniel Baxter still couples the peacock and the turkey in an aristocratic environment:

> Peacocks beene Birds of rare qualitie,
> Of shining Feathers, pride and Majestie,
> . . . .
> Sabaean Queene for estimation,
> Presented these to mightie Salomon.
> The Turkie-cocke, a Crauen by nature,
> Is excellent meate, and of Large stature.
> (sig. H3r)

In Thomas Heywood's *The English Traveller* (c. 1627), the scapegrace Young Lionel, bent on consuming his father's estate, has the following exchange with his steward Reignald:

> *Young Lionel*: This night I haue a purpose to be Merry,
>   Iouiall and Frollicke, how doth our cash hold out?
> *Reignald*: The bag's still heauy.
> *Y. Lio.*: Then my heart's still light.
> *Reig.*: I can assure you, yet tis pretty deepe,
>   Tho scarce a mile to th'bottome.
> *Y. Lio.*: Let mee haue
>   to Supper, let me see, a Ducke—
> *Reig.*: Sweet Rogue.

Y. Lio.: A Capon—
Reig.: Geld the Rascall.
Y. Lio.: Then a Turkey—
Reig.: Now spit him for an Infidell.
Y. Lio.: Green Plouer, Snite,
    Partridge, Larke, Cocke, and Phessant.
Reig.: Nere a Widgin?
Y. Lio.: Yes, wait thy selfe at Table.

(sig. B4r)

In each of these cases the aristocratic associations remain, but only under pressure. Sancho Panza would forgo the opportunity to eat turkey in favor of a humble but unaffected repast of bread and onion. Baxter's turkey still appears in the company of peacocks, but it is "Crauen by nature." Young Lionel's call for a capon and a turkey amply demonstrates the grand style of dining he is determined to maintain, but it also enables Reignald's sotto voce insolence about gelding and infidels. The overall impression is of a bird whose cultural meaning has undergone a split between a residual investment in aristocratic ritual and newer, more downmarket connections. These latter preserve the turkey's original affiliation with privilege and grandeur, now reconfigured as empty pretension, cowardice, vanity, self-indulgence, and gluttony. Thus, in Shakespeare's *Henry V*, Gower introduces the "counterfeit cowardly knave" Ancient Pistol, who is ambling unaware toward his humiliation at the hands of Fluellen, with a fowl simile: "Why here he comes, swelling like a turkey-cock" (5.1.69–70; 14–15). The ensuing action deflates Pistol's complacency, with the sequel already signaled by Fluellen's contemptuous retort: "'Tis no matter for his swelling nor his turkey-cocks" (5.1.16–17). In the event Pistol's swollen pretense of heroism encounters its symbolic antithesis in the bloody, swollen pate he receives from Fluellen's cudgel. In like fashion, the turkey-cock of Pistol's bravado—a grand, inflated dish indeed—discovers its gastronomic counterpart in the leek that Fluellen feeds him later in the scene. This latter item marks a predictable bit of poetic justice, since it is the same vegetable that Pistol had earlier promised to "knock about [Fluellen's] pate" as an expression of his contempt for all things Welsh (4.1.54). In the final encounter between these two rivals the leek also very much functions as a parodic dish of shame, fed to Pistol perforce in a caricature of courtly hospitality. Thus, whereas Pistol addresses Fluellen with the familiar and insulting "thou" throughout the leek-eating scene, Fluellen responds ironically in the polite register, in a mockery of the formalities that obtain between host and dinner guest: "You say very true, scald knave. . . . I will desire you to . . . eat your victuals. Come, there is sauce for it. [*Strikes him.*] You call'd me yesterday mountain-squire, but I will make you to-day a squire of low degree. I pray you fall to; if you can mock a leek, you can eat a leek" (5.1.32–38). The scene anticipates Sancho Panza's symbolic opposition between turkey and onion, but where Cervantes' squire imagines the onion to mark a space of humble freedom—specifically, freedom from the oppressive formalities of aristocratic dining—Fluellen's leek presides over the opposite: a carefully formalized ritual of public shaming.

At the same time, if in a more diffuse way, Gower's turkey-cock simile also enacts a valediction to the comic characters and themes of the second tetralogy as a whole. By the last act of *Henry V*, Falstaff has died, forsaken by his prince, and Bardolph has suffered hanging for his theft of church property. To fill the dramaturgical vacuum created by Falstaff's disappearance from *Henry V*, Pistol has been "moved into his place" (T. W. Craik 36) as the centerpiece of that play's comic action, and in his encounter with Fluellen, Pistol appears for the last time in the play. As a result, Fluellen's humiliation of the ancient resonates, marking the sad, demoralized end of all the tetralogy's transgressive energies. Perhaps it is coincidence, but the only other reference to turkeys in any of the four plays occurs early in *1 Henry IV*; there the carriers to be robbed by Falstaff and his companions at Gadshill bestir themselves at the inn where they have lodged for the night, and one of them discovers that his cargo of live birds has not been fed: "God's body, the turkeys in my pannier are quite starv'd. What, ostler! A plague on thee! hast thou never an eye in thy head?" (2.1.26–28). Here the turkeys—Estienne's "cofers to cast oates into"—serve as a minor but suitably mundane and gluttonous feature of Falstaff's comic exploits at Gadshill, providing a prelude to the four-play sequence of comic action whose end will be occasioned by Pistol's turkey-cockish self-inflation. Likewise, the specific exploits framed by these references to turkeys also speak to one another through a complex process of mimicry and deformation. After all, the robbery at Gadshill is made possible by a counterfeit bravado much like Pistol's in *Henry V*, and like Pistol in *Henry V*, Falstaff is exposed as a craven braggart when a disguised Prince Hal and Poins set upon him and his fellows. However, unlike Pistol, Falstaff manages to stave off the reckoning for his cowardice, claiming that he fled from Gadshill after recognizing his assailants through their disguises: "Why, hear you, my masters, was it for me to kill the heir-apparent? Should I turn upon the true prince?" (2.4.268–70).

Pistol, by contrast, lacks the acumen and effrontery to effect such a reversal: "Old I do wax, and from my weary limbs / Honor is cudgell'd" (5.1.84–85). Slinking back to England to turn bawd and cutpurse, he signals the final exhaustion of the Falstaffian impulse.

In *Twelfth Night*, Shakespeare invokes the turkey to similar effect as an emblem of self-inflated folly, but this time the image acquires more rank-specific connotations. Disgusted with the steward Malvolio's social pretensions, Maria and Sir Toby Belch famously convince him that his mistress, Olivia, is in love with him. As the jest begins, Maria instructs Sir Toby, Sir Andrew Aguecheek, and Fabian to conceal themselves where they may observe the steward's conduct: "Malvolio's coming down this walk. He has been yonder i' the sun practicing behavior to his own shadow this half hour. Observe him, for the love of mockery" (2.5.16–18). As he comes into view, the conspirators eavesdrop on Malvolio's meditations and punctuate them with indignant asides:

> *Malvolio*: 'Tis but fortune, all is fortune. Maria once told me she
> [Olivia] did affect me. . . . Besides, she uses me with a more exalted
> respect than anyone else that follows her. What should I think on't?
> *Sir Toby*: Here's an overweening rogue!
> *Fabian*: O, peace! Contemplation makes a rare turkey-cock of him.
> How he jets under his advanc'd plumes!
> *Sir Andrew*: 'Slight, I could so beat the rogue!
> *Sir Toby*: Peace, I say!
> *Malvolio*: To be Count Malvolio! . . . There is example for't: the Lady of
> the Strachy married the yeoman of the wardrobe.
>
> (2.5.23–40)

Where Pistol pretends to martial honor, Malvolio aspires to social distinction; where Pistol fantasizes about beating his betters, Malvolio dreams of marrying them. The two cases provide differently inflected versions of the same obscene impulse: an inappropriate drive to self-promotion, manifested through inept acts of mimicry. Both cases receive the same general treatment: humiliation in its root sense of lowering, a shamefully public putting-in-place. If Shakespeare finds the turkey-cock fitting as an image of the pretensions in question, that is perhaps because the turkey has begun to experience its own symbolic devaluation in the late sixteenth century, with its initial aristocratic associations reconfigured as empty appearance, vain puffery.

Ironically, the turkey has been preceded in this negative valuation, as in its more positive ones, by the peacock. In the twenty-first century the most recognizable of the peacock's old symbolic connections remains its association with pride and vanity. As Victoria Dickenson has noted, "Aristotle called the peacock 'jealous and conceited,' and in Cesare Ripa's late sixteenth-century *Iconologia*, it featured in the emblem for 'Arrogance'" (175). Thus in the turkey-cock imagery of Shakespeare we may perhaps observe another level of inter-species cultural transference, as the New World bird acquires the symbolic associations of the Old World fowl with which it was initially confused. However, elsewhere the turkey gains new semiotic values all on its own, and these have much to do with the greed and gluttony of the lower social ranks. For instance, Andrew Barker's *True and certaine report of the beginning, proceedings, ouerthrowes, and now present estate of Captaine Ward and Danseker* (1609) describes how Ward, the most notorious English pirate of his day, boards a bark in search of treasure, only to discover that this has already been offloaded. Furious, Ward and his followers search the vessel, "[i]n which search, there was presently laid open to their Rauening eies, a couple of Venison-Pasties, diuers Turkey-pies, Capons, Hens, and such other choice viands. . . . At the sight of which, Ward raps out oathes like pellets out of a peece, . . . and cals, come, lets bee merrie my hearts, . . . lets be merrie, & freely fat ourselues with their fodder. . . . Who would bee a boord of the Lyons whelpe, with bare and hungrie allowance of colt fish and naked cheese, and may as we do thrust up their armes to the elbow in a Venison pastie?" (sigs. B2v–B3r). In the absence of gold, the food serves here as an object and emblem of the pirate's rapacity. Similarly, in 1595 the ever-edifying Thomas Beard exhorts his readers to shun the vice of drunkenness, reporting how "Two servants of a Brewer in Ipswich, drinking for a rumpe of a Turkey, strugling in their drinke for it, fell into a scalding Caldron backwards; whereof the one died presently, the other lingringly, and painfully, since my coming to Ipswich" (423). A century later Lady Dainty in William Burnaby's *The Reform'd Wife* can speak with horror of a visit she has just paid to Lady Thrivewell, who "thinks there is no other Welcome but Eating and Drinking": "At the Sight of her Table I was ready to swoon, coming out of the Air! . . . At the upper End sat her Ladiship, and at each Elbow a Daughter with Arms like Plough-Men, and Cheeks like Milk-Maids—They were enough to beat one down with their Breath— . . . The Table, (or rather Larder) was fill'd with *Westphalia* Hams, Pullets, and Turkey-Pies; with a great *Cheshire* Cheese, that rival'd everyone in bulk but her Ladiship, and a large Tankard of Ale, enough to destroy a Dozen Porters" (25).

As her charactonym implies, Lady Dainty has her own foibles, but even so, her description here carries the force of a commonly recognized caricature. In part it feels like a tattered recollection of the old style of manorial banqueting, with its upper-table seating arrangements and its groaning tables. However, Lady Dainty makes it clear that this old model of the food of privilege no longer represents the fashionable standard: "To see the Titles of Quality join'd with such Mob Dispositions! Well, there's nothing distinguishes the Commons so much as their Eating" (26). Her passing insult presupposes a sea change in the prevailing code of English manners, a change well documented by scholars from Norbert Elias to Patricia Fumerton.[9] And this change also presumes a shift in human-animal relations, which undergird the notions of social exclusivity that codes of manners seek to define and enforce. Thus the foodstuffs on Lady Thrivewell's table are marked as irredeemably base in terms of their quantity and their individual quality: the only foreign item is ham from Westphalia, that province still endowed with a reputation for boorish rusticity some sixty years later, when Voltaire made it the setting for the opening section of *Candide*. As for the turkey pies that populate Lady Thrivewell's table, they seem utterly shorn of exoticism, consistent with the plebeian associations of Cheshire cheese and ale, ploughmen and milkmaids and porters.

Burnaby ends this scene of his comedy by paraphrasing Horace's *Epistles* 2.1: at the theater Lady Dainty remarks that "the Audience is much the more Entertaining Sight, and tho' they call the Stage the Image of the World, yet the Box and the Galleries are certainly the truer Picture" (27). The Horatian passage in question has a distinguished pedigree in English writing, appearing on the title page of Ben Jonson's *Bartholomew Fair* in 1631, and its reappearance in Burnaby's play says something about the long shadow Jonson's work cast over the Restoration stage. As it happens, that is not the only debt to Jonson in *The Reform'd Wife*. In fact, Lady Thrivewell's turkey pies also make a preliminary appearance in *Bartholomew Fair*, where they help to introduce the play's most wicked satirical caricature: the hypocritical Puritan minister Zeal-of-the-Land Busy. Before Busy even appears on Jonson's stage, the widow Dame Purecraft, whose favors he pursues, needs him to resolve a question of reformed doctrine. After a bit of a search, Purecraft's son-in-law, John Littlewit, finds the Puritan in a proleptically compromised position, "fast by the teeth, i' the cold Turkey-pye, i' the cupbord, with a great white loafe on his left hand, and a glass of *Malmesey* on his right" (1.6.34–36). Jonson is fond of heraldic and emblematic devices, which he sometimes parodies to good effect with the language of gourmandise and the lower bodily stratum; *Every Man Out of His Humour* (1599), for instance, snidely revises the motto ("Non Sans Droit") of Shakespeare's recently acquired coat of arms: "*Not without mustard*" (3.4.86). Littlewit's discovery of Busy falls into this same category of writing, comprising a kind of unseen impresa: the Puritan's ministerial pretensions are signaled by the Eucharistic bread and wine, and yet the turkey pie intervenes between these two items in a way that hijacks their meaning, steering it away from the regions of the sacred and instead positioning it squarely within the realm of carnal appetites.

Nothing could be more appropriate to a play like *Bartholomew Fair*, which may be the English literary world's most grandly executed tribute to the sin of gluttony. At heart the story of a group outing to a food stand located in a fairground, Jonson's comedy presents the craving for food as a synecdoche for much broader desires. In this context roast pig rather than turkey provides the play with its most prominent comestible symbol; as Littlewit urges his wife, who has already led their entire household to Bartholomew Fair in order to satisfy her pregnant craving for pork, "now you ha' begun with Pigge, you may long for any thing" (3.6.8–9). Busy's turkey pie appears at a particularly delicate point in the play's catenation of desire, just as Dame Purecraft has summoned her spiritual guide to pronounce on the lawfulness of eating pig at the fair. In the event Busy approves the motion with a virtuoso display of exegetical skill: "Pigge, it is a meat, . . . and may be long'd for and so consequently eaten . . . : but in the *Fayre*, and as a *Bartholmew*-pig, it cannot be eaten, for the very calling it a *Bartholmew*-pigge, and to eat it so, is a spice of *Idolatry*, . . . but . . . there may be a good vse made of it, too, now I thinke on't: by the publike eating of Swines flesh, to professe our hate, and loathing of *Iudaisme*. . . . I will therefore eate, yea, I will eate exceedingly" (1.6.51–97). Busy's interpretive gymnastics in this passage help define his character as a whole; his symbolic pig wrestling typifies the process whereby he contorts scriptural teaching into "a sophistical defence of his own appetites" (Stallybrass and White 64). Yet this same self-aggrandizing combination of the sacred and the profane appears before Busy ever sets foot onstage, in his wordless communion with a turkey pie.

As Jealous as a Turkey

The initial association with India and the Middle East, only later superseded by identifications with the New World; the affiliation with traditional foods of privilege, especially the peacock, and the culinary order they presuppose; the additional connection with aristocratic values in their negative dimension, for example, pride and vanity; and the increasing emphasis on these latter qualities, gradually reconfigured as the foolish and gluttonous pretension of the lower social ranks—these are the principal topoi through which western writers understood the turkey between its introduction to Europe in the early sixteenth century and its full establishment there as a domesticated species sometime in the mid- to late seventeenth century. To these one could add certain secondary associations whose origins are not always so easy to trace. For instance, by the mid-seventeenth century the turkey had also acquired something of a reputation for jealousy. In Shakespeare and Fletcher's *Two Noble Kinsmen*, for instance, a minor character frets that by taking a holiday, "I am sure / To have my wife as jealous as a turkey" (2.3.29–30). Margaret Cavendish's poem "Of a Travelling Thought" (1653) depicts the thought in question entering an imaginary poulterer's shop in an imaginary city: "There lay *wild Geese*, though *black* and heavy meat / Yet some grosse appetite lik'd them to eat. / The *cholerick Turkey*, and the *Peacocks* pride, / The *foolish dotterels* lay there close beside" (191–92). By 1648 James Shirley's *Wit's Labyrinth* lists "You are as jealous as a Turkey" as a proverbial expression (43).

Cavendish's familiar juxtaposition of the turkey and the peacock might encourage one to view the former's choler as an extension of the latter's pride, in which case the turkey's jealousy could be understood as one more instance of cross-species transference, with the peacock's pride reconfigured as jealousy when it is assimilated to the cognate species. However, the peacock has no pronounced reputation for jealousy—apart, perhaps, from its mythical association with Juno, a goddess not unfamiliar with the emotion—while other birds are renowned for jealous behavior. For instance, Pliny describes male doves as "very churlish" to their mates, "offering them wrong and hard measure; so jealous be they of the hens" (*Historie* 1:290). In 1675 Joseph Blagrave writes of the female "solitary-sparrow" as being "very jealous, both of her Eggs and young Ones" (103). Bartholomaeus Anglicus likewise repeats Aristotle to the effect that the sparrow "is iealous of his wife, & fighteth oft for her" (sig. 2I7v). And so on: the reputation for jealousy is not so clearly attributed to particular species of birds as to provide a traceable pattern of influence.

Yet even here one might suspect that early modern writers approach the turkey through a set of prefabricated perceptions, a repertoire of habits of thought that largely delimit—if they do not entirely predetermine—the new bird's potential for meaning. The attribution of jealousy to particular species of animal is so common a practice among early writers of natural history as to comprise a general reflex for the writers themselves, a reflex that the scientific tradition from Descartes forward will stigmatize as anthropomorphic. The charge of anthropomorphism insists that by seeing turkeys as jealous or by understanding them as a kind of peacock or by thinking of peacocks as a food of privilege, we say more about ourselves than about the object of our attention, and one object of the new science, from Bacon and Descartes forward, has been to redress this imbalance. The difference, as Carolyn Merchant and others have shown,[10] may in the end prove more tactical than strategic; Bacon is just as interested in rendering nature serviceable to humanity as is any medieval cook preparing a peacock in its own feathers. However, in the materials this chapter has surveyed, we may discern an older notion of nature and an older mode of natural history, in which we cause the natural world to speak to us in our own voice, about ourselves, and tell us what we already know, even in the midst of all that is rich and strange and new.

Chapter 5

"Vulgar Sheepe"

By the 1500s England's sheep grazed placidly behind a thick fog of classical and ecclesiastical metaphor. The effect was most baneful, of course, for people of literary temperament, many of whom seemed unable to distinguish the flesh-and-blood beasts from their figurative counterparts. For instance, the sheep, lambs, rams, wethers, and ewes that populate the works of Shakespeare are overwhelmingly of the figurative variety, illustrating with anesthetic regularity a conventional series of concepts: pathetic helplessness, endangered innocence, sacrificial submission, bleating obedience, errant stupidity. These qualities, in order, may be exemplified as follows: Talbot, seeing his fellow soldiers driven back by the French, exclaims, "Hark, countrymen, either renew the fight, / Or tear the lions out of England's coat; / Renounce your soil, give sheep in lions' stead" (*1 Henry VI* 1.6.27–29); when Henry VI entails his crown upon Richard, Duke of York, in preference to his own son, Queen Margaret claims that he might as well leave "The trembling lamb environed with wolves" (*3 Henry VI* 1.1.242); Malcolm imagines Macduff delivering him to Macbeth like "a weak, poor, innocent lamb / T'appease an angry god" (*Macbeth* 4.3.16–17); Cassius complains that Caesar "would not be a wolf, / But that he sees the Romans are but sheep" (*Julius Caesar* 1.3.104–5); Proteus declares that "a sheep doth very often stray, / And if the shepherd be a while away" (*Two Gentlemen of Verona* 1.1.74–75).

These are the basic morphemes of what we might call early modern "sheepspeak"—a specific instance of the "system of psycho-sociological differences" that Lévi-Strauss viewed as structuring human interaction with the animal world more generally (207; see 204–8). To think with sheep is preeminently to invoke these categories, but it is also to invoke them in connection with a secondary set of associations that function more clearly on the level of literary allusion. For instance, Shakespeare twice refers to the classical tradition wherein Ajax, driven mad by his jealousy of Odysseus, attacks a herd of sheep before committing suicide (2 *Henry VI* 5.1.25–27; *Love's Labour's Lost* 4.3.6–7).[1] Aesop, in turn, provides early modern writers with a rich variety of sheep stories, many of which presuppose the inveterate dyad of sheep (or lamb) and wolf. Caxton's 1483 Aesop (with additional material from Rinuccio, Avianus, Petrus Alphonsus, and Poggio Bracciolini) features three fables of "The Wolf and the Lamb" (75, 93, 192), a fable of "The Wolves and the Sheep" (114), and one of "The Wolf, the Shepherd, and the Hunter" (123). Not included among these was another bit of the Aesopic corpus of particular influence: the fable of "The Wolf in Sheep's Clothing" (Perry 1:500). This last was already so widely dispersed in classical times that Christ could allude to it in the Sermon on the Mount: "Beware of false prophets, which come to you in sheepes cloathing, but inwardly they are rauening wolues" (Matthew 7.15). As for Shakespeare, his sheep and lambs appear often in the company of wolves, as in the passages already cited from 3 *Henry VI* and *Julius Caesar*. In 2 *Henry VI*, Queen Margaret specifically recalls Aesop, exclaiming of Richard of Gloucester, "Is he a lamb? his skin is surely lent him, / For he's inclin'd as is the ravenous wolves" (3.1.77–78). Yet by Shakespeare's day England was famously rid of its wolves; as Keith Thomas notes, while they "seem . . . to have survived on the North Yorkshire Moors and other high parts of England until the fifteenth century" (*Man* 273n), nonetheless "at the beginning of the early modern period England was distinctive among European countries because she had no wolves" (273). To this extent Shakespeare's various wolf/sheep pairings cannot be regarded as a reflection of contemporary environmental circumstances; instead, they acquire the character of a literary convention.

If this chapter begins with a survey of the various breeds of symbolic sheep that populate the early modern English literary imagination, this is in necessary contrast to my purpose, which is to search for literary evidence of their living, ruminating counterparts. As this opening survey suggests, such evidence practically disappears beneath the accumulated sediment of ovine metaphor, allusion, anecdote, and cliché. This effect is not confined to traditional belletristic texts. Edward Topsell opens his discussion of sheep in *The Historie of Foure-footed Beastes* by rehearsing the animal's different names in Hebrew, Arabic, Chaldee, Persian, Greek, Latin, French, Italian, Spanish, German, and Illyrian; he then retails various bits of travelogue and bestiary lore, in the process citing (among others) Homer, Herodotus, Strabo, Varro,

Aelian, Nicomachus, Oppian, Leo Africanus, and holy writ; he recounts selected regional ceremonies and traditions relating to the care, treatment, and
exchange of sheep; and then, on the fourth of his fifty-odd folio pages devoted
to the animal, he declares, "[T]hus much I thought good to expresse before
the generall nature of sheepe, of the diuers and strange kinds in other nations,
that so the studious Reader, may admire the wonderfull workes of God, as
in all beasts so in this . . . : and for as much as their story to be mingled with
the others would have been exorbitant and farre different from the common
nature of vulgar sheepe, and so to have been mixed amongest them, might
haue confounded the Reader: It was much better in my opinion to expresse
them altogether" (601).

It is a wonderful moment of *recusatio*, as Topsell declines to speak of
that whereof he has already spoken. However, even his promise of future relief goes unfulfilled; the following pages contain more references to classical
authors (Pliny appears in the very next paragraph, Virgil, Ovid, and others
on the next page), more ethnographic detail, more, in fact, of everything.
Yet despite all this verbiage and erudition, Topsell can still complain twenty
pages later,

> Horses, Dogs, and almost euery creature, haue gotten fauour in
> Gentlemens wits, to haue their natures described, but the silly
> sheepe better euery way then they, and more necessary for life, could
> neuer attaine such kindnesse, as once to get one page written or
> indighted for the safegard of their natures, I do therefore by these
> presence from my soule and spirit, inuite all Gentlmen and men
> of learning, . . . to giue their mindes to know the defects of this
> beast. . . . *Columella* and *Varro* two great Romanes, . . . being men
> of excellent wits and capacitie, yet had their names been forgotten
> & they neuer remembred, if they had not written of rustick and
> countrey matters. . . . Therefore it shall be no disgrace for any man
> of what worth soeuer to bestow his wits vpon the sheep. (618–19)

One is reminded of Buffon's critique of Aldrovandi, made famous by Foucault: "Let it be judged after that what proportion of natural history is to be
found in such a hotch-potch of writing. There is no description here, only
legend" (quoted in Foucault 39). Topsell seems to see the problem, even as
he conceives its solution in terms of classical literary precedent. Here, as in
Shakespeare, the sheep is less an animal than a textual effect.

Given such circumstances, it makes sense that the two most successful current scholars of literary sheep in early modern England should both conceive of their subject as, in Hamlet's sense of the word, a tropical beast. Julian Yates traces "the figure of a speaking sheep, individuated from the flock, summoned to the table talk of its human masters, and made to speak the truth about labor," as this figure migrates from More's *Utopia* to Philip K. Dick's *Do Androids Dream of Electric Sheep?* (2). Likewise, Paul Yachnin presents *The Winter's Tale* as an exploration of "the Christian metaphor of the virtuous human community as a flock of sheep" (216–17). In both cases these scholars respond, like Topsell, to the preeminently figurative status of sheep in early modern England, a status so densely elaborated as to render their character as living beings secondary and virtually coincidental. By contrast, the present study responds to Erica Fudge's insistence that "the animals within [Renaissance] texts . . . be interpreted as animals and not simply as symbols of something else" (*Brutal Reasoning* 4).

Fudge's call for scholarship to "interpret . . . animals as animals" in early modern England (*Brutal Reasoning* 176) may not fully theorize the form such interpretation would take, but her work provides abundant evidence that "human beings are inextricably linked with nonhumans" in the period (189). In what follows I propose to trace the remnants of this linkage as they figure in traditionally literary texts of the Elizabethan and Jacobean period; in the development of contemporary nonbelletristic genres such as the husbandry manual; and ultimately in the English landscape, as such texts register its transformation in Tudor and Stuart times. Ironically, this line of study begins with a particular kind of nonhuman animal, only to end with people. In the process it also traces the impact of their interrelation, as this becomes manifest in the quality of their shared environment.

Sheep-Biting Rascals

To study how early modern English writers dealt with sheep, one could do worse than to start with the concordances. Consider, for instance, the two most successful nondramatic poets of the sixteenth and seventeenth centuries. Edmund Spenser's works contain seventy-five instances of the word "sheep" or its plural and possessive variants, together with thirty-six occurrences of "lamb," "lambs," or "lamb's" (Osgood 468, 758). By contrast, John Milton's English poems include three instances of "sheep" along with four instances of "lamb" and its variants (Bradshaw 195, 314). The difference is breathtaking, especially for two poets so close to one another in time and equally renowned for their appropriations of the pastoral mode.[2] One might seek to redress the balance on Milton's behalf by surveying his English prose works too, but even these yield only two further instances of "lamb" and twenty-three usages of "sheep" and its immediate variants (Sterne 738, 1224–25).

I have already suggested that Milton's experiments with genre include the development of a "horseless epic," purged of the form's traditional chivalric associations. One could almost as easily credit him with the creation of a sheepless pastoral mode, in which these conventional markers of the *locus amoenus* recede into virtual invisibility. For Spenser, on the other hand, the sheep functions mostly in its traditional capacity as an attribute of the pastoral landscape and a sign of the pastoral mode; of the 111 occurrences of "sheep" and "lamb" cited above, 71 appear in *The Shepheardes Calender, Colin Clouts Come Home Again*, and book 6 of *The Faerie Queene*. (Fifteen more instances occur in "Mother Hubberds Tale," where they perform a similar generic function as conventional attributes of the beast fable.)

One can readily understand the horselessness of Milton's epics as reflecting the poet's express dissatisfaction with the martial focus of traditional epic verse. The scarcity of sheep in his pastoral poetry, on the other hand, is not quite so easy to account for. One explanation may involve the structural nature of Renaissance pastoral, which links the pagan bucolic tradition of Greece and Rome to the vocational discourse of Christian obedience. This linkage, of course, comprises the master trope of early modern sheepspeak; far more ubiquitous and powerful than allusions to Aesop or Ajax's madness, it provided the early modern world with its single best means of transforming sheep from animals into symbols. Following Maureen Quilligan's claim that "[a] sensitivity to the polysemy in words is the basic component of the genre of allegory" (*Language of Allegory* 33), this linkage also becomes densely allegorical, combining the profane and the sacred, body and spirit in a complex, open-ended pun. However, allegory has famously been a problem for Milton, from Doctor Johnson's strictures on the war in heaven to Quilligan's claim that the originality of *Paradise Lost* lies in the "audacious unallegorical literalness" of its narrative (*Milton's Spenser* 132).[3] By discarding the standard zoological attributes of pastoral, Milton, it could be argued, dismisses the body of allegory in favor of its spirit—a procedure consistent with his broader tendency to debunk the classical tradition while simultaneously appropriating its genres and gestures for altered purposes.

Later in this chapter I offer a second explanation for Milton's relative non-treatment of sheep. For now, however, let it suffice that he and Spenser provide us with an instructive opening contrast: two poets famous for their engagement with pastoral, one of whom employs sheep primarily for their conventional value as signifiers of the mode and the other of whom scarcely employs them at all. At the risk of further complication, it is worth introducing Shakespeare's patterns of usage into this overview as well, for they vary considerably from their equivalents in Spenser and Milton. There are fifty-three lambs and forty-seven sheep in Shakespeare, almost as many as in Spenser, but they are dispersed throughout his works in a way that frustrates any definitive identification with a specific genre. There are no heavy concentrations of usage in traditionally pastoral plays such as *The Winter's Tale* and *As You Like It*, as the example of Spenser might lead one to expect. True, sheep tend to be slightly more numerous in the comedies, where they appear in *The Comedy of Errors*, *Two Gentlemen of Verona*, *The Taming of the Shrew*, *Love's Labour's Lost*, *Much Ado about Nothing*, *As You Like It*, *Twelfth Night*, and *The Merchant of Venice*. However, they also do turns in tragedies such as *Hamlet*, *King Lear*, *Macbeth*, *Julius Caesar*, *Coriolanus*, *Titus Andronicus*, and *Romeo and Juliet*; in histories such as the three installments of *Henry VI*, *Richard III*, *King John*, *Richard II*, and *Henry V*; in problem comedies such as *Measure for Measure* and *Troilus and Cressida*; in romances such as *Cymbeline*, *The Tempest*, and *The Winter's Tale*; in both epyllia; and in the sonnets (Spevack 4:1868, 5:2880). Sheep do seem to occur a bit more frequently in the early work; there are eleven in *Two Gentlemen of Verona* and six in *Love's Labour's Lost*. However, apart from these modest spikes, the words "sheep" and "lamb" are distributed evenly across the entire range of the poet's career and without respect to genre or subject matter, with at least one and no more than four usages in each of the other works mentioned above. To judge by the mundane exercise of counting them, sheep seem never to have been far from Shakespeare's mind.

Of course, this sort of numerical assessment can take us only so far toward understanding how sheep worked in early modern English cultural and literary imaginations. Sooner or later we must attend to specific contexts, a process made especially difficult in this case by the high density of formalized and figurative reference already noted. Spenser's sheep, for instance, do all the same symbolic things that Shakespeare's do. They stand for martial fecklessness, as when, in book 6 of *The Faerie Queene*, the Salvage Man defends himself against Turpine's followers, "Whom he likewise right sorely did constraine, / Like scattred sheepe, to seeke for safetie" (6.6.38.5–6). They represent endangered innocence, as when Colin implores Pan to "save from mischiefe the unwary sheepe" (*Shepheardes Calender*, December.10). They serve as sacrificial victims, as when Hobbinoll promises to present Elisa with "a milkwhite lamb" as an offering of love and obedience (*Shepheardes Calender*, April.96). They represent pliant gullibility, as when Diggon Davie complains of evil shepherds who "bene ydle and still, / And ledde of theyr sheepe what way they wyll" (*Shepheardes Calender*, September.80–81). They wander and lose their way, as Thomalin understands in the March eclogue of *The Shepheardes Calender*, where he worries repeatedly that his own "sheepe would stray" or "chaunce to swerve" (34, 44). They appear over and over in the company of wolves; indeed, the November eclogue even manages to combine wolves and straying flocks in Colin's complaint that "The beastes in forest wayle as they were woode, / Except the wolves, that chase the wandering sheepe" (135–36). Like Shakespeare's wolves, Spenser's sometimes don sheep's clothing, as, for instance, one to which Diggon refers in the September eclogue, a beast that "ever at night wont to repayre / Unto the flock, when the welkin shone faire, / Ycladde in clothing of seely sheepe" (186–88).

I am not arguing for the inferiority of this language as literature, nor am I suggesting that Shakespeare, Spenser, and their compatriots were incapable of dealing with sheep on the level of literal reference. I also am not arguing that their figurative references to sheep lack any basis in observable ovine behavior, as if sheep never strayed from their flocks or wolves never ate them. I simply note that whatever basis these topoi may have had in empirical observation (and some, such as the convention of the wolf in sheep's clothing, had none at all) remained subordinate and indeed coincidental to their status as discursive markers. In positing this distinction, I simply follow the practice of the *OED*, whose entry on sheep begins by invoking "the ruminant genus *Ovis*" (s.v. "sheep," sb. 1) before quickly passing on to enumerate various "[s]imilative (often passing into figurative) uses" of the word (s.v. "sheep," sb. 2). I argue that, by contrast to these figurative animals, certain other early modern sheep betray a relatively recent assimilation to the period's discursive regime; they display, in other words, a traceable connection to the distinct circumstances of early modern grazing, animal husbandry, and related activities. While the following examples cannot pretend to be exhaustive, they do offer a different way of thinking with sheep, one that helps us to glimpse their material presence within sixteenth- and seventeenth-century English culture.

One such cluster of usages develops around certain sheep-related social and legal practices. Most beginning students of medieval literature are familiar, for instance, with the scene in the Wakefield *Second Shepherds' Pageant* wherein the shepherds in question catch their neighbor Mak in the theft of a sheep and toss him in a blanket by way of punishment (628). Within the symbolic economy of the play, this moment marks a transition from justice to mercy, from the law of the Old Testament to the promise of the New, and it therefore contrasts sharply with the shepherds' earlier threats to "hang" Mak's wife Gill and "do thaym [both] to dede" if they are caught with the stolen animal (596, 621). However, for all that, these earlier threats have no basis in Old Testament law, which stipulates, to the contrary, "If a man steale an oxe or a sheepe and kill it or sell it, he shall restore fiue oxen for the oxe, and foure sheepe for the sheepe," and "If the theft be found with him aliue, (whether it be oxe, asse, or sheepe) hee shall restore the double" (Exodus 22.1, 4). Instead, the punishment of death for grand larceny (that is, theft of more than a shilling) originates with Henry I, who "decreed that all thieves taken in the act"—like Mak and Gill—"should be hanged" (Pollock and Maitland 2:496), and whose precedent in this regard extended, albeit with exceptions, into the early modern period. To this extent, when *The Second Shepherds' Pageant* turns from the law to the gospel, it is, in fact, turning away from a specifically English version of the law.

That, at least, is the theory of how punishment for larceny worked. In practice, magistrates had a good deal of flexibility in applying the death penalty to cases of manifest theft, with the result that the standard punishment "fluctuated between death and mutilation" (Pollock and Maitland 2:496). The less severe penalty thus appears in *2 Henry VI*, again in connection with the theft of sheep. There, as Jack Cade inaugurates his rebellion with a public account of his supposedly noble birth and inherent virtues, his followers supply a sotto voce counterpoint to his exaggerated claims:

> *Cade.* I am able to endure much.
> *Dick. [Aside.]* No question of that; for I have seen him whipt three
>   market-days together.
> *Cade.* I fear neither sword nor fire.
> *Smith. [Aside.]* He need not fear the sword, for his coat is of proof.
> *Dick. [Aside.]* But methinks he should stand in fear of fire, being burnt
>   i' th' hand for stealing of sheep.
>
>   (4.2.56–63)

Like the episode with Mak and his wife, this passage occurs in a comic and deflationary context perhaps partly determined by the association of sheep with such *genera humilia* as pastoral. However, the association is also clearly popular and contemporary, and in both cases it involves a noteworthy pattern of substitution. For Dick the butcher and Smith the weaver, Cade's sheep theft represents the truth behind his pretensions to aristocratic descent; likewise, the sheep stolen by Mak and Gill and hidden in their child's cradle stands in for that child, and by further extension for the infant Christ, whose birth provides the main matter of *The Second Shepherds' Pageant*. In both cases these patterns of replacement return us to the very modes of figuration and symbolism that this essay has sought to step beyond. It is almost as if the place-holding function were a part of the nature of early modern sheep themselves—as if the principle of fungibility had itself become intrinsic to early modern sheepishness.

Sheep stealing—like theft of livestock more generally—was "a lucrative offence in the middle ages" that remained profitable in the early modern period (Ireland 318), and it presented both the offender and the authorities with a series of problems regarding the sheep's status as a distinct, identifiable animal. To begin with, "I cannot simply place my neighbour's sheep in my field and hope that no-one notices"; likewise, "I might try to conceal" or "disguise" them, but these expedients are unreliable and at best temporary (Ireland 318). On the whole, the best way to dispose of livestock is "to transform them into money or goods" via the act of sale or barter (Ireland 318). To this extent, one could say, the act of sheep stealing aims to transform a unique and distinguishable beast into a nonunique, fungible commodity. Thus it makes a certain sense that both Cade's and Mak's sheep theft should occur in the context of exchanges that render the nature of identity unstable. A cigar may sometimes be just a cigar, but one begins to suspect that there may be no such thing as a nonsymbolic sheep.

At any rate, similar transformations occur in a later context that also involves issues of theft and imposture. Long known as one of Shakespeare's most deeply pastoral plays,[4] *The Winter's Tale* also deploys sheep in ways that suggest their connection to contemporary law and popular culture. The play's bucolic final acts open with a trip to market, as the Clown who is ostensibly Perdita's brother goes forth to buy spices for an upcoming sheep-shearing festival. These provisions—"saffron to color the warden pies; mace; dates; . . . nutmegs," and so forth (4.3.45–47)—will feast the shearers (4.3.42), who are clearly "additional workers" of the sort typically hired by substantial sheep farmers at shearing time (Bowden 669). That the Clown and his father have achieved such affluence is made clear in this same scene, in terms that once again entail the economic convertibility of sheep, as the Clown tries to reckon the anticipated income from their shearing: "Let me see: every 'leven wether tods, every tod yields pound and odd shilling; fifteen hundred shorn, what comes the wool to? . . . I cannot do it without the compters" (4.3.32–36). The herd of fifteen hundred wethers signals prosperity in itself, without any further calculation; that the Clown attempts such calculation anyway, and fails, says even more about the substantial nature of the family's holdings. In this context the trip to market represents a conventional business expense,[5] funded presumably with the proceeds from last year's shearing, which will now be invested against future profits as well. In legitimate as well as illegitimate commerce, the sheep operates as a placeholder for other kinds of wealth.

However, the Clown's main function in this scene is not to serve as a representative of successful legitimate commerce but instead to enact its exploitation by scoundrels. The play's scoundrel par excellence is, of course, Autolycus, who here accosts the Clown and, claiming to have been robbed (by himself, no less), relieves him both of his cash and of potentially useful information about the upcoming feast. This action effectively restages the fable of the wolf in sheep's clothing, as Autolycus assumes the role of victim in order to victimize others. Thus it also ends, appropriately, in the same way it began, with reference to sheep; as the Clown heads on to market, Autolycus declares to his retreating back, "I'll be with you at your sheep-shearing too. If I make not this cheat bring out another, and the shearers prove sheep, let me be unroll'd, and my name put in the book of virtue!" (4.3.119–22). Not only does "the picking of the Clown's pocket prefigure the 'sheep-shearing' scene that follows" (McFarland 132), but from the legal standpoint pickpocketing and illicit sheep shearing are, in fact, the same offense. The former "was debarred of the benefit of clergy so early as by the statute of 8 Eliz. c. 4" in the same cases wherein sheep theft is accounted a felony without benefit of clergy—that is, when the larceny exceeds "the value of twelvepence" (Blackstone 4:241). As for the latter, it was specifically accounted a felony not only to steal sheep but also "to kill sheepe, and take theyr skinnes, or to pull wool from sheeps backs" (Pulton 131). Autolycus's idea of theft as fleecing here encounters its material counterpart in the Jacobean notion of fleecing as theft.

Autolycus traces his onomastic lineage back to the grandfather of Ulysses whose own father was Mercury, the god of thieves.[6] (Shakespeare's Autolycus is "litter'd under Mercury" [4.3.25].) However, his more immediate dramatic ancestry derives from medieval vice and trickster figures such as Mak of *The Second Shepherds' Pageant*. This being so, it seems somehow right that both these characters should perpetrate sheep-related crimes and that these crimes should involve transformations of identity whereby a sheep is alleged to be a human infant or human beings are alleged to be sheep. That these transformations also parallel the processes of exchange whereby sheep are translated into goods and currency, both within *The Winter's Tale* and in the early modern English agrarian and criminal (and literary) economies more generally, simply underscores the importance of such symbolic transactions for our understanding of early modern ovinity. Barbara Mowat has remarked that the "vocations" of Autolycus and the Clown—"a rogue" and "a wealthy owner of sheep," respectively—"can hardly be seen as coincidental" (68); rather, they embody tensions in the economic life of early modern England whereby sheep become implicated in various morally and legally questionable activities. As Leonard Mascall observes at the outset of his third book on *The Gouernment of Cattell*, "The shepheard ought to be of a good nature, wise, skilfull, countable, and right in all his doings, wherein few are to be found at this day, . . . for by their idlenes and long rest they grow now to waxe . . . ill mannered, whereof breeds many theeuish conditions, being pickers, lyars, & stealers, and runners about from place to place, with many other infinite euils" (197). After all, the fleecing of sheep was a common metaphor for the cheating of simpletons, in early modern England as now; as Webster's Lodovico observes, "Great men sell sheep thus to be cut in pieces / When first they have shorn them bare and sold their fleeces" (1.1.63–64). However, the metaphor was less dead four hundred years ago than it is today; beyond the usual symbolic patterns, the cases cited all display some recognizable connection to a lived reality in which real people interacted with real animals. This renders them unusual among literary sheep of the period.

This point can be illustrated with one more crime-related figurative usage, in this case one that has not survived into late modern English. The noun "sheep-biter" and its participial variant "sheep-biting" first enter the language in Tudor and Stuart times; the *OED*'s earliest recorded instance of the former dates from 1548, whereas its first example of the latter comes from *Measure for Measure*. In fact, Shakespeare uses the words twice in his plays. In *Measure for Measure*, Lucio insults the disguised Duke Vincentio (who has just accused him of defamation) by tearing at his friar's hood and exclaiming, "[Y]ou bald-pated, lying rascal, . . . [s]how your sheep-biting face, and be hang'd an hour!" (5.1.351–55). In *Twelfth Night*, likewise, Sir Toby refers to Malvolio as a "niggardly rascally sheep-biter" who deserves to "come by some notable shame" (2.5.5–6). These constructions both accord with the *OED*'s definition of the words as denominating "a malicious or censorious fellow" (s.v. "sheep-biter," sb. 2.a.) who engages in "thieving" or "sneaking" (s.v. "sheep-biting," vbl. sb.). As it happens, the *OED* also— and unsurprisingly—describes these forms as a figurative transference from earlier usage, in which the noun "sheep-biter" refers to "[a] dog that bites or worries sheep" (s.v. "sheep-biter," sb. 1). This, in turn, is precisely the sort of behavior in which one "Adam the Waynwriht" allegedly indulged his dogs in 1317 in Wakefield, where a certain Thomas Fernoule brought charges against him because those dogs, "at the instigation of [Adam's] children, killed a sheep of his worth 2ˢ" (Baildon et al. 4:168). Here, as with Autolycus's fleecing of the Clown, a specific sheep-related criminal activity provides the basis for a metaphorical usage. The latter usage has endured, whereas the former has not, but both can be traced in specific ways to the material practices of early modern English agrarian culture. In this sense they help to put us in touch with what Topsell called the era's "vulgar sheepe."

Honey-Stalks

A second set of references worth our study relates to what we would now call veterinary medicine. These images conjure up the idea of the diseased sheep, or flock, in ways that speak both to the long-standing figurative correspondence between ovine and human communities and to the more recent development, in early modern England, of a systematic discourse of agricultural management and animal husbandry. Topsell speaks directly to the need for the latter when, in a passage from *The Historie of Foure-footed Beastes* quoted earlier, he calls for gentlemen to publish books about sheep "to the safeguard of their natures." He is calling, specifically, for a prophylactic and therapeutic medical discourse: a literature whose object is "to know the defects of this beast, but also to inuent the best remedies that nature can afford" for its ailments (619). With its growing emphasis on empirical observation, seventeenth-century natural history proves receptive to his appeal.

Despite his sometimes retrograde habits of natural-history writing, Topsell leads the way into a detailed study of the maladies of sheep. He catalogs a series of ovine health hazards that include "venomous meates or Hearbes," "colds,"

"Scabs," "the Pox, or the Blisters," "the warts, and cratches," "the falling sick-nesse," "the paines in the eies," "phlegme," "the swelling in the iawes," "the cough, and paine in the lungs," "sighing, and shortness of breath," "loathing," "fluxes," "the melt," "the sicknesse of the Spleene," "Feauers," "pestilence," and "Lice and Tikes," offering preventives and remedies—in some cases more than one—for all of them (611–18). However, Topsell's efforts in this direc-tion are hardly unique. In 1577, thirty years ahead of Topsell's work, Conrad von Heresbach's *Vier Bücher zur Landwirtschaft* had already been translated into English by Barnabe Googe under the title *Fovre Bookes of Husbandry*; there Heresbach offers remedies for the scabs ("wash . . . them with Urine, and after annoynt . . . them with Brimstone, and Oyl" [143a]), "the murreyne of the Loongs" (143b), "Eating of woormes, or venemous grasse" (144a), the "woorme in [the] foote" (143b), "the cough" (143b), and so forth. Earlier than Googe's translation of Heresbach, Thomas Tusser advised his readers on how to protect their sheep from "[t]he flie . . . and wormes" (C3r). Earlier even than Tusser, John Fitzherbert described how to make "a medicine to salue pore mens shepe" (f. 21) The final book of Leonard Mascall's *Gouernment of Cattell*, which first appeared in 1591, devotes a full section to "The Rem-edies and Medicines for Sheepe and other Catell" (213). Shortly after Topsell, Gervase Markham's *Cheape and Goode Husbandry* (1614) gave the subject ten pages of detailed discussion. And so on.

These publications bespeak a rapid growth of interest in the interrelated topics of agriculture, animal husbandry, farm management, and veterinary medicine, a growth that scholars have also related to such concurrent develop-ments as the realignment of agricultural economies, the emergence of nation-alism, and the advent of the new science. Anthony Low posits the occurrence of a "georgic revolution" in seventeenth-century England, an event "with social, ideological, economic, and technological ramifications as well as liter-ary consequences" (12). Stefano Perfetti has argued that the new "science of animals" in early modern Europe "found its expression in new literary genres and epistemic practices" (ms. 1). Wendy Wall has implicated Markham's hus-bandry manuals in the production of "a national myth of the land . . . that called into being national subjects by renaming their activities in terms of the collective unit of Englishness" ("Husbandry" 770). In such narratives the vocabularies of economics, natural history, and national sovereignty develop through a process of mutual implication that also manifests itself in more tra-ditionally belletristic literature. Given that British sheep produce the British wool that produces the British economy that produces the British Empire, we should not be surprised to find sheep involved in this same process.

In *Titus Andronicus*, for instance, Tamora prepares to solicit Titus's aid in defending Rome, which is under assault by an army of Goths led by Titus's son Lucius. When the emperor Saturninus expresses doubt that Titus will "entreat his son" on Rome's behalf, Tamora replies,

> I will enchant the old Andronicus
> With words more sweet, and yet more dangerous,
> Than baits to fish, or honey-stalks to sheep,
> When as the one is wounded with the bait,
> The other rotted with delicious feed.
>
> (4.4.89–93)

Editors have made little of this passage, generally resting content to gloss "honey-stalks" as clover.[7] Alan Hughes's revised New Cambridge edition of the play provides more information here than most, noting that "'Rot' is a liver disease of sheep" (137n92) and that, according to the *OED*, "Shakespeare is the only writer" to use the phrase "honey-stalks" as a name for clover blossoms (137n90). However, if Shakespeare is the only writer to use the phrase, and if Shakespeare's usage of it requires an explanatory gloss, where does the gloss come from? How, for that matter, does the *OED* know the meaning of Shakespeare's unique phrase?

As it happens, both the *OED* and Shakespeare's modern editors get the gloss from Samuel Johnson, who first provides it, without any specific attribution, in his 1765 edition of Shakespeare's works: "Honey-stalks are clover flowers, which contain a sweet juice. It is common for cattle to overcharge themselves with clover, and so die" (Shakespeare, *Dramatick Works* 7:55n9). From there it has migrated into standard editorial usage, but not without at least some dissent. For instance, John Monck Mason objects in 1785, "Clover has the effect that Johnson mentions, on black cattle but not on sheep. Besides, these *honey-stalks*, whatever they may be, are described as rotting the sheep, not as bursting them, whereas clover is the wholesomest food you can give them" (306). So the standard explanation of Shakespeare's phrase is introduced without attribution, 150 years after the poet's death, by a highly influential literary scholar whose attainments in the field of veterinary medicine remain somewhat less well attested, and whose explanation in this case encountered disagreement fairly early on. If editors have held on to Johnson's gloss, one suspects, they have done so mostly for want of an alternative.

On the other hand, if we turn to early English husbandry manuals for help with the passage, we may at first be disappointed, for they do not mention "honey-stalks." However, they are much exercised about other unwholesome feeds, especially those that impart excessive moisture to animals. For instance, Mascall counsels that "in Winter & Spring time, ye ought for to keepe [sheep] close, till the day haue taken all the gelly or netty rime from the earth, for in time the gelly is on the grasse, [it] doth ingender . . . heauinesse of the head, and a looseness of the belley" (*Cattell* 208–9). Markham advises against feeding sheep on "lowe and moyst grounds, which are infectious" (68). Gabriel Plat declares, "Sheep that feed upon such grounds as yeeld silkish soft grasse, are sooner rotted, then those that feed upon a drier, and a hard grasse" (62). Heresbach warns shepherds not to put their flocks out to graze "tyll the sunne haue drawen up the deawe, and hurtfull vapours of the ground" (140). In general these writers seem concerned about the noxious effects of dew on tender ovine bellies.

Notable among the dews in question is one sort with loose biblical associations, which Topsell describes as follows: "In India . . . it raineth many times a dew like liquid honey falling vppon the hearbs and grasse of the earth: wherefore the shepheards lead their flocks vnto those places, wherewithal their cattle are much delighted. . . . Such a kind of dew the Haebrewes call *Manna*, the Grecians *Aeromelos*, and *Drosomelos*: the Germans *Himmelhung*: and in English Honny-Dew; but if this bee eaten vpon the herbs in the month of May, it is very hurtful vnto them" (603). Elsewhere, Topsell warns, "If in the spring time Sheepe do eate of the dew called the Hony-dew, it is poyson vnto them and they dye thereof" (611). Thirty years later Plat remarks that "some are of the opinion, that Honey-dewes cause" sheep to become "rotten" (70). As for clover, by contrast, Markham declares it "most wholesome for sheep" (79).

My immediate point about Tamora's words should be clear by now. The husbandry manuals suggest that those words do not involve a reference to clover at all, but rather that "honey-stalks" is a convenient nonce formulation referring to any vegetation laden with honeydew and therefore noxious to sheep. However, if we stay with the husbandry manuals for a moment longer, we may discover something else worth noting: specifically, that the husbandry writers do not seem clear about what "honey-dew" is supposed to be. Instead, their use of the term tends to conflate three different things: the biblical manna of Exodus 16 (as in the passage from Topsell cited above); the aphid secretions identified by the *OED* as the term's principal referent (and illustrated by a passage from Googe's Heresbach [s.v. "honeydew," sb. 1]); and the plant nectar gathered by bees in the production of honey. This last substance, in turn, is conventionally identified with the honeydews troublesome to sheep; thus Plat dismisses the argument that honeydews cause rot in sheep by noting that "there are more honey-dewes in sound yeares for Sheepe, then in rotten yeares" and that "when Sheepe are most subject to this disease [that is, rot], the Bees are likewise most subject to die in the Winter time with famine" (70). This honeydew is both etymologically and semantically identical to mildew—or "Meldew," as Markham calls it (79).[8] As Plat explains,

> Mildew . . . is thus caused: When the flowers . . . are in their pride, . . . the Sunne . . . exhaleth some part of their sweetnesse, and converteth the same into Common Aire, which in the night is condensed, and falleth into dew . . . ; This dew being unctuous and clammie, . . . getteth power to suffocate, and strangle the vegetative vertue of the Corne . . . ; and to the end that all things might be conducible to the generall profit; I will spend a few lines in commendation of this creature of God, the Bee; who getteth her riches totally, out of nothing but what else would be lost; for whatsoever she getteth, is that which the flowers by their attractive vertue draw to them in the night, out of the dew that falleth. (59–60)

This mildew, which strangles and rots vegetation, likewise engenders rot in sheep.

For his part, Shakespeare's fascination with rot is well attested. As Robert Appelbaum has pointed out (18–27), it acquires a persistent culinary dimension that asserts itself memorably in Hamlet's vision of his father's "funeral bak'd-meats" appearing at his mother's wedding feast (1.2.180); likewise, Appelbaum has noted the anticipation of this image that occurs in *Titus Andronicus* when Titus bakes Tamora's sons into a pie (27–28). We are now in a position to see Tamora's "honey-stalks" as another instance of this same preoccupation with decay and putrescence, elaborated this time through the vocabulary of animal husbandry. Once again the image anticipates a complementary moment in *Hamlet*, where the prince draws Gertrude's attention to two portrait miniatures, one of his father and the other of his uncle: "Look you now what follows: / Here is your husband, like a mildewed ear, / Blasting his wholesome brother" (3.4.63–65). Here, Claudius is translated into a metaphorical version of Tamora's honey-stalks, communicating his corruption to Hamlet Sr. much as Tamora imagined conveying hers to Titus. Hamlet's participle "blasting" clearly draws on its verb's sense "To blow or breathe on balefully or perniciously" (*OED*, s.v. "blast," v. 7), which in turn derives from the corresponding noun, meaning "A sudden infection destructive to vegetable or animal life" (*OED*, s.v. "blast," sb. 6). Given the density of Hamlet's image, he could be imagining his father either as a plant or as a grazing animal; in either case he is employing the language of animal husbandry that Shakespeare explored earlier, in *Titus*, to similar effect.

Such imagery, though fairly unusual, is not confined to Shakespeare; other writers, too, draw on the vocabulary of ovine disease. Fresh from the stocks in *Bartholomew Fair*, Ben Jonson's Justice Overdo persists with his project of reforming the fair's manners, insisting that "The shepherd ought not, for one scabbed sheep, to throw by his tar-box" (3.3.26–27). Frustrated in her amorous designs, John Fletcher's Amaryllis in *The Faithfull Shepherdesse* seeks the assistance of a local shepherd "whose nigh starved flocks / Are alwayes scabby" (B4v); later in the same play the swain Perigot swears that he loves Amaryllis and insists, "if I falsely swear, / Let [Pan] not guard my flocks, let Foxes tear / My earliest Lambs, and Wolves while I do sleep / Fall on the rest, a Rot among my sheep" (E4v). However, this imagery finds its most memorable expression in Milton's "Lycidas": "The hungry Sheep look up, and are not fed, / But swoln with wind, and the rank mist they draw, / Rot inwardly, and foul contagion spread" (Riverside 125–27). Commenting on this passage, Stella Revard has seen in it an allusion to the plague of 1637, which "many thought . . . was a judgment of God upon the people of England and their unworthy clergy" (255). However, any such reference has also been relayed through the intervening language of the early modern husbandry manuals, as has the poem's preceding complaint "As killing as the Canker to the Rose, / Or Taint-worm to the weanling Herds that graze, / . . . / So, *Lycidas*, thy loss to Shepherds ear" (45–49). Googe's translation of Heresbach prescribes a remedy for "the Taint, or Stingworme" (134b) and, like most husbandry manuals, tends to present it primarily as a threat to cattle and horses. (Markham does observe, however, that "Sheep are as subject to wormes in their guts and stomackes as any other cattell whatsoeuer" [78].)

As for the "rank mist" that spreads "rot" and "contagion" to Milton's "hungry Sheep," it is clearly conceived as a kind of devotional mildew.

If these passages prove notable because they employ concepts and language that circulate widely in contemporary agricultural treatises, they deserve further attention for their frequent translation of this material into the spiritual and ethical register. From Tamora's image of honeyed deceit, through Overdo's penal tar box and Perigot's false oath, to Milton's wind-swollen flock, the idea of ailing ovine bodies seems to encounter its representational double in the diseased human conscience and the corrupted human soul. Like the stolen and fleeced sheep of *The Second Shepherds' Pageant* and *The Winter's Tale*, these ailing creatures derive their meaning from a specific set of agrarian conditions; they attest to a distinct way of experiencing the relation between human beings and domestic animals. Yet, in the process, they are abstracted from those same conditions, conscripted into a signifying order that in effect denatures them. In a move that is the opposite of reification, real sheep lose their materiality and are reconstituted within the realm of the symbolic. An ovine body becomes a figurative placeholder for the human soul.

A comparable transformation occurs in one more set of early modern sheep images drawn from contemporary agriculture: those relating to the phenomena of enclosure and engrossing. Recent scholarship has been particularly drawn to this material, which provides a convenient point of purchase for ecocritical discussions of environmental transformation and degradation. Especially popular is Raphael Hythloday's complaint, in Sir Thomas More's *Utopia*, that the proponents of enclosure "are not content, by leading an idle and sumptuous life, to do no good to their country; they must also do it positive harm," allowing their sheep to "devour human beings themselves and devastate and depopulate fields, houses, and towns" (4:19). Joan Thirsk describes this as "the best remembered of all the diatribes against depopulation" that emerged from the enclosure controversy of the early 1500s (238), and Julian Yates has pointed out how it effects "a perverse reversal of pastoral (and pastoral care)" such that "metaphorical shepherds [the 'abbots' and other 'holy men' Hythloday blames for the spread of enclosure] have literalized their flocks and been transformed into wolves" (17). Topsell cites More while complaining that "depopulation and destroying of townes" have made it "so that for Christians now you haue sheepe" (625). Elsewhere passing references to enclosure may not always carry such a clear ethical and spiritual charge; when Shakespeare's Katharine tells Boyet in *Love's Labour's Lost*, "My lips are no common, though several they be" (2.1.223), the jest is brief and relatively innocent. However, More's and Topsell's sentiments resonate, as when William Harrison blames the "enclosures" of "the abbots and prelates of the clergy" for causing "the chief decay of men and of tillage in the land" (258). Here again the vulgar sheep of early modern England make a fleeting appearance on the printed page, only to disappear once more into an enveloping haze of metaphor.

Dignity of Sheep

Among metaphors, none attaches itself more insistently to the sheep of early modern Europe than the cluster of tropes that depict Christ as a sacrificial lamb and/or shepherd to the flock of his believers. The symbolic investment here is enormous, so much so that it transcends devotional discourse and sacred occasions, leading to the appearance of such imagery in other contexts entirely. Topsell, for instance, is much exercised to assert "the dignity of sheep" (620). "[T]he aboundance of the names thereof in the Haebrew tongue," he maintains, "is a notable testimony of the singular account which God himselfe made of this beast" (598), and elsewhere he invites "the studious Reader" to "admire the wonderfull workes of God, as in all beasts so in this, to whom in holy Scripture he hath compared both his Sonne and his Saints" (601). Again, in his discussion of lambs, Topsell insists that "the greatest honour thereof is for that it pleased God to call his blessed Son our Sauiour by the name of a Lamb in the Old Testament, a Lambe for sacrifice, & in the new Testament, styled by Iohn Baptist, the Lambe of God that taketh away the sinnes of the world" (641).

Oddly, this effusion follows hard upon a different kind of remark altogether: "Their [that is, lambs'] flesh is nourishable and conuenient for food, but yet inferior to weather mutton, for that it contayneth more moysture then heate" (641). Elsewhere, too, Topsell juxtaposes the animal symbology of Christ's sacrifice with the mundane business of eating and drinking. Thus he observes that

> in many houses . . . there is a kind of Venison made of the flesh of Rammes, which is done by this meanes: First they take the Ramme (and beate him with stripes on all parts till the flesh grow redde, for such is the nature of the blood, that it wil gather to the sicke affected

places, and there stande to comfort them, so by this meanes after
the Ramme is killed the flesh looketh like Venison: but as in other
discourses, namely Hares and Conies, wee haue already shewed our
hatred of all cruell meates, so also I vtterly dislike this, for it be not
sufficient to kill and eat the beast, but first of all put it to Tyranni-
cal torments, I cannot tell what wil suffice, except we will deale with
beastes, as PILATE did with CHRIST, who was first of all whipped and
crowned with thornes, and yet afterward did crucifie him. (622)

In an early moment of Keith Thomas's "compassion for the brute creation"
(143), Topsell voices his abhorrence of culinary refinements that involve un-
necessary animal suffering. In the process, too, he effects an unexpected
reversal such that the suffering animal serves as a figurative substitute for
Christ, the metaphorical Lamb of God. Taken to its logical conclusion, this
pattern of reciprocal metaphor endows "a kind of Venison made of the flesh
of Rammes" with the redemptive properties of the Eucharist.

Elsewhere the gastronomical qualities of sheep's flesh function in a parallel if debased register as a marker of sexual appetite. As a common euphe-
mism for "prostitute," the noun "mutton" resounds jocularly through the
surviving canon of early English drama. In *Doctor Faustus*, Lechery describes
himself as "one that loves an inch of raw mutton better than an ell of fried
stockfish" (2.2.153–54); in *The Two Gentlemen of Verona*, Speed cheekily refers
to Julia, his master's beloved, as "a lac'd mutton" (1.1.97). In *Friar Bacon and
Friar Bungay*, Robert Greene gives this language an ecclesiastical spin; as
Margaret, thinking her beloved Lacy has forsaken her, bids farewell to her
father and prepares to enter a convent, the gentleman Ermsby jests, "The
old lecher hath gotten holy mutton to him: a Nunne" (4.1.1895–96). It is
an odious witticism, forcing the carnal and the spiritual together under the
implicit shadow of incest, but its juxtaposition of the salacious and the sacred
occurs repeatedly, figured in terms of the ingestion of sheep's flesh and often
connected with issues of dietary prohibition and regulation. Thus, Falstaff
facetiously accuses Mistress Quickly of "suffering flesh to be eaten in [her]
house, contrary to the law" (*2 Henry IV* 2.4.344–45)—a charge that speaks
ambiguously to the Boar's Head Tavern's reputation for catering to two rather
different kinds of appetite. As for Mistress Quickly, she shrugs off the charge
in a way that specifies the dietary restriction it entails: "What's a joint of
mutton or two in a whole Lent?" (2.4.346–47). Perhaps it is not much to her,
but to Lucio in *Measure for Measure*, the prohibited consumption of sheep's

flesh betokens both sexual hypocrisy and political malfeasance; Duke Vincentio, he insists, has never been afflicted with Angelo's moral prissiness: "The
Duke . . . would eat mutton on Fridays. He's now past it, yet . . . he would
mouth with a beggar, though she smelt brown bread and garlic" (3.2.181–84).
For his defamatory pains, we may recall, Lucio is rewarded by enforced mar-
riage to "a whore" (5.1.515), a punitive dietary regimen that makes fish days
look like liberty incarnate.

No literary moment speaks more clearly to the entangled sacred and
profane associations of early modern sheep's flesh than act 2, scene 2 of
Thomas Middleton's *Chaste Maid in Cheapside*, not least because this scene
bypasses questions of plot development, preferring to operate instead at
the level of thematic relevance. In it the complacent cuckold Allwit encounters two Promoters on a London street: informers charged with polic-
ing the Lenten prohibitions against the consumption or sale of flesh. For
Middleton's original audience of 1613, these figures would have been only
too familiar; the year had seen a disappointing harvest (Marcus 99), and
the resulting austerity measures led to severe enforcement of the Lenten
dietary restrictions. Given the generally sardonic tone of Middleton's play,
it comes as no surprise that the Promoters in question should prove thor-
oughly corrupt, accepting bribes, on one hand, while stuffing themselves
with confiscated meat, on the other: "This Lent will fat the whoresons up
with sweetbreads, / And lard their whores with lamb-stones; what their
golls / Can clutch goes presently to their Molls and Dolls" (2.2.67–69). As
for Allwit, he recognizes the informers at once for what they are—"Sheep-
biting mongrels, hand-basket freebooters" (2.2.99), "planted" in the street
"To arrest the dead corpses of poor calves and sheep" (2.2.62)—and much
of the scene's humor derives from the adroitness with which he arouses and
then mocks their greed by pretending to be a gullible visitor to the wicked
city, in search of "veal and green-sauce" (2.2.80).

Yet, Allwit's fun pales beside its sequel. After he leaves the stage, there
appears a nameless Wench *"with a basket, and a child in it under a loin of
mutton"* (2.2.136 s.d.), and spotting the piece of meat, the Promoters set
upon her at once. In apparent distress, she insists that her mistress has
medical permission to eat meat during Lent and promises to fetch confir-
mation if the Promoters will simply watch over her basket of mutton in the
meantime. More than happy to take command of her forbidden edibles,
the Promoters send her off on her errand, only then to discover the true
contents of her basket:

Second Promoter: Look what market she hath made.
First Promoter: Imprimis, sir, a good fat loin of mutton.
   What comes next under this cloth? Now for a quarter
   Of lamb.
Second Promoter: Now for a shoulder of mutton.
First Promoter: Done!
Second Promoter: Why, done sir!
First Promoter: By the mass, I feel I have lost;
   'Tis of more weight, i'faith.
Second Promoter: Some loin of veal?
First Promoter: No, faith. Here's a lamb's head,
   I feel that plainly; why, I'll yet win my wager.
[He takes out a baby.]
Second Promoter: Ha?
First Promoter: 'Swounds, what's here?
Second Promoter: A child!
First Promoter: A pox of all dissembling cunning whores!
Second Promoter: Here's an unlucky breakfast!

(2.2.159–69)

Scholars have noted the almost contrapuntal parallelism between this scene and the sheep-stealing episode from the Wakefield *Second Shepherds' Pageant* (Dutton xix). Where Mak and Gill disguise a sheep as a child, Middleton's Wench disguises a child as a sheep; where Mak and Gill steal the disguised sheep; Middleton's Wench abandons the disguised child; where the sheep's discovery reveals Mak's crime and leads to his symbolic punishment, the child's discovery confirms the Wench's successful evasion of responsibility for her actions; both plays use their sheep to shadow their respective themes of death and resurrection. The patterns are so neat as to imply imitation, and yet there is nothing in Middleton's play to suggest that he wrote with the Wakefield *Pageant* in mind, or even that he was at all familiar with the Wakefield *Pageant*. Instead, it makes better sense to regard both plays as expressing a shared set of cultural conditions governing the relation between humanity and ovinity, such that the two categories entail and distill into one another at their extremities of reference. This feature of their behavior helps to explain why the present chapter, which has taken as its starting point the effort to identify the literal, material presence of animals in early modern writing, should do so repeatedly, only to discover in the process that these literal animals are somehow always being reabsorbed into metaphor.

In a way that recalls the dilemma of certain early Protestant exegetes vis-à-vis the four senses of scripture, one is forced to conclude at last that there is no sustainable distinction between the literal and the figurative capacities of early modern animals—that these beasts are nowhere more themselves than when standing for what they are not. Bruno Latour begins *We Have Never Been Modern* by identifying what he calls "hybrids of nature and culture" (10): constructs, problems, and events (the AIDS phenomenon, for instance, or global warming) that escape modern disciplinary categorization by functioning in ways that are "simultaneously real, social, and narrated" (7). Part of his point is that these hybrids emerge as such when viewed through the lens of modern disciplinarity—that the modern investment in a subdivided and specialized regime of knowledge production has proved ill-equipped to address issues whose nature and consequences are spread out across the entire map of knowledge. In this respect the early modern sheep surveyed here offer a case in point; from Latour's perspective they may indeed be early, but their refusal to accommodate themselves to specific registers of discourse or genre (literal as opposed to metaphorical usage, the husbandry manual as opposed to pastoral verse) marks them as resistant to the notion of modernity. My point is not to adopt Latour's critique of modern disciplinarity, as compelling as this may be in many of its particulars. Rather, I wish simply to point out the difficulty inherent in recent exhortations for scholarship "to interpret [early modern animals] as animals and not simply as symbols of something else" (Fudge, *Brutal Reasoning* 4). Not only does this impulse neglect the possibility that animals might participate "as animals" in networks of meaning that are "simultaneously real, social, and narrated," but it also marks one more recurrence of the "reflex . . . to look back to nature" as a cure for one's spiritual and political and epistemological and ecological malaise (Watson, *Back to Nature* 20), a reflex that Robert N. Watson has located in the various regressive intellectual projects to emerge from the breakup of the medieval *consensus fidei*.[9] From Watson's standpoint as well as Latour's, the emphasis on biological literalism in animal studies emerges as one more expression of modern intellectual anxieties and limitations. It also fails to do justice to the richness of animal being as this is represented in the textual records surveyed here.

Sheepless Pastoral

Finally, let us return to the sheep in *The Second Shepherds' Pageant* and *A Chaste Maid in Cheapside*. As pointed out earlier, scholars are quick to note their similarities, but there are important differences, too, and these have received rather less attention. For one thing, the two animals embody very dissimilar notions of community. Mak's sheep theft may lead to exposure and punishment, but the punishment itself is drastically mitigated; as the three offended shepherds toss him in a blanket, their own vengeful impulses melt away, and they find themselves overcome by the urge to sleep. This sleep, in turn, prepares them for Christ's nativity as an angel appears and summons them to attend on the Lamb of God: "At Bedlem go se / There ligys that fre / In a crib full poorely, / Betwix two bestys" (643–46). The animal presence here seems to mark a turn away from fallen vindictiveness and toward an ethic of common creatureliness: a kind of animal fellowship in which resentments are set aside and the intimate unity of creation is reaffirmed.

This affirmation may be extracted easily enough from the principal source of *The Second Shepherds' Pageant*, which is, after all, the Gospel of Luke. However, the corresponding scene from *A Chaste Maid in Cheapside* displays rather different literary associations, and these in turn betray a markedly different sense of community. The Wench's trick on the Promoters draws on the genre of rogue literature and concy-catching pamphlets, and for its part, this genre arises to deal with a distinct set of social circumstances related to the rapid urbanization of early modern society. As Katharine Eisaman Maus has put it, "Whereas the inhabitant of a small village would have been acquainted with the same limited group of neighbors from birth, the city-dweller had to interact with a dramatically larger number and variety of people. The changes were qualitative as well as quantitative. The new urbanite needed to learn to manage a wider spectrum of familiarities: from almost anonymous interactions with unknown persons, to casual attachments with acquaintances, to the intimate relationships among family members and close friends" (24). As Maus goes on to observe, the "coseners" of early modern rogue literature "self-consciously exploit rustic modes of identity formation based on kinship relations, reputation among one's neighbors, and reciprocal acts of hospitality," in the process "counterfeit[ing] social intimacy" with others—the gulls they exploit—"for whom that intimacy involves obligations" (25). To this extent, "[t]he wiliness of [early modern] thieves is . . . a distinctively urban trait, a product of the distance between emerging and traditional ways of life" (25).

As it happens, Maus's description applies perfectly to the Promoters in *Chaste Maid*. Creatures of the city, they exploit their relative familiarity with urban ways and the relative ignorance of others. Thus when Allwit announces himself as "a stranger both unto the city / And to her carnal strictness" (2.2.75–76), the First Promoter responds with predatory glee: "[*Aside to Second Promoter*] Come hither, Dick; a bird, a bird!" (2.2.78). Yet the point of Middleton's scene is not to dramatize the Promoters' wiliness but rather to display their gullibility. His real scam artists, as it turns out, are Allwit and the Wench, who secure their reputations as such by preying not on naive rustics but rather on the urban gamesters. Theirs is a second-order model of thieves' cunning based not on "counterfeiting social intimacy" of the traditional, rural variety but instead on simulating rural *credulity*. When the Wench first appears with a loin of mutton protruding conspicuously from her basket, she almost inspires the Promoters' pity: "Look, look! Poor fool, she has left the rump uncovered too, / More to betray her" (2.2.139–40). In this context her insistence that the Promoters swear an oath to keep the basket until she returns from her spurious errand to obtain "true authority from the higher powers" (2.2.151) can look only like evidence of even greater ingenuousness: "What a strange wench 'tis!" (2.2.155). Then the Promoters discover, to their chagrin, that it is they who have been gulled:

> *First Promoter*: 'Swounds, what's here?
> *Second Promoter*: A child!
> *First Promoter*: A pox of all dissembling cunning whores!
> *Second Promoter*: Here's an unlucky breakfast!
> *First Promoter*: What shall's do?
> *Second Promoter*: The quean made us swear to keep it too.
> *First Promoter*: We might leave it else.
>
> (2.2.167–71)

In the twenty-odd years that separate Greene's coney-catching pamphlets from *Chaste Maid*, the culture of early modern London has evolved sufficiently to accommodate this new form of social predation, specifically enabled by urban anomie. To succeed at their cozenage, Allwit and the Wench must not only understand the difference between traditional, rural modes of relation based on ties of personal obligation and mutual trust, on the one hand, and newer forms of casual and anonymous urban relation, on the other; they must also understand the new urban sensibility enough to recognize the weaknesses of its predatory style. Indeed, in comparison to Allwit and the Wench, the Promoters come to appear almost endearingly rustic. If nothing else, they feel strangely bound by their oath to retain the contents of the Wench's basket, and this residual sense of obligation makes them seem, for a moment at least, positively naive. Middleton's London belongs not to them but to their cozeners, for whom anomie has become the social norm to be exploited, and in this environment it seems appropriate that Mak's living sheep has been translated into a hunk of butchered meat. Its carcass becomes metonymic of broader losses and dismemberments: the atrophy of people's organic relation to a place or collective, the dissolution of long-established standards of behavior, the fragmentation of the social fabric. These are the conditions that make city comedy possible and even necessary; yet they also make sheep, in a sense, *im*possible: that is to say, the conditions of separation, specialization, and fragmentation that typify the world of *Chaste Maid* also impair the old organic, integrated modes of relation between communities of human beings and of animals, while in the process subjecting the two communities to mutually sequestrated economies of scale. Middleton's London is only half the picture here; as the city grows and metamorphoses into a recognizably modern urban configuration, that growth is enabled also by the concomitant growth of enclosed pasturage for sheep. As human populations expand in the city, they also decline in the country, where sheep become reciprocally more numerous:

> In 1521 the tenants of Sir William Fyllol in the settlements along the Winterborne valley south of Dorchester complained . . . that their lands were overrun by sheep. . . . It is clear that their pleas were in vain, for all along the valley there is a string of deserted village sites. . . . At Iwerne Courtnay, a chalkland manor near Blandford Forum . . . , a manorial survey of 1553 records that the arable lands had been enclosed in 1548 and that as a result half the tenants had left. . . . Similar piecemeal enclosures of common arable fields on the lower slopes of the chalk downs occurred in Wiltshire, Hampshire, and Sussex, and, for example, by 1640 twelve out of the forty-two Sussex downland parishes were fully enclosed. . . . At Frome Whitfield (Dorset) the parish was almost completely deserted by the later sixteenth century, there was no resident parson and "the church is filled up with hay and corn and is so far in decay that it is like to fall down." (Bettey 41)

Early in this chapter I suggested that the relative sheeplessness of Milton's exercises in pastoral might be explained in part as an exemplary adjustment to classical influence: a typical case of the poet invoking classical precedent by "The meaning, not the Name" (*Paradise Lost* 7.5); the sense, not the signifier; the spirit, not the body. I had promised to offer another explanation too, and this involves the poet's identity as an early modern urban intellectual. Born on Bread Street five years before the debut of *Chaste Maid in Cheapside*, Milton grew up in the city that Middleton depicts. Apart from his days at Cambridge and his grand tour of 1638–39, he spent virtually his entire life in and around London, just as the city embarked upon its grand transformation into one of the world's largest and most celebrated metropoles. As one might expect, pastoral thus occupies a site of desire in the Miltonic corpus, but it is a site no longer characterized as a united, organic community of human and nonhuman animals; indeed, like many sophisticated conceptions of pastoral, it hardly seems grounded at all in actual experience of the animal world. For Milton, pastoral functions instead as a realm of spiritual longings and spiritual fulfillments, a space of mental abstraction, and thus a world uncongenial to Topsell's "vulgar sheepe."

O Blazing World

During their years of Interregnum exile, Margaret and William Cavendish, then marquis and marchioness of Newcastle, maintained a circle of acquaintance extending to the foremost Anglo-French intellectuals of the day, among them Thomas Hobbes, Pierre Gassendi, and René Descartes.[1] Later, in her *Philosophical Letters* of 1664, Lady Margaret would attack the theories of Hobbes and Descartes, and for their part, all three of these men had mutual differences as well. However, in the summer of 1648 the three philosophers frequented the Cavendish household; John Aubrey reports Edmund Waller as saying that "W. Lord Marquisse of Newcastle was a great patron of Dr. Gassendi and M. Des Cartes, as well as Mr. Hobbes, and that he hath dined with them all three at the Marquiss's table in Paris" (2:2.626). Also present at any such meal (or meals) must have been Lady Margaret, and a meeting with Descartes seems particularly appropriate for a woman whose interest in philosophy and experimental science was as keen as her passion for letters. In terms of the present study, the encounter between French philosopher and English writer marks a natural end point: a coming together of nations and of disciplines at the dawn of a new intellectual dispensation.

As for Margaret Cavendish, after lying almost dormant for three centuries her literary reputation has gained unprecedented influence over the past fifty years, largely thanks to the efforts of feminist scholars who have seen her as a forerunner in the literary struggle against patriarchy. The censure she incurred in her own day from figures such as Samuel Pepys and Dorothy Osborne has been refashioned as a badge of honor, the sign of a woman ahead of her time in "emancipating herself from seventeenth-century female bondage" (Meyer 16).[2] She has been described as "an eloquent 'feminist'" *avant la lettre* (Mendelson 54)—even if the key term here is given in scare quotes. In addition, her interest in the new science has been correlated to her insistence that "the social order could expand to accommodate the intellectual equality of women," with the result that at least one reader has insisted, "Cavendish's work shows how the radical implications of one area of thought can reinforce and strengthen the subversive tendencies of another, quite different attack on authority" (Sarasohn 289, 290).

Still better for present purposes, Cavendish's feminism and her interest in science find a parallel in her progressive attitudes toward animals and the natural world. As Keith Thomas has put it, Cavendish "rejected the whole anthropocentric tradition, . . . arguing that men had no monopoly of sense or reason" (*Man* 128). More recently her views have been described as "remarkably similar to modern criticisms of human anthropocentrism" (Edwards, *Horse and Man* 20), and she has been credited with "originating a sensibility that we might call ecological" (Bowerbank 62). Contesting masculine bigotry, expressing an ethic of care for animals and the environment, writing bizarre tales that anticipate more-recent forms of science fiction and utopia, Cavendish cuts a brave and distinctive figure. We may perhaps be forgiven for succumbing to the narcissistic temptation to see her as one of us.

Still, forgivable or not, the temptation *is* narcissistic. It is also less than wholly accurate. Despite her bold protofeminist pronouncements, "[t]he Duchess of Newcastle did not conceal her contempt for women of the lower orders; . . . [i]n real life she expressed more empathy for wild animals than for the poor in her midst" (Mendelson 6). Politically a Tory reactionary, she was moved by "a desire to restore past nature (and privilege) under the power of the crown and aristocracy" (Bowerbank 74). In her writing, too, she "echoed the conventional ideas about women in many prefaces" (Crawford 228), while her protagonists often remain "conventionally feminine" in terms of their motives and aspirations (Mendelson 23). Even her choice of literary genres is less forward-looking than it might at first appear, being marred by a "tendency to express her ideas in trite literary forms that had already become old-fashioned by the mid-seventeenth century" (Mendelson 38). In all these respects Cavendish's reputation as a progressive is compromised, her legacy strangely mixed.

The same may also be said of Cavendish's interventions on the subject of species difference. In some ways these do indeed seem the stuff of future animal-rights philosophy and ecocriticism; yet if this is so, it is in large part because of the very retrograde character of her thought and work. Typical in this respect is her convoluted prose narrative *The Blazing World*, first published in 1666 along with her *Observation upon Experimental Philosophy*. In form, this work feels strangely like a late twentieth-century technoutopia along the lines of *Star Trek*, in which diverse species join together to engineer an ideal life for one another with the aid of their respective talents and occasional bits of novel and convenient machinery. However, the work's lineage allies it more closely still to traditions of romance and travelogue that date back to classical times and encompass such notable antecedents as Mandeville's *Travels* and More's *Utopia*. Here again, for Cavendish, the road to the future leads oddly through the past.

The tale's anonymous female protagonist, kidnapped by an amorous merchant and carried aboard his ship, survives when the rest of the crew and passengers perish of exposure after the ship drifts into arctic regions. Reaching the North Pole, she and the ship are strangely translated to the pole of a parallel world, and once there she immediately encounters evidence of species difference: "[T]he distressed Lady . . . at last perceived land, but covered all with snow: from which came walking strange creatures, in shape like bears, only they went upright as men; those creatures coming near the boat, catched hold of it with their paws, that served them instead of hands; some two or three of them entered first . . . ; at last having viewed and observed all that was in the boat, they spoke to each other in a language which the Lady did not understand, and having carried her out of the boat, sunk it" (Cavendish, *Blazing World* 126–27). Further cross-species encounters quickly ensue. The bear-men carry the lady "into another island of a warmer temper, in which were men like foxes . . . who received their neighbours the bear-men with great civility and courtship" (127); the bear-men and fox-men together take her to visit another species of "men which had heads, beaks, and feathers like wild-geese, only they went in an upright shape" (128); and so on until the entire assembly conveys the lady to the world's emperor. The emperor, in turn, is so taken with her that in the course of one brief paragraph he at first attempts to worship her and then settles for the second-best expedient of making her his wife, with "absolute power to rule and govern all that world as she pleased" (132).

This elaborate narrative frame develops quickly, within the space of a few pages, and thereafter *The Blazing World* settles into a self-gratifying mode of escapist fantasy, replete with elaborate descriptions of the lady's costume as Empress; the two chapels she causes to be built for reformation of the world's religious practice; and the intimate relationship she develops with her spiritual amanuensis, who turns out to be none other than Margaret Cavendish,

Duchess of Newcastle. However, within this context the Blazing World's various nonhuman (or is it quasi-human?) inhabitants take up a surprising amount of space, as the Empress organizes them into distinct professional groups:

> The rest of the inhabitants of that world, were men of several different sorts . . . ; some were bear-men, some worm-men, some fish- or mear-men, otherwise called syrens; some bird-men, some fly-men, some ant-men, some geese-men, some spider-men, some lice-men, some fox-men, some ape-men, some jackdaw-men, some magpie-men, some parrot-men, some satyrs, some giants, and many more, which I cannot all remember; and . . . each followed a profession as was most proper for the nature of their species, which the Empress encouraged them in, . . . and to that end she erected schools, and founded several societies. (133–34)

Cavendish herself famously attended a meeting of the Royal Society at Gresham College on May 30, 1667, roughly a year after the publication of *The Blazing World*. That visit came only "after much debate, *pro* and *con*," within the society, "it seems many being against it" (Pepys 8:243). In *The Blazing World*, on the other hand, the Empress's establishment of "several societies" may be read as a proleptic reversal of such resistance, with the Royal Society transformed into the Empress's creation and its members into her creatures. Thus, much of Cavendish's narrative summarizes the various reports presented to the Empress by the different societies she has commissioned to study different sorts of natural phenomena.

When it comes to these reports, it seems misguided to view the Empress's government as an egalitarian one in which "even the lowly worm-men were recognized for their particular expertise and were numbered among her valued advisors" (Bowerbank 74). To my ear, the Blazing World's learned societies sound more like a doubly encoded revenge on the scientific institutions from which Cavendish was excluded by gender. On one hand, the presiding figures of those institutions are subjected to a translation of species that compromises the very humanity on whose distinction and privileges the scientific community insisted, and which it sought to confirm in many cases through experimentation on so-called "lesser" animals. On the other hand, such cross-species translation elides these same scientific worthies with the natural world, so that they embody the scientific ideal of Bruno Latour's modern constitution: an ideal whereby "natural forces are . . . endowed or entrusted with meaning" (28–29). Thus, Cavendish is able to dominate and rebuke figures who condescended to her and sneered at her in real life, while claiming the authority of nature for her own philosophical theories. In one notable case, for instance, she calls upon the bear-men, "which were her experimental philosophers," to "observe [the celestial bodies] through such instruments as are called telescopes" (*Blazing World* 140). However—just as Cavendish had argued in the *Observations upon Experimental Philosophy*[3]—these instruments "caused more differences and divisions amongst them, than ever they had before" (140), and so the Empress "began to grow angry at their telescopes, that they could give no better intelligence; for, said she, now I do plainly perceive, that your glasses are false informers, and instead of discovering the truth, delude your senses, wherefore I command you to break them" (141).

Having thus asserted Cavendish's own views on the value of magnifying instruments, the episode then veers into comedy as the bear-men,

> exceedingly troubled at her Majesty's displeasure concerning their telescopes, kneeled down, and in the humblest manner petitioned that they might not be broken, for, said they, we take more delight in artificial delusions, than in natural truths. Besides, we shall want employment for our senses, and subjects for arguments; for were there nothing but truth, and no falsehood, there would be no occasion for to dispute, and by this means we should want the aim and pleasure of our endeavours in confuting and contradicting each other; neither would one man be thought wiser than another, but all would either be alike knowing and wise, or all would be fools, wherefore we most humbly beseech your Imperial Majesty to spare our glasses, which are our only delight, and as dear to us as our lives. (142)

The Empress responds to this plea with an exquisite mixture of compassion and condescension, allowing the bear-men to keep their telescopes "upon condition, that their disputes and quarrels should remain within their schools, and cause no factions or disturbances in state, or government" (142). Thus, Cavendish defends her scientific views, exposes her detractors as self-serving charlatans, and—unkindest cut of all—agrees even so to tolerate their behavior, provided they confine themselves to a life of academic irrelevance.

The exchange has its wit and poetic justice, but as symbolic payback for the author's exclusion from serious academic circles it also feels a little sad, even childish, if one agrees with Auden that one ceases to be a child when one realizes that telling one's trouble does not make it better. In any case, the scene hardly offers a meaningful protofeminist alternative to the "mechanistic view of nature" that Carolyn Merchant has identified with Cavendish's male scientific contemporaries (290).[4] Instead, it operates mainly as an expression of "a woman's 'will to power,'" formulated as "the chronicle of her extraordinary ambitions" and set against the pervasive backdrop of "a power struggle between the sexes" (Mendelson 22–23). This struggle provides the principal recurring theme of Cavendish's belletristic work—and, in a different way, of her philosophical work as well. On the level of literary character, its signal innovation lies not in the bear-men and bird-men of *The Blazing World* but instead in the solipsistic, spiritual, same-sex relation at the tale's heart: the intimate bond between the Empress and Margaret Cavendish herself.

Intimate femme-femme relationships, engaging the themes of transgender and platonic love and sometimes configured with an immediate erotic frisson, are staples of Cavendish's fiction and drama.[5] One might instance Lady Happy and the Princess of *The Convent of Pleasure* ([1668] where the relationship is cross-gendered after the fact) or Travellia and the Queen of Amity in "Assaulted and Pursued Chastity" (1656). In *The Blazing World* this sort of relationship acquires a particularly involuted quality, as the Empress, resolving to engage the services of a scribe in order to produce a "Cabbala" (181), summons for that purpose the spirit of the Duchess of Newcastle. In a lengthy exchange the Duchess persuades the Empress to make the Cabbala "poetical or romancical" in nature, and the Empress, pleased at this, adopts the Duchess as "her favourite," the two women developing "such an intimate friendship . . . that they became platonic lovers, although they were both females" (183). In effect, Cavendish's fictional creation (the Empress) presides over Cavendish's own translation into a fictional character (the Empress's scribe), with Cavendish as scribe serving as the midwife for her own birth as a textual artifact.

In sum, while Cavendish's *Blazing World* does present nonhuman animals as literary characters, the real characterological innovation of her work lies in another place entirely: in her staging of herself. The tale's animal-men—like its endless scientific ruminations—are largely beside the point; they function in conventional ways, either as dismissive caricatures (on the order of Baldwin's cats and the Protestant reformers' parrots) or as servant figures (in the manner of Shakespeare's horses or the Eucharistic Agnus Dei). The real purpose of Cavendish's writing, in both its philosophical and belletristic variants, is that of self-creation, which is to say self-promotion. The record here is well attested. There is Pepys's famous declaration that "[t]he whole story of this Lady is a romance, and all she doth is romantic" (8:163). There is Cavendish's own, equally well-known, insistence that "I endeavour . . . to be as singular as I can; for . . . I had rather appear worse in singularity, than better in the mode" (*Blazing World* 218). There is a consensus among contemporary scholars that "Cavendish self-consciously produced herself as a fantastic and singular woman" (Lilley xii). More acutely, there is Elizabeth Spiller's recognition that "Cavendish makes the creation of a textual self a key concern of her texts" (139–40). My point, in keeping with these observations, is simply this: that in staging herself as "fantastic and singular," Cavendish fashions herself into a living, breathing literary character, and that she acknowledges as much by introducing herself as both character and scribe in the plot of her *Blazing World*.

Of course, there are moments in Cavendish's work that seem to presage a modern ecological and animal-rights consciousness, even as they gesture back to earlier formations of thought. When the immaterial spirits of the Blazing World inform the Empress that "nature is but one infinite self-moving, living, and self-knowing body" (176), for instance, we seem to encounter an emphatic rejection of seventeenth-century mechanistic philosophy. When, in response to the Empress's question "whether man was a little world," these same spirits inform her that "if a fly or worm was a little world, then man was so too" (169–70), we may see their response as foreshadowing twenty-first-century challenges to the distinction between human and nonhuman animals. However, if Cavendish dismisses the species barrier between man and fly, it is because this barrier holds relatively little importance for her. Indeed, the *Blazing World*'s entire array of bear-men, fox-men, bird-men, lice-men, parrot-men, worm-men, and so forth may be understood as a way of rendering the traditional species boundary so nuanced as to be immaterial. These creatures, as we eventually learn, do differ from conventional nonhuman animals, just as they differ from human beings; when the Empress asks her spirits "whether in the beginning and creation of the world, all beasts could speak?," they respond "that no beasts could speak, but only those sorts of creatures which were fish-men, bear-men, worm-men and the like, which could speak in the first age, as well as they do now" (170). Thus the formation of intermediate categories between worm and man, bear and man, and so on, has the effect of replacing a single sharp distinction (human/nonhuman) with an infinite series of much finer ones (human/bear-human/louse-human/

bear/louse/fish-human/fish, and so forth). In the end, none of these differences seems to matter much to Cavendish, but it would be wrong to conclude therefore that *no* difference matters to her.

One difference does matter, manifestly and obsessively, to her. Cavendish's entire body of work is conceived to produce and confirm this sole distinction above all others, and to identify it as the only difference that really counts: the difference separating her—as author, thinker, woman, personality, spirit—from the rest of creation. Nothing else holds such intense, recurring fascination for her. She formulates this as a difference of imagination, creative potential, or, as she likes to put it, "fancy." Thus, *The Blazing World* comes to focus on the intimate kinship between the Duchess of Newcastle and her imaginary creation/companion, the Empress—a kinship figured precisely through their ability to create personal, imaginary realities. The Duchess, wishing to govern a realm like the Blazing World but finding none available in the physical universe, determines to "despise all the worlds without me, and create a world of my own" (186); in this she sets the pattern for her creation/patroness, the Empress, who likewise resolves "to make a world of her own invention" (188). It is the inward turn, straight from Descartes, extracting an irreducibly unique identity from the subject's own interior life, and in this respect Cavendish shows herself to be very much a woman of her time and milieu. However, where Descartes employs the inward turn as an instrument of skepticism, to dismiss ungrounded opinions about the nature of the universe and therefore achieve a supposedly firmer understanding of external reality, Cavendish uses it as an instrument of self-gratification, to *invent* realities, and most particularly the reality of her own character. Thus the affinity and the opposition of these two extraordinary seventeenth-century figures: where Descartes's legacy attaches him firmly to a cause (scientific skepticism) and certain accompanying principles (the cogito, the *bête-machine*), the one cause to which Margaret Cavendish, Duchess of Newcastle, is most clearly and consistently attached—despite the intimations of feminism, ecology, and animal-rights thinking in her work—is none other than Margaret Cavendish, Duchess of Newcastle.

In the service of this cause, Cavendish's notion of the species divide has narrowed to encompass a very few select individuals—herself, her literary/spiritual creations and companions, her husband, and King Charles II being the most notable of these. The only distinction of kind that really matters to her is the one that separates these few choice spirits from hoi polloi, and one may profitably understand her work as an extended elaboration and advertisement of this distinction. In other words, her work exists first and foremost as literary self-promotion, and to this extent it is very much ahead of its time, heralding the development of a literary profession stocked with "originals" (to use one of Smollett's favored phrases for his literary characters). These figures—from Cavendish and Doctor Johnson to Norman Mailer and Harold Bloom—seem to have stepped out of the pages of their own books, to have become characters in their own right. Their colorful interiority has provided the subject matter for such books as Boswell's *Life of Johnson*, Wilde's *De Profundis*, Joyce's *Portrait of the Artist as a Young Man*, Orwell's *Down and Out in Paris and London*, Hunter S. Thompson's *Fear and Loathing in Las Vegas*, and many more; the list is as capacious as one's own reading and memory. Figures such as these—one might call them authors-as-characters—populate any undergraduate literature syllabus or graduate student's reading list. Their distinctness makes them worth studying. They are, as we like to put it, a breed apart.

In the present book, I have tried to reach some understanding of how this breed emerged into literary life out of what came before it. In the process, I have suggested that the literary profession plays a noteworthy role in developing and maintaining the species barrier—a barrier without which the modern literary character (to say nothing of the author-as-character) could not emerge into recognizable being. More generally, I have been interested in the creatures forced to the margins of existence by this new literary species—the talking birds, spiritual stallions, tortured cats, and transfigured sheep that held a place in our society before we began to set ourselves more forcefully apart from them. As for how—or even whether—the literary profession may be uncoupled from its alliance with species difference, I offer no suggestions; as set forth at the outset of this book, this project is descriptive rather than ameliorative in nature. That being the case, we might rightly conclude with one last broad observation, in this case relating to historical developments in the history of genre.

I have cast the emergence of modern literary character as implicated in the emergence of new literary fashions more generally, especially the rise of the novel in eighteenth- and nineteenth-century English writing. However, if we survey the individual animal characters evaluated in this book, we may see that they enact a rather different, albeit parallel, history of genre in which modes of discourse associated with romance and travelogue, fable and beast epic are steadily denigrated and debunked. The rational horses of Pulci, Boiardo, and Ariosto; the miraculous articulate parrots of Cantimpré and

Mandeville; the clever foxes (and less clever cats) of Aesop and the *History of Reynard*—these figures fall casualty to the march of literary progress in the west, and so too do the modes of literary production hospitable to them.

Beyond this, one might also note that the representative genres of nonhuman character—romance, fable, travelogue, beast epic—fall victim, very broadly, to the increased prestige of a newly empowered set of literary genres that includes polemic, parody, and satire. The wise horses of the Italian romance writers give way in part to the mockery of Cervantes and in part to a new model of sacred epic, forged by Tasso and Milton, that itself encompasses a repertoire of subgenres including satire and parody (as in Milton's war in heaven). The miraculous parrots of medieval travelogue yield place to the vacuous, repetitive birds of Reformation polemic, with their mindless iteration of set liturgical forms. The cats and foxes of beast epic and fable are parodied by Baldwin and manhandled by Stevenson. The Eucharistic lamb of *The Second Shepherds' Pageant* encounters its replacement in the cynical world of *A Chaste Maid in Cheapside*. In each case an old model of nonhuman character is muscled aside along with an old set of favored literary forms, and in each case the same newly ascendant regime of polemic, parody, and satire does the muscling.

We are left with one final question: how does this satirical regime relate to the eventual ascendancy of the novel? If the novel becomes the signature genre of human character in the Cartesian sense of the phrase, then what is the role of satire and polemic and parody in its installation as such? To begin with, it hardly seems coincidental that the eighteenth century, the period of English literary history that ends with the novel securely established as the most vibrant and representative of literary forms, is also sometimes known as the age of satire. There seems, indeed, to be a kind of symbiosis between the two genres, and a broad final hypothesis could be that this has to do with the two genres' placement relative to issues of literary character. To put it simply, in the realm of literary representation satire is to the novel what the *bête-machine* is to the cogito in the realm of Cartesian philosophy. For Descartes, the assumption that nonhuman animals lack consciousness throws into particular relief the inner-directed skepticism that forms the basis of his philosophy. By the same token, that skepticism comprises the unique defining faculty of the human, the distinction of kind that separates *Homo sapiens* from all other earthly life. For the European writers leading up to and following Descartes, satire—like the *bête-machine* theory—provides an essential instrument for the denial of character, an instrument applied indiscriminately to horses and parrots, cats and sheep, Catholics and Native Americans, women and servants. This instrument proves essential in large part because it clears a space within which writers are freed to elaborate the inner-directed characters that become the stock-in-trade of the classic realist novel. On this logic satire continues to function in its traditionally accepted sense as an instrument of enforcement. However, what it enforces here is not a standard of justice or a vision of morality but rather the commonly understood species distinction between human and nonhuman animals. It is this distinction, finally, that makes the modern novel possible.

Notes

1. For the association of talking animals with children's literature, see Cosslett passim, who dates this convention's emergence from "the mid-eighteenth century" (1). Also see Bowerbank 135–60.

2. One could add concurring testimony from more-recent theorists on the subject. Deidre Shauna Lynch quotes with approval John Frow's assertion that "literary character remains the 'most problematic and . . . undertheorized of the basic categories of narrative theory'" (Lynch 1; Frow 227). James Phelan's *Reading People, Reading Plots* presents itself as an analysis and attempted solution of "the main problem of character" (20–21). The third chapter of Martin Price's *Forms of Life* is subtitled "Problems of Character" (Price 37). Elizabeth Fowler complains that "[o]ur tools for the study of literary character are surprisingly primitive compared to those we have developed for . . . other formal aspects of fiction" (3).

3. For the utilitarian argument, see Singer 1–23. For the Kantian argument and its variance with utilitarianism on the question of rights, see Regan 218–28, 349–57.

4. Theophrastus's numerous lost works, as listed by Diogenes Laertius, also include nine different treatises on animals, as well as works on comedy, acting, poetry, meter, "Introduction and Narrative," and "Mankind" (489–503; 5.42–50).

5. For the notion of paradigm shift and its relation to preceding crises of understanding, see Kuhn 66–91.

6. See Raymond Williams 196–97 for a discussion of the etymology of the word "character," which he relates to the parallel development of the noun "personality."

7. See White passim.

8. See *De Anima* 76–77, 83–85; 413b2–27, 414b29–415a14.

9. For the seventeenth-century debates, see Boehrer, "Milton" passim. For Aristotle's "troublingly ambiguous" (69) denial of the deliberative faculty to animals, see Steiner 62–76.

10. For Descartes's subscription to this view, see Regan 10.

11. *OED*, s.v. "pet," sb. 1. See Boehrer, "Shylock" 153–54.

12. See *Oxford Latin Dictionary* (hereafter *OLD*), s.v. "familia," sb. 6: "(leg.) Estate (consisting of the household property)."

13. For the history of these prosecutions, see Evans passim. For a recent treatment of the subject, see Ferry ix–xvi.

CHAPTER I

1. For an overview of the textual history and literary influence of the *Quatre fils*, see Combarieu du Grès and Subrenat 16–19.

2. For Aristotle's original distinction of the rational soul from the vegetative or sensitive, see *De Anima* 2.3 (559–60). For the rational soul's relation to Aristotle's zoological observations, see Steiner 70–76. For early modern reception of the doctrine of the rational soul, see Fudge, *Brutal Reasoning* 48–50.

3. See Watson, "Horsemanship" passim. Watson's application to Shakespeare of the *Phaedrus*'s model of equine representation also owes something to Giamatti, "Headlong Horses," which employs the same paradigm in a reading of Pulci, Boiardo, and Ariosto. However, Giamatti passes over all of the moments of equine characterization in these authors that I touch on here, largely, I believe, because these moments (e.g., Baiardo's flight in Cantos 1–2 of the *Furioso*) draw on a different tradition of animal representation that does not entirely assimilate to the Platonic use of the horse as an emblem of unbridled desire.

4. See Plato, *Phaedrus* 246a–247b.

5. For the decline of horse-based military leadership in its practical and ideological dimensions in early modern England, see Peter Edwards, *Horse and Man* 119–80; Davis 4–20.

6. For the sexual dimension of the horse-rider image and its relation to husbandly authority within the household, see Roberts 63–68; Willems 192–93.

7. For this insistence, see, for instance, Leo of Naples 17; *Historia de Preliis Alkexandri Magni* 17; *The Wars of Alexander* 750–87.

8. For the authorship of *The Two Noble Kinsmen*, see Shakespeare, *Riverside Shakespeare* 1689–90; Shakespeare, *Complete Works* 1604–5; Wells and Taylor 1279; Jowett 113–14.

9. For an early account of Morocco the intelligent horse, see Dando passim. For a recent discussion, see Fudge, *Brutal Reasoning* 123–46.

10. For Boiardo's nameless flying horse, which unexpectedly carries off Gradasso, King of Sericana, see *Orlando innamorato* (ed. Scaglione) 3.7.24–28.

11. For Milton's reactions to Ariosto, see Flannagan passim; Sims passim.

12. For a discussion of Plutarch's argument, its reappearance in the debate of 1615, and its relevance for Milton's work, see Fudge, *Brutal Reasoning* 101–4; Boehrer, "Milton" passim.

13. See Leo of Naples 17; *Historia de Preliis Alkexandri Magni* 17; *The Wars of Alexander* 750–87.

CHAPTER 2

1. *Canterbury Tales*, General Prologue 146–50.

2. For the monograph, see Boehrer, *Parrot Culture*. For representative articles and book chapters, see Walters, Redfern 80–104, Dundas, and Brown 221–66 For the essay collection, see Courtney and James passim. This last records the proceedings of the conference "Parrot Play: The Trickster in the Text," hosted by Open University at Milton Keynes on February 10, 2005.

3. See Boehrer, *Parrot Culture* 23–49.

4. Here and throughout, translations are mine unless otherwise ascribed in the list of works cited.

5. For the association of parrots with the earthly paradise, see Boccaccio, *Genealogia* 4.49; and Mandeville 195–98; this carries over to Gesner 2P1r. For the connection with Mount Gilboa (from 2 Samuel 1.21, whence also their supposed intolerance of water), see Neckam 1.37; Cantimpré 5.109; Boccaccio, *Eclogues* 5.43–45.

6. For associations with the Virgin, see *OED*, s.v. "popinjay," sb. 4.a; *Middle English Dictionary* (hereafter *MED*), s.v. "papejai" sb.a.; Lydgate, "Balade in Commendation of Our Lady" 81.

7. For the discovery of parrots by early explorers of the New World, see Boehrer, *Parrot Culture* 50–60.

8. See *Oh read ouer D. John Bridges* [The Epistle], sig. E4v, in *The Marprelate Tracts*.

9. For other recent versions of the story, also unattributed, see Eisler 268; http://petcaretips.net/nistory-pet-bird.html. Indeed, I have found only one post-Renaissance account of this tale that offers any source at all: Emma Phipson's *Animal-Lore of Shakespeare's Time* (214). Unfortunately, Phipson's source (Wright 288–89) cites no source.

10. For secular versions of the parrot in early modern satire and insult, see Boehrer, *Parrot Culture* 65–69; Boehrer, *Shakespeare among the Animals* 121–29. Representative instances include Shakespeare's *1 Henry IV* 2.4.97–99 (1596–98) and *Much Ado about Nothing* 1.1.138 (1598–99), but other examples of such usage are common.

11. For previous discussion of the parrot motif in *Volpone*, see Boehrer, *Parrot Culture* 66–68; Boehrer, *Shakespeare among the Animals* 127–29.

12. Tilley's *Proverbs* offers historical citations dating from 1534 to 1678 to illustrate various forms of this expression (522–23).

13. For a full account of Pepperberg's research and its implications, see *The Alex Studies* passim.

CHAPTER 3

1. The entry appears in 1562–63: "Recevyd of Thomas Colwell for his lycense for pryntinge of a playe entituled DYCCON of Bedlam &c. iiiid." See Arber 1.206.

2. For this identification, see also Spivak 323–27; Bevington, *From "Mankind" to Marlowe* 33.

3. "There is . . . far more dev il in this play than in . . . later 'nocturnals.' The constant groping in holes and heaps of rubbish, and the constant references to turds . . . show the presence of the devil. . . . [T]he most devilish part of the human body is the arse-hole, as the proverb says, and as Chaucer's Summoner knew. The villagers are living in devilish darkness" (Robinson 61).

4. See Shakespeare, *New Variorum Edition* 12.34n249.

5. See Cressy 141–70; Hutton, *Stations* 393–407; Hutton, *England* 182–87.

6. Cat historians have mistakenly claimed that this event occurred on Elizabeth's coronation day in 1558. See, e.g., Rogers 39; Van Vechten 69.

7. Relayed to me in personal correspondence dated December 15, 2005.

8. For a summary of the arguments in favor of Stevenson's authorship, see Bradley 197–202. William D. Wolf wrote in 1978, "Today, the general consensus is that the play belongs to William Stevenson" (113). In the quarter-century since Wolf's remark, the consensus has gone unchallenged.

9. For a summary of these customs, see Kozikowski 9–10.

10. See, for instance, 4.2.886, 4.2.894, 5.2.996, 5.2.1123.

11. King 394. For discussion of the work's plot structure, whose "large number of narrative frames within frames makes the tripartite *paragena* preceding *The Adventures of Master F. J.* look simple indeed" (Kinney, *Humanist Poetics* 116), see Kinney, *Humanist Poetics* 115–16; Bonahue passim.

12. For a broader discussion of such rhetoric, with additional examples, see Thomas, *Man* 152–59.

CHAPTER 4

1. For instance, see Columbus 77, 84.

2. For early names of the turkey and their derivations, see Schorger 464, 466; Chiappeli, Allen, and Benson 2:598–600; Albala 233.

3. For Geertz's version of the tale, see *The Interpretation of Cultures*, 28–29. It has been repeated in various forms by authors from Thoreau to Stephen Hawking, but it does not appear to be traceable to a particular source.

4. For classical descriptions of the guinea fowl, see Aristotle, *Historia* 2:225; Varro 479–81; Pliny, *Natural History* 3:339–41.

5. For instance, see Horace, satire 2.2.23–27.

6. See also White 149. For the origin of this tale, see Augustine 21.4.

7. For a brief discussion of these rituals, see Bergman 62–63.

8. Albala 110. For a good example of this placement, see Ben Jonson's *Epigrammes* 101, 9–11.

9. See Elias 48–104; Fumerton passim.

10. For instance, see Merchant 164–91.

CHAPTER 5

1. The tradition relates that Ajax lost his mind when the armor of Achilles was given to Odysseus in preference to him. Its earliest appearance is in *The Odyssey* 11.541–67, where the slaughter of sheep is not mentioned. This latter feature of the tale provides the setting for Sophocles' *Ajax*, where the hero has returned from a night attack on the Greeks who have insulted him; misled by Athena, he has been tricked into attacking sheep and cattle instead (*Ajax* 1–73).

2. The extensive scholarship on Spenser's and Milton's engagements with pastoral cannot be fully summarized in passing; however, specific comparisons of their treatment of the mode occur in Snyder 19–75; Mallette passim; and Rosenberg passim.

3. For Johnson's remarks on allegory in *Paradise Lost*, see his *Lives of the Poets* in *Selected Poetry and Prose* 439–40.

4. See, for instance, McFarland 122–45; Lindheim 187–236.

5. For a calculation of the average cost of such expenses in seventeenth-century England, see Bowden 669–70 and 665, table 28.

6. See Garber 843; Mowat 60–61. In Homer, Odysseus's grandfather is simply "befriended" by Hermes, "For to him he burned acceptable sacrifices of the thighs of lambs and kids" (19.397–98). In Ovid's *Metamorphoses* (ed. Miller), Autolycus figures as the son of Mercury and Chione (11.314–19).

7. For instance, see Evans 1090n92; Bate 242n90; Shakespeare, *Complete Works* 997n91; Greenblatt 2:129n7.

8. The *OED* derives the first syllable of "mildew" from the Old Teutonic *melip*, or honey, and lists "honey-dew" as the word's first—and now obsolete—sense (s.v. "mildew," sb. 1).

9. See Watson, *Back to Nature* passim, esp. 3–35, for the full extension of this complex argument.

CONCLUSION

1. See Kargon 60–76.

2. For the hostile reactions, see Pepys 8:243–44; Osborne 41.

3. See Cavendish, *Observations* 58–60; Spiller 151–61.

4. For Merchant's view of Cavendish—whom she credits with developing an antimechanistic philosophy that assumed "nature was self-knowing and perceptive" (271)—see 270–72.

5. For cross-dressing and femme-femme intimacy in Cavendish's work, see Traub 177–80.

Works Cited

PRE–1700

A. W. *A Book of Cookrye*. London, 1591.

Acosta, José de. *Natural and Moral History of the Indies*. Ed. Jane E. Mangan. Trans. Frances López-Morillas. Durham: Duke University Press, 2002.

Aelian. *Ex Aeliani historia per Petrum Gyllium Latini facti . . . libri XVI. De vi et natura animalium*. Paris, 1533.

Albertini, Francesco. *Opusculum de Mirabilibus Novae Urbis Romae*. Ed. August Schmarsow. Heilbronn: Gebrüder Henninger, 1886.

Aldrovandi, Ulisse. *Ornithologiae hoc est de auibus historiae libri XII*. 3 vols. Bologna, 1599.

Ames, William. *The Marrow of Sacred Divinity Drawn out of the Holy Scriptures*. London, 1642.

Amours, F. J., ed. *Scottish Alliterative Poems in Rhyming Stanzas*. Edinburgh: William Blackwood and Sons, 1897.

Anglicus, Bartholomaeus. *Batman vppon Bartholome his booke De proprietatibus rerum*. Trans. Stephen Batman. London, 1582.

Arber, Edward, ed. *A Transcript of the Registers of the Company of Stationers of London: 1554–1640 A.D.* 5 vols. London, 1875. Repr., New York: Peter Smith, 1950.

Ariosto, Lodovico. *Orlando furioso*. Ed. Lanfranco Caretti. Milan: Riccardo Ricciardi, 1954.

———. *Orlando Furioso*. Trans. Sir John Harington. Ed. Robert McNulty. Oxford: Clarendon, 1972.

Aristotle. *De Animalibus Historia*. Trans. A. L. Peck. 3 vols. Cambridge: Harvard University Press, 1965–91.

———. *On the Soul, Parva Naturalia, On Breath*. Trans. W. S. Hett. Cambridge: Harvard University Press, 1957.

Ascham, Roger. *The Scholemaster*. Ed. R. J. Schoeck. Don Mills, Ontario: J. M. Dent and Sons, 1966.

Astley, John. *The Art of Riding*. 1584. Facs., Amsterdam: Da Capo, 1968.

Attersoll, William. *The Badges of Christianity: Or a Treatise of the Sacraments Fully Declared out of the Word of God*. London, 1606.

Aubrey, John. *Letters of Eminent Persons in the Seventeenth and Eighteenth Centuries.* 2 vols. London, 1813.

Augustine, Saint. *The City of God.* Trans. Rev. March Dods. Edinburgh, 1864. Facs., http://etext.lib.virginia.edu/toc/modeng/public/AugCity.html.

Aulus Gellius. *The Attic Nights of Auluas Gellius.* Trans. J. C. Rolfe. 3 vols. Cambridge: Harvard University Press, 1984.

Babington, Gervase. *A Profitable Exposition of the Lords Prayer.* London, 1588.

Baldwin, William. *Beware the Cat: The First English Novel.* Ed. William A. Ringler, Jr., and Michael Flachmann. San Marino, Calif.: Huntington Library, 1988.

Ball, Thomas. *The Life of the Renowned Doctor Preston.* London, 1883.

Barber, Richard, ed. and trans. *Bestiary, Being and English Version of the Bodleian Library, Oxford M.S. 764.* Woodbridge: Boydell, 1993.

Barker, Andrew. *A true and certaine report of the beginning, proceedings, ouerthrowes, and now present estate of Captaine Ward and Danseker.* London, 1609.

B[axter], N[athaniel]. *Sir Phillip Sidneys ourania that is, Endimions song and tragedy.* London, 1606.

Beard, Thomas. *The theatre of Gods judgements.* London, 1642.

Blagrave, Joseph. *New additions to the art of husbandry.* London, 1675.

Boccaccio, Giovanni. *Eclogues.* Trans. Janet Levarie Smarr. New York: Garland, 1987.

———. *Genealogiae.* 1494. Repr., New York: Garland, 1976.

Boiardo, Matteo Maria. *Orlando innamorato.* Ed. Aldo Scaglione. 2 vols. Turin: Unione Tipografico-Editrice Torinese, 1963.

———. *Orlando Innamorato: Orlando in Love.* Trans. Charles Stanley Ross. West Lafayette, Ind.: Parlor Press, 2004.

Braithwaite, Richard. *A Strappado for the Diuell.* London, 1615.

Burnaby, William. *The reform'd wife.* London, 1700.

Butler, Samuel. *Hudibras.* London, 1761.

Cadamosto, Alvise da. *The Voyages of Cadamosto and Other Documents on Western Africa in the Second Half of the Fifteenth Century.* Trans. G. R. Crone. London: Hakluyt Society, 1937.

Cantimpré, Thomas of. *De Rerum Natura.* Ed. Luis Garcia Ballester. 2 vols. Granada: University of Granada, 1974.

Cartwright, Thomas. *A Confutation of the Rhemists Translation, Glosses and Annotations of the New Testament.* 1618. Facs., Amsterdam: Theatrum Orbis Terrarum, 1971.

Castiglione, Baldesar, *The Book of the Courtier.* Trans. George Bull. Harmondsworth: Penguin, 1967.

Cavendish, Margaret, Duchess of Newcastle. *Margaret Cavendish: The Blazing World and Other Writings.* Ed. Kate Lilley. London: Penguin, 2004.

———. *Observations upon Experimental Philosophy.* Ed. Eileen O'Neill. Cambridge: Cambridge University Press, 2001.

———. *Poems, and fancies written by the Right Honourable, the Lady Margaret Newcastle.* London, 1653.

Caxton, William. *Caxton's Aesop*. Ed. R. T. Lenaghan. Cambridge: Harvard University Press, 1967.

———. *The History of Reynard the Fox*. Ed. Donald B. Sands. Cambridge: Harvard University Press, 1960.

Cervantes, Miguel de. *Don Quixote: The Ormsby Translation, Revised*. Trans. John Ormsby. Ed. Joseph R. Jones and Kenneth Douglas. New York: W. W. Norton, 1980.

La chanson des quatre fils Aymon. Ed. Fernand Castets. Montpellier: Coulet et Fils, 1909.

Chaucer, Geoffrey. *The Riverside Chaucer*. Ed. Larry D. Benson. Boston: Houghton Mifflin, 1997.

Clarke, John. *Paroemioliogia Anglo-Latina*. London, 1639.

Columbus, Christopher. *The Log of Christopher Columbus*. Trans. Robert H. Fuson. Camden, Maine: International Marine Publishing, 1992.

Correspondence of the Family of Hatton. Ed. Edward Maunde Thompson. 2 vols. Westminster: Camden Society, 1878.

Córtes, Hernán. *Fernando Cortes: His Five Letters of Relation to the Emperor Charles V*. Trans. Francis Augustus MacNutt. 2 vols. Cleveland: Arthur H. Clark, 1908.

Crouch, Humphrey. *A Whip for the Back of a Backsliding Brownist*. N.p., [1640?].

Dando, John. *Maroccus Exstaticus, or Bankes Bay Horse in a Trance*. London, 1595.

Descartes, René. *A Discourse on the Method*. Trans. Ian Maclean. Oxford: Oxford University Press, 2006.

Díaz, Bernal. *The Conquest of New Spain*. Trans. J. M. Cohen. London: Penguin, 1963.

Diogenes Laertius. *Lives of Eminent Philosophers*. Trans. R. D. Hicks. 2 vols. Cambridge: Harvard University Press, 1959.

Dom Zara del Fogo: A Mock-Romance. London, 1656.

Duchesne, Joseph. *Le pourtraict de la santé*. Paris, 1606.

Estienne, Charles. *Maison Rustique, or The Countrie Farme*. Trans. Richard Surflet. London, 1600.

Evelyn, John. *The Diary of John Evelyn*. Ed. E. S. de Beer. 6 vols. Oxford: Clarendon, 1955.

Fitzherbert, John. *The boke of husbandry*. London, 1556.

Fletcher, John. *The Faithfvll Shepherdesse*. London, 1634.

Foxe, John. *Actes and Monuments of these latter and perilous dayes touching matters of the Church*. 7 vols. New York: AMS, 1965.

Gammer Gurton's Needle. In *Four Tudor Comedies*, ed. William Tydeman, 207–88. Harmondsworth: Penguin, 1984.

The Geneva Bible: A Facsimile of the 1599 Edition. Ozark, Mo.: L. L. Brown, 1990.

Gesner, Conrad. *Historia Animalium Liber III: Qui est de avium natura*. Frankfurt, 1604.

Gibbons, A., ed. *Ely Episcopal Records*. Lincoln: James Williamson, 1891.

Greene, Robert. *The Plays and Poems of Robert Greene*. Ed. J. Churton Collins. 3 vols. Oxford: Clarendon, 1905.

Haddon, Walter. *Against Ierome Osorius Byshopp of Siluane in Portingall.* Trans. James Bell. London, 1581.

Harrison, William. *The Description of England.* Ed. Georges Edelin. Washington, D.C.: Folger Shakespeare Library, 1994.

Heresbach, Conrad von. *Fovre Bookes of Husbandry.* Trans. Barnabe Googe. 1577. Facs., Amsterdam: Da Capo, 1971.

Heywood, Thomas. *The English traueller.* London, 1633.

Historia de Preliis Alexandri Magni. In *The Romances of Alexander,* trans. Dennis M. Kratz, 1–82. New York: Garland, 1991.

Hoccleve, Thomas. *Hoccleve's Works: II. The Minor Poems in the Ashburnham MS Addit. 133.* Ed. Israel Gollancz. London: Early English Text Society, 1925.

The Holy Bible. Revised Standard Version. New York: New American Library, 1962.

Homer. *The Iliad.* Trans. Richmond Lattimore. 1951. Repr., Chicago: University of Chicago Press, 1974.

———. *The Odyssey.* Trans. A. T. Murray. Rev. George E. Dimock. 2 vols. Cambridge: Harvard University Press, 1995.

Horace. *Horace: Satires and Epistles.* Ed. Edward P. Morris. 1939. Repr., Norman: University of Oklahoma Press, 1968.

Horman, William. *Vulgaria.* London, 1519. Repr., Amsterdam: Theatrum Orbis Terrarum, 1975.

Jewel, John. *A Defense of the Apologie of the Churche of Englande.* London, 1567.

Jonson, Ben. *Ben Jonson.* Ed. C. H. Herford, Percy Simpson, and Evelyn Simpson. 11 vols. Oxford: Clarendon, 1925–52.

Krämer, Heinrich, and Jakob Sprenger. *The Malleus Maleficarum.* Trans. Montague Summers. 1928. Repr., New York: Dover, 1971.

La Chesnaye, Nicolas de. *La condamnacion de Bancquet.* In *Le théatre Français avant la Renaissance,* ed. Edouard Fournier, 216–71. Paris, 1880.

Lemaire de Belges, Jean. *Les épîtres de l'Amant Vert.* Ed. Jean Frappier. Lille: Librairie Giard, 1948.

Leo of Naples. "Historia de Preliis." In *The Romances of Alexander,* trans. Dennis M. Kratz, 135–88. New York: Garland, 1991.

Luther, Martin. *Selected Writings of Martin Luther.* Ed. Theodore G. Tappert. 4 vols. Philadelphia: Fortress Press, 1967.

Lydgate, John. *Poems.* Ed. John Norton-Smith. Oxford: Clarendon, 1966.

Macrobius. *Ambrosii Theodosii Macrobii Saturnalia . . . [et] in Somnium Scipionis.* Ed. Jacob Willis. 2 vols. Leipzig: B. G. Teubner, 1963.

Mandeville, John. *Mandeville's Travels.* Ed. M. C. Seymour. Oxford: Clarendon, 1967.

Markham, Gervase. *Cheape and Goode Husbandry.* London, 1614.

Marlowe, Christopher. *The Plays of Christopher Marlowe.* Ed. Leo Kirschbaum. Cleveland: Meridian, 1962.

The Marprelate Tracts [1588–1589]. 1588–89. Facs., Leeds: Scolar Press, 1967.

Martial. *Epigrams.* Trans. D. R. Shackleton Bailey. 3 vols. Cambridge: Harvard University Press, 1993.

————. *Martialis Epigrammata.* Ed. D. R. Shackleton Bailey. Stuttgart: B. G. Teubner, 1990.

Martyr, Peter *The Decades of the New World or West India.* Trans. Richard Eden. London, 1555.

————. *De Orbe Novo.* Trans. Francis Augustus MacNutt. 2 vols. 1912. Repr., New York: Burt Franklin, 1970.

Mascall, Leonard. *The Gouernment of Cattell.* London, 1620.

————. *The Husbandlye ordring and Gouernmente of Poultrie.* London, 1581.

Mather, Increase. *Remarkable Providences Illustrative of the Earlier Days of American Colonisation.* 1856. Repr., New York: Arno Press, 1977.

Middleton, Thomas. *"Women Beware Women" and Other Plays.* Ed. Richard Dutton. Oxford: Oxford University Press, 1999.

Milton, John. *John Milton: Complete Poems and Major Prose.* Ed. Merritt Y. Hughes. Indianapolis: Odyssey, 1957.

————. *The Riverside Milton.* Ed. Roy Flannagan. Boston: Houghton Mifflin, 1998.

Montaigne, Michel de. *The Complete Essays of Montaigne.* Trans. Donald Frame. Stanford, Calif.: Stanford University Press, 1958.

[Montauban, Renaud de] *The right plesaunt and godly historie of the foure sons of Aimon.* [Trans. William Caxton.] London, 1554.

More, Sir Thomas. *The Complete Works of Thomas More.* Ed. Edward Surtz and J. H. Hexler. 8 vols. New Haven, Conn.: Yale University Press, 1965.

Murrell, John. *Mvrrell's Two Books of Cookerie and Carving.* London, 1638.

Nashe, Thomas. *The Works of Thomas Nashe.* Ed. Ronald B. McKerrow. 4 vols. Oxford: Basil Blackwell, 1958.

Neckam, Alexander. *De Naturis Rerum et De Laudibus Sapientiae.* Ed. Thomas Wright. London: Longman, Green, Longman, Roberts, and Green, 1863.

Norden, John. *A Load-Starre to Spiritual Life.* London, 1614.

Osborne, Dorothy. *The Letters from Dorothy Osborne to William Temple.* Ed. G. C. Moore Smith. Oxford: Clarendon, 1928.

Ovid. *Heroides and Amores.* Trans. Grant Showerman. Cambridge: Harvard University Press, 1978.

————. *Metamorphoses.* Trans. Rolfe Humphries. Bloomington: Indiana University Press, 1955.

————. *Metamorphoses.* Trans. Frank Justus Miller. 2 vols. Cambridge: Harvard University Press, 1984.

Oviedo, Gonzalo Fernández de. *Natural History of the West Indies.* Trans. Sterling Stoudemire. Chapel Hill: University of North Carolina Press, 1959.

Page, Samuel. *A Godly Learned Exposition, Together with Apt and Profitable Notes on the Lords Prayer.* London, 1631.

Pepys, Samuel. *The Diary of Samuel Pepys.* Ed. Robert Latham and William Matthews. 11 vols. Berkeley: University of California Press, 1970.

Perry, Ben Edwin, ed. *Aesopica.* 2 vols. Urbana: University of Illinois Press, 1952.

Pico della Mirandola, Giovanni. *Oration on the Dignity of Man.* Trans. A. Robert Caponigri. Chicago: Regnery Gateway, 1956.

Pigafetta, Antonio. "First Voyage around the World." In *Magellan's Voyage around the World: Three Contemporary Accounts,* ed. and trans. Charles E. Nowell, 79–268. Evanston, Ill.: Northwestern University Press, 1962.

Plat, Gabriel. *A Discovery of Infinite Treasure, Hidden since the Worlds Beginning.* London, 1639. Facs., Amsterdam: Theatrum Orbis Terrarum, 1974.

Plato. *Euthyphro, Apology, Crito, Phaedo, Phaedrus.* Trans. Harold North Fowler. London: Heinemann, 1923.

———. *The Republic.* Trans. H. D. P. Lee. Harmondsworth: Penguin, 1955.

Pliny the Elder. *The historie of the world: Commonly called, The naturall historie of C. Plinius Secundus.* Trans. Philemon Holland. 2 vols. London, 1634.

———. *Natural History.* Trans. H. Rackham. 10 vols. Cambridge: Harvard University Press, 1938–63.

Prynne, William. *Histriomastix.* 1633. Repr., New York: Garland, 1974.

Pulci, Luigi. *Morgante.* Ed. Franca Ageno. Milan: Riccardo Ricciardi, 1955.

———. *Morgante: The Epic Adventures of Orland and His Giant Friend Morgante.* Trans. Joseph Tusiani. Bloomington: Indiana University Press, 1998.

Rabelais, François. *Oeuvres complètes.* Ed. Pierre Jourda. 2 vols. Paris: Garnier, 1962.

The right plesaunt and goodly historie of the foure sons of Aimon. Trans. William Caxton. London, 1554.

Rhodiginus, Caelius [Lodovico Ricchieri]. *Lvdovici Caelii Rhodigini Lectionvm Antiqvarvm Libri Triginta.* Frankfurt, 1599.

Scappi, Bartolomeo. *Opera.* Venice, 1622.

The Second Shepherds' Pageant. In *Medieval Drama,* ed. David Bevington, 383–408. Boston: Houghton Mifflin, 1975.

Shakespeare, William. *The Complete Works of Shakespeare.* Ed. David Bevington. New York: Pearson Longman, 2004.

———. *The Dramatick Works of William Shakespeare.* Ed. Samuel Johnson. 9 vols. Boston, 1807.

———. *A New Variorum Edition of Shakespeare.* Ed. Horace Howard Furness. 15 vols. 1899. Repr., New York: American Scholar Publications, 1966.

———. *The Norton Shakespeare.* Gen. ed. Stephen Greenblatt. 4 vols. New York: W. W. Norton, 1997.

———. *The Oxford Shakespeare: The Complete Works.* Gen ed. Stanley Wells and Gary Taylor. 2nd ed. Oxford: Clarendon, 2005.

———. *The Riverside Shakespeare.* Ed. G. Blakemore Evans et al. Boston: Houghton Mifflin, 1997.

———. *Titus Andronicus.* Ed. Alan Hughes. Cambridge: Cambridge University Press, 2006.

Shirley, James. *Hyde Park.* In *Drama of the English Renaissance,* vol. 2, ed. Russell A. Fraser and Norman Rabkin, 743–70. New York: Macmillan, 1976.

———. *Wits labyrinth, or, A briefe and compendious abstract of most witty, ingenious, wise, and learned sentences and phrases.* London, 1648.

Sidney, Sir Philip. *The Countess of Pembroke's Arcadia (The New Arcadia).* Ed. Victor Skretkowicz. Oxford: Clarendon, 1987.

————. *The Poems of Sir Philip Sidney*. Ed. William Ringler. Oxford: Clarendon, 1962.

————. *Sidney's Defense of Poesy*. Ed. Lewis Soens. Lincoln: University of Nebraska Press, 1970.

Skelton, John. "Speke, Parrot." In *The Poetical Works of John Skelton,* vol. 2, ed. and rev. Alexander Dyce, 1–25. 1843. Repr., New York: AMS Press, 1965.

Sophocles. *Ajax; Electra; Oedipus Tyrannus*. Trans. Hugh Lloyd-Jones. Cambridge: Harvard University Press, 1994.

Spenser, Edmund. *Spenser's Complete Poetical Works*. Ed. R. E. Neil Dodge. Boston: Cambridge University Press, 1908.

Stow, John. *The Annales; or, Generall chronicle of England*. London, 1615.

Stubbes, Philip. *The Anatomie of Abuses*. 1583. Facs., New York: Garland, 1973.

Surtees Society. *The Publications of the Surtees Society, Volume 4: Testa Eboracum, or Wills Registered at York, Part I*. London: J. B. Nichols and Son, 1836.

Taillevent. *Le viandier de Guillaume Tirel dit Taillevent*. Ed. Baron Jérôme Pichon and Georges Vicaire. Geneva: Slatkine Reprints, 1967.

Tasso, Torquato. *Godfrey of Bulloigne: A Critical Edition of Edward Fairfax's Translation of Tasso's "Gerusalemme liberata," Together with Fairfax's Original Poems*. Trans. Edward Fairfax. Ed. Kathleen M. Lea and T. M. Gang. Oxford: Clarendon, 1981.

————. *Opere*. Ed. Bruno Maier. 5 vols. Milan: Rizzoli Editore, 1963.

————. *Rinaldo*. Trans. John Hoole. London, 1792.

Theophrastus. *Theophrastus: Characters; Herodas: Mimes; Sophron and Other Mime Fragments*. Ed. and trans. Jeffrey Rusten and I. C. Cunningham. Cambridge: Harvard University Press, 2002.

Topsell, Edward. *The Historie of Fovre-Footed Beastes*. London, 1607. Repr., Amsterdam: Theatrum Orbis Terrarum, 1973.

Trapp, John. *A Commentary or Exposition upon All the Epistles and the Revelation of John the Divine*. London, 1647.

Tusser, Thomas. *A Hundreth Good Pointes of Husbandrie*. 1557. Facs., Amsterdam: Da Capo, 1973.

Tyndale, William. *An Answere vnto Sir Thomas Mores Dialoge*. Ed. Anne M. O'Donnell and Jared Wicks. Washington, D.C.: Catholic University of America Press, 2000.

————. *The Obedie[n]ce of a Christen Man*. [Antwerp, 1528.] Facs., Amsterdam: Theatrum Orbis Terrarum, 1977.

Varro. *On Agriculture*. With Marcus Portius Cato, *On Agriculture*. Trans. William Davis Hooper. Rev. Harrison Boyd Ash. Cambridge: Harvard University Press, 1934.

Vasari, Giorgio. *Le vite de' piu eccellenti pittori, scultori e architettori*. 7 vols. Florence: Salani Editore, 1963.

Vaughan, William. *The Sovles Exercise in the Daily Contemplation of Our Saviours Birth*. London, 1641.

Walter of Châtillon. *The "Alexandreis" of Walter of Châtillon*. Trans. David Townsend. Philadelphia: University of Pennsylvania Press, 1996.

The Wars of Alexander. Ed. Hoyt N. Duggan and Thorlac Turville-Petre. Oxford: Oxford University Press, 1989.

Webster, John. *The White Devil.* In *English Renaissance Drama: A Norton Anthology,* ed. David Bevington et al., 1659–1832. New York: W. W. Norton, 2002.

White, T. H., ed. and trans. *The Book of Beasts, Being a Translation from a Latin Bestiary of the Twelfth Century.* 1954. Repr., New York: Dover, 1984.

Willughby, Francis. *The Ornithology of Francis Willughby.* London, 1678.

Wriothesley, Charles. *A Chronicle of England during the Reigns of the Tudors.* Ed. William Douglas Hamilton. Westminster: Camden Society, 1877.

Xenophon. *Scripta Minora.* Trans. G. W. Bowersock. Cambridge: Harvard University Press, 1984.

POST-1700

Adamson, J. H. "The War in Heaven: The Merkabah." In *Bright Essence: Studies in Milton's Theology,* ed. W. B. Hunter, C. A. Patrides, and J. H. Adamson, 103–14. Salt Lake City: University of Utah Press, 1971.

Agamben, Giorgio. *The Open: Man and Animal.* Trans. Kevin Attell. Stanford, Calif.: Stanford University Press, 2004.

Albala, Ken. *Eating Right in the Renaissance.* Berkeley: University of California Press, 2002.

Appelbaum, Robert. *Aguecheek's Beef, Belch's Hiccup, and Other Gastronomic Interjections: Literature, Culture, and Food among the Early Moderns.* Chicago: University of Chicago Press, 2006.

Ascoli, Albert Russell. *Ariosto's Bitter Harmony: Crisis and Evasion in the Italian Renaissance.* Princeton, N.J.: Princeton University Press, 1987.

Aussy, Pierre J. B. d'. *Histoire de la vie privée des français.* Paris: SenS, 1999.

Baildon, W. P., et al., eds. *Court Rolls of the Manor of Wakefield.* 6 vols. York: Yorkshire Archaeological Society Record Series, 1901–45.

Bakhtin, Mikhail. *Rabelais and His World.* Trans. Helene Iswolsky. Bloomington: Indiana University Press, 1984.

Bate, Jonathan, ed. *Titus Andronicus.* London: Routledge, 1995.

Bedini, Silvio. *The Pope's Elephant.* Nashville: J. S. Sanders and Company, 1998.

Bergman, Charles. "A Spectacle of Beasts: Hunting Rituals and Animal Rights in Early Modern England." In *A Cultural History of Animals in the Renaissance,* gen. ed. Linda Kalof and Brigitte Resl; ed. Bruce Boehrer, 53–73. Oxford: Berg, 2007.

Berry, Alice Fiona. *The Charm of Catastrophe: A Study of Rabelais's "Quart livre."* Chapel Hill: North Carolina Studies in the Romance Languages and Literatures, 2000.

Berry, Ralph. *Shakespeare and the Awareness of the Audience.* London: Macmillan, 1985.

Bettey, Joseph. "Downlands." In *The English Rural Landscape,* ed. Joan Thirsk, 27–49. Oxford: Oxford University Press, 2000.

Bevington, David. *From "Mankind" to Marlowe.* Cambridge: Harvard University Press, 1962.

Blackstone, Sir William. *Commentaries on the Laws of England*. 4 vols. New York: Garland, 1978.

Boehrer, Bruce. "The Horseless Epic." *Milton Quarterly* 43.1 (March 2009): 1–16.

———. "Milton and the Reasoning of Animals: Variations on a Theme by Plutarch." *Milton Studies* 39 (2000): 50–73.

———. *Parrot Culture: Our 2500-Year-Long Fascination with the World's Most Talkative Bird*. Philadelphia: University of Pennsylvania Press, 2004.

———. *Shakespeare among the Animals: Nature and Society in the Drama of Shakespeare and His Contemporaries*. New York: Palgrave, 2002.

———. "Shakespeare and the Social Devaluation of the Horse." In *The Culture of the Horse: Status, Discipline, and Identity in the Early Modern World,* ed. Karen Raber and Treva J. Tucker, 91–111. New York: Palgrave, 2005.

———. "Shylock and the Rise of the Household Pet: Thinking Social Exclusion in *The Merchant of Venice*." *Shakespeare Quarterly* 50.2 (Summer 1999): 152–70.

Bonahue, Edward T., Jr. "'I know the place and the persons': The Play of Textual Frames in Baldwin's *Beware the Cat*." *Studies in Philology* 91.3 (Summer 1994): 283–300.

Bowden, Peter. "Agricultural Prices, Farm Profits, and Rents." In *The Agrarian History of England and Wales,* vol. 4, gen. ed. H. P. R. Finberg, ed. Joan Thirsk, 593–695. Cambridge: Cambridge University Press, 1967.

Bowerbank, Silvia. *Speaking for Nature: Women and Ecologies of Early Modern England*. Baltimore, Md.: Johns Hopkins University Press, 2004.

Bowers, Terence N. "The Production and Communication of Knowledge in William Baldwin's *Beware the Cat*: Toward a Typographic Culture." *Criticism* 33.1 (Winter 1991): 1–29.

Bradley, Henry. "Critical Essay." In *An Historical View of the Beginnings of English Comedy,* vol. 1, ed. Charles Mills Gayley, 197–204. New York: Macmillan, 1926.

Bradshaw, John. *A Concordance to the Poetical Works of John Milton*. Hamden, Conn.: Archon, 1965.

Brand, John. *Observations on the Popular Antiquities of Great Britain*. 3 vols. London: George Bell and Sons, 1908.

Brillat-Savarin, Jean Anthelme. *The Physiology of Taste, or Meditations on Transcendental Gastronomy*. Trans. M. F. K. Fisher. 1949. Repr., Washington, D.C.: Counterpoint, 1994.

Boyce, Benjamin. *The Theophrastan Character in England to 1642*. Cambridge: Harvard University Press, 1947.

Brand, C. P. *Torquato Tasso: A Study of the Poet and of His Contribution to English Literature*. Cambridge: Cambridge University Press, 1965.

Brown, Laura. *Fables of Modernity: Literature and Culture in the English Eighteenth Century*. Ithaca, N.Y.: Cornell University Press, 2001.

Brown, Laura Feitzinger. "Brawling in Church: Noise and the Rhetoric of Lay Behavior in Early Modern England." *Sixteenth Century Journal* 34.4 (Winter 2003): 955–72.

Calin, William C. *The Old French Epic of Revolt: "Raoul de Cambrai," "Renaud de Montauban," "Gormond at Isembard."* Geneva: Librairie E. Droz, 1962.

Campbell, Thomas. *A philosophical survey of the south of Ireland*. London, 1777.

Carey, John, and Alastair Fowler, eds. *The Poems of John Milton*. 2 vols. London: Longman, 1968.

Cartwright, Kent. "*Gammer Gurton's Needle*: Towards a Dramaturgy of Empathy." *Renaissance Papers* (1993): 117–40.

Cave, Terence. *The Cornucopian Text: Problems of Writing in the French Renaissance.*" Oxford: Clarendon, 1979.

Champollion-Figeac, Aimé. *Louis et Charles, Ducs d'Orleans*. Paris: Comptoir des Imprimeurs-Unis, 1844.

Chiappelli, Fredi, Michael J. B. Allen, and Robert L. Benson, eds. *First Images of America: The Impact of the New World on the Old*. 2 vols. Berkeley: University of California Press, 1976.

Cimber, L. *Archives curieuses de l'histoire de France*. 12 vols. in 4. Paris: Beauvais, membre de l'Institut Historique, 1834.

Cohn, Dorrit. *Transparent Minds: Narrative Modes for Presenting Consciousness in Fiction*. Princeton, N.J.: Princeton University Press, 1978.

Colie, Rosalie L. "Reason and Need: *King Lear* and the 'Crisis' of the Aristocracy." In *Some Facets of "King Lear": Essays in Prismatic Criticism*, ed. Rosalie L. Colie and F. T. Flahiff, 185–219. Toronto: University of Toronto Press, 1974.

———. *Shakespeare's Living Art*. Princeton, N.J.: Princeton University Press, 1974.

Combarieu du Grès, Micheline de, and Jean Subrenat, eds. *Les quatre fils Aymon, ou Renaud de Montauban*. Paris: Gallimard, 1983.

Cosslett, Tess. *Talking Animals in British Children's Fiction, 1786–1914*. Aldershot: Ashgate, 2006.

Courtney, Julia, and Paula James, eds. *Parrot Play: The Trickster in the Text*. Lampeter: Edwin Mellen Press, 2006.

Craik, Katherine A. "'The Material Point of Poesy': Reading, Writing, and Sensation in Puttenham's *The Arte of English Poesie*." In *Environment and Embodiment in Early Modern England,* ed. Mary Floyd-Wilson and Garrett A. Sullivan, Jr., 153–70. New York: Palgrave, 2007.

Craik, T. W. "Introduction." In William Shakespeare, *King Henry V,* ed. T. W. Craik, 1–111. London: Routledge, 1995.

Crawford, Patricia. "Women's Published Writings 1600–1700." In *Women in English Society 1500–1800,* ed. Mary Prior, 211–31. London: Methuen, 1983.

Cressy, David. *Bonfires and Bells: National Memory and the Protestant Calendar in Elizabethan and Stuart England*. London: Weidenfeld and Nicolson, 1989.

Crist, Eileen. *Images of Animals: Anthropomorphism and Animal Mind*. Philadelphia: Temple University Press, 1999.

Darnton, Robert. *The Great Cat Massacre and Other Episodes in French Cultural History*. New York: Vintage, 1985.

Davis, R. H. C. "The Medieval Warhorse." In *Horses in European Economic History: A Preliminary Canter,* ed. F. M. L. Thompson, 4–20. Leeds: British Agricultural History Society, 1983.

Deleuze, Gilles, and Félix Guattari. *A Thousand Plateaus: Capitalism and Schizophrenia.* Trans. Brian Massumi. Minneapolis: University of Minnesota Press, 1988.

Derrida, Jacques. "The Animal That Therefore I Am (More to Follow)." Trans. David Wills. *Critical Inquiry* 28.2 (Winter 2002): 369–418.

Dickenson, Victoria. "Meticulous Depiction: Animals in Art, 1400–1600." In *A Cultural History of Animals in the Renaissance,* gen. ed. Linda Kalof and Brigitte Resl; ed. Bruce Boehrer, 165–99. Oxford: Berg, 2007.

Dunbar, Henry. *A Complete Concordance to the Odyssey of Homer.* Ed. Benedetto Marzullo. Hildesheim: Georg Olms, 1971.

Duncan, Douglas. *"Gammer Gurton's Needle* and the Concept of Humanist Parody." *Studies in English Literature* 27.1 (Spring 1987): 177–93.

Dundas, Judith. *"Vox Psittaci*: The Emblematic Significance of the Parrot." In *Florilegio de estudios de emblemática,* 291–98. Inclán: Sociedad de Cultura Vale Inclán, 2004.

Dutton, Richard, ed. *"Women Beware Women" and Other Plays.* Oxford: Oxford University Press, 1999.

Duval, Edwin M. *The Design of Rabelais's "Quart livre de Pantagruel."* Geneva: Librairie Droz, 1998.

Eagleton, Terry. *Marxism and Literary Criticism.* Berkeley: University of California Press, 1974.

Edwards, Karen L. *Milton and the Natural World: Science and Poetry in "Paradise Lost."* Cambridge: Cambridge University Press, 1999.

Edwards, Peter. *Horse and Man in Early Modern England.* London: Hambledon Continuum, 2007.

———. *The Horse Trade of Tudor and Stuart England.* Cambridge: Cambridge University Press, 1988.

Egan, Gabriel. *Green Shakespeare: From Ecopolitics to Ecocriticism.* London: Routledge, 2006.

Eisler, Colin. *Dürer's Animals.* Washington, D.C.: Smithsonian Institution Press, 1991.

Elias, Norbert. *The Civilizing Process: The History of Manners and State Formation and Civilization.* Trans. Edmund Jephcott. Oxford: Blackwell, 1994.

Evans, E. P. *The Criminal Prosecution and Capital Punishment of Animals: The Lost History of Europe's Animal Trials.* 1906. Repr., London: Faber and Faber, 1987.

Fedden, Katharine, trans. *Manor Life in Old France: From the Journal of the Sire de Gouberville for the Years 1549–1562.* New York: Columbia University Press, 1933.

Ferry, Luc. *The New Ecological Order.* Trans. Carol Volk. Chicago: University of Chicago Press, 1995.

Fish, Stanley. *John Skelton's Poetry.* New Haven, Conn.: Yale University Press, 1965.

Flannagan, Roy. "Reflections on Milton and Ariosto." *Early Modern Literary Studies* 2.3 (1996): 4.1–16. http://purl.oclc.org/emls/02-3/flanmilt.html.

Forsyth, Neil. *The Satanic Epic.* Princeton, N.J.: Princeton University Press, 2003.

Foucault, Michel. *The Order of Things: An Archaeology of the Human Sciences.* New York: Vintage, 1973.

Fowler, Elizabeth. *Literary Character: The Human Figure in Early English Writing.* Ithaca, N.Y.: Cornell University Press, 2003.

Frame, Donald M. *François Rabelais: A Study.* New York: Harcourt Brace Jovanovich, 1977.

Frazer, Sir James George. *The Golden Bough.* 12 vols. London: Macmillan, 1919.

Freeman, James A. *Milton and the Martial Muse: "Paradise Lost" and European Traditions of War.* Princeton, N.J.: Princeton University Press, 1980.

Frow, John. "Spectacle Binding: On Character." *Poetics Today* 7.2 (1986): 227–50.

Frye, Roland Mushat. *Milton's Imagery and the Visual Arts: Iconographic Tradition in the Epic Poems.* Princeton, N.J.: Princeton University Press, 1978.

Fudge, Erica. *Brutal Reasoning: Animals, Rationality, and Humanity in Early Modern England.* Ithaca, N.Y.: Cornell University Press, 2006.

———. "Saying Nothing Concerning the Same: On Dominion, Purity, and Meat in Early Modern England." In *Renaissance Beasts: Of Animals, Humans, and Other Wonderful Creatures,* ed. Erica Fudge, 70–86. Champaign: University of Illinois Press, 2004.

Fumerton, Patricia. *Cultural Aesthetics: Renaissance Literature and the Practice of Social Ornament.* Chicago: University of Chicago Press, 1991.

Garber, Marjorie. *Shakespeare after All.* New York: Pantheon, 2004.

Gaskell, Elizabeth. *North and South.* 2 vols. London: Chapman and Hall, 1855.

Gebhart, Emile. *La renaissance italienne et la philosophie de l'histoire.* Paris: Librairie Leopold Cerf, 1887.

Geertz, Clifford. *The Interpretation of Cultures.* New York: Basic Books, 1973.

Giamatti, A. Bartlett. "Headlong Horses, Headless Horsemen: An Essay on the Chivalric Epics of Pulci, Boiardo, and Ariosto." In *Italian Literature: Roots and Branches,* ed. Giose Rimanelli and Kenneth John Atchity, 265–308. New Haven, Conn.: Yale University Press, 1976.

Girard, René. *Violence and the Sacred.* Trans. Patrick Gregory. Baltimore, Md.: Johns Hopkins University Press, 1972.

Givry, Grillot de. *The History of the Devil and the Idea of Evil.* Trans. J. Locke. 1931. Repr., New York: Dover, 1971.

Goldberg, Jonathan. *James I and the Politics of Literature: Jonson, Shakespeare, Donne, and Their Contemporaries.* Baltimore, Md.: Johns Hopkins University Press, 1983.

Goossens, Jan. "The Ill-Fated Consequence of the Tomcat's Jump, and Its Illustration." In *Reynard the Fox: Social Engagement and Cultural Metamorphoses in the Beast Epic from the Middle Ages to the Present,* ed. Kenneth Varty, 113–24. New York: Berghahn, 2000.

Grant, Teresa. "The Uses of Animals in English Early Modern Drama, 1558–1642." Doctoral thesis, Cambridge University, 2001.

Greenblatt, Stephen. *Will in the World: How Shakespeare Became Shakespeare.* New York: W. W. Norton, 2004.

Gresham, Stephen. "William Baldwin: Literary Voice of the Reign of Edward VI." *Huntington Library Quarterly* 44 (1981): 101–16.

Guttery, D. R. *The Great Civil War in Midland Parishes: The People Pay.* Birmingham: Cornish Brothers, 1951.

Haraway, Donna. *The Companion Species Manifesto: Dogs, People, and Significant Otherness.* Chicago: Prickly Paradigm Press, 2003.

Harbison, Craig. *Jan van Eyck: The Play of Realism.* London: Reaktion Books, 1991.

Harris, Tim. *London Crowds in the Reign of Charles II: Propaganda and Politics from the Restoration to the Exclusion Crisis.* Cambridge: Cambridge University Press, 1987.

Harrison, Fraser. *Strange Land: The Countryside; Myth and Reality.* London: Sidgwick and Jackson, 1982.

Hatton, Caroline. "La lame en vers de l'Amant Vert." http://www.columbia.edu/cu/french/graduate/conferences/Penassword/HattonCabstract.htm.

Hole, Christina. *English Sports and Pastimes.* 1949. Repr., New York: Books for Libraries Press, 1968.

Hults, Linda C. "Baldung and the Reformation." In *Hans Baldung Grien: Prints and Drawings,* ed. James H. Marrow and Alan Shestack, 38–59. Chicago: University of Chicago Press, 1981.

Hutton, Ronald. *The Rise and Fall of Merry England: The Ritual Year, 1400–1700.* Oxford: Oxford University Press, 1994.

———. *The Stations of the Sun: A History of the Ritual Year in Britain.* Oxford: Oxford University Press, 1996.

Ireland, Richard W. "Law in Action, Law in Books: The Practicality of Medieval Theft Law." *Continuity and Change* 17.3 (2002): 309–31.

Izacke, Richard. "A perfect Catalogue of all the Sheriffs of the County of Devon." In *Remarkable Antiquities of the City of Exeter,* n.p. London, 1734.

Jeanneret, Michel. *A Feast of Words: Banquets and Table Talk in the Renaissance.* Trans. Jeremy Whitely and Emma Hughes. Chicago: University of Chicago Press, 1991.

Johnson, Samuel. *Samuel Johnson: Selected Poetry and Prose.* Ed. Frank Brady and W. K. Wimsatt. Berkeley: University of California Press, 1977.

Jowett, John. "Varieties of Collaboration in Shakespeare's Problem Plays and Late Plays." In *A Companion to Shakespeare's Works, Volume IV: The Poems, Problem Comedies, Late Plays,* ed. Richard Dutton and Jean E. Howard, 106–28. Oxford: Blackwell, 2003.

Juniper, Tony. *Spix's Macaw: The Race to Save the World's Rarest Bird.* London: Fourth Estate, 2002.

Kahn, Coppélia. *Roman Shakespeare: Warriors, Wounds, and Women.* London: Routledge, 1997.

Kargon, Robert Hugh. *Atomism in England from Hariot to Newton.* Oxford: Clarendon, 1966.

King, John N. *English Reformation Literature: The Tudor Origins of the Protestant Tradition.* Princeton, N.J.: Princeton University Press, 1982.

Kinney, Arthur F. *Humanist Poetics: Thought, Rhetoric, and Fiction in Sixteenth-Century England.* Amherst: University of Massachusetts Press, 1986.

———. *John Skelton: Priest as Poet.* Chapel Hill: University of North Carolina Press, 1987.

Kittredge, George Lyman. *Witchcraft in Old and New England*. Cambridge: Harvard University Press, 1929.

Knight, G. Wilson. *Chariot of Wrath: The Message of John Milton to Democracy at War*. London: Faber and Faber, 1942.

Knights, L. C. *Explorations: Essays in Criticism Mainly on the Literature of the Seventeenth Century*. New York: George W. Stewart, 1947.

Kozikowski, Stanley J. "Comedy Ecclesiastical and Otherwise in *Gammer Gurton's Needle*." *Greyfriar: Siena Studies in Literature* 18 (1977): 5–18.

Kuhn, Thomas S. *The Structure of Scientific Revolutions*. 2nd ed. Chicago: University of Chicago Press, 1970.

Latour, Bruno. *We Have Never Been Modern*. Trans. Catherine Porter. Cambridge: Harvard University Press, 1993.

Leland, John. *Joannis Lelandi antiquarii: De rebus Britannicis collectanea*. 6 vols. London, 1770.

L'Estoile, Pierre de. *Memoir-journaux de Pierre de L'Estoile*. 11 vols. Paris: Alphonse Lemerre, 1888.

Lévi-Strauss, Claude. *The Savage Mind*. Chicago: University of Chicago Press, 1966.

Lewalski, Barbara. *The Life of John Milton*. Oxford: Blackwell, 2000.

Lewis, C. S. *English Literature in the Sixteenth Century Excluding Drama*. Oxford: Clarendon, 1954.

Licht, Meg. "Elysium: A Prelude to Renaissance Theater." *Renaissance Quarterly* 49.1 (Spring 1996): 1–29.

Liddell, H. G., and Robert Scott. *Greek-English Lexicon*. Oxford: Oxford University Press, 1996.

Lilley, Kate. "Introduction." In *The Blazing World and Other Writings*, ed. Kate Lilley London: Penguin, 2004.

Lindheim, Nancy. *The Virgilian Pastoral Tradition from the Renaissance to the Modern Era*. Pittsburgh: Duquesne University Press, 2005.

Lodge, David. *Nice Work*. London: Secker and Warburg, 1988.

———. *Small World*. New York: Warner Books, 1984.

Loisel, Gustave. *Histoire des menageries de l'antiquité à no.s jours*. 3 vols. Paris: Octave Doins et fils, 1912.

Low, Anthony. *The Georgic Revolution*. Princeton, N.J.: Princeton University Press, 1985.

Lynch, Deidre Shauna. *The Economy of Character: Novels, Market Culture, and the Business of Inner Meaning*. Chicago: University of Chicago Press, 1998.

Mallette, Richard. *Spenser, Milton, and Renaissance Pastoral*. Lewisburg, Pa.: Bucknell University Press, 1981.

Marcus, Leah. *The Politics of Mirth: Jonson, Herrick, Milton, Marvell, and the Defense of Old Holiday Pastimes*. Chicago: University of Chicago Press, 1986.

Marichal, Robert. "Quart Livre: Commentaires." In *Etudes Rabelaisiennes*, 1:151–202. Geneva: Librairie E. Droz, 1956.

Martin, Catherine Gimelli. *The Ruins of Allegory: "Paradise Lost" and the Metamorphosis of Epic Convention*. Durham, N.C.: Duke University Press, 1998.

Mason, John Monck. *Comments on the Last Edition of Shakespeare's Plays.* 1785. Facs., New York: AMS, 1973.

Maus, Katharine Eisaman. *Inwardness and Theater in the English Renaissance.* Chicago: University of Chicago Press, 1995.

McFarland, Thomas. *Shakespeare's Pastoral Comedy.* Chapel Hill: University of North Carolina Press, 1972.

Mendelson, Sara Heller. *The Mental World of Stuart Women: Three Studies.* London: Harvester Press, 1987.

Merchant, Carolyn. *The Death of Nature: Women, Ecology, and the Scientific Revolution.* New York: HarperCollins, 1983.

Meyer, Gerald Dennis. *The Scientific Lady in England 1650–1760: An Account of Her Rise, with Emphasis on the Major Roles of the Telescope and Microscope.* Berkeley: University of California Press, 1955.

Miola, Robert. *Shakespeare's Rome.* Cambridge: Cambridge University Press, 1983.

Moesen, Annemie. "De Kattenfeesten te Ieper : Ein analyse van de Kattenstoet en het Kattenwerpen aan de hand van de theorie van Hobsbawm." Doctoral thesis, University of Maastricht, 2005.

Monnas, Lisa. "Silk Textiles in the Paintings of Jan van Eyck." In *Investigating Jan van Eyck,* ed. Susan Foister, Sue Jones, and Delphine Cool, 147–62. Turnhout: Brepols, 2000.

Mosley, Charles, ed. *Burke's Peerage.* 2 vols. Chicago: Fitzroy Dearborn, 1999.

Mowat, Barbara. "Rogues, Shepherds, and the Counterfeit Distressed: Texts and Infra-contexts of *The Winter's Tale* 4.3." *Shakespeare Studies* 22 (1994): 58–76.

M'Queen, Rev. Donald. "Curious and learned reflections . . . on antient customs." *Gentleman's Magazine* 65.1.2 (February 1795): 123–25.

Norbrook, David. *Writing the English Republic: Poetry, Rhetoric, and Politics, 1627–1660.* Cambridge: Cambridge University Press, 1999.

Osborn, James M. *Young Philip Sidney, 1572–1577.* New Haven, Conn.: Yale University Press, 1972.

Osgood, Charles G. *A Concordance to the Poems of Edmund Spenser.* Washington, D.C.: Carnegie Institution, 1915.

Orwell, George. *The Collected Essays, Journalism, and Letters of George Orwell.* Ed. Sonia Orwell and Ian Angus. 4 vols. New York: Harcourt, Brace and World, 1968.

Paster, Gail Kern. *The Body Embarrassed: Drama and the Disciplines of Shame in Early Modern England.* Ithaca, N.Y.: Cornell University Press, 1993.

Peck, A. L., trans. *Aristotle: History of Animals.* 3 vols. Cambridge: Harvard University Press, 1993.

Pepperberg, Irene. *The Alex Studies: Cognitive and Communicative Abilities of Grey Parrots.* Cambridge: Harvard University Press, 1999.

Perfetti, Stefano. "Philosophers and Animals in the Renaissance." In *A Cultural History of Animals in the Renaissance,* 6 vols., gen. ed. Linda Kalof and Brigitte Resl; ed. Bruce Boehrer, 147–64. Oxford: Berg, 2007.

Phelan, James. *Reading People, Reading Plots: Character, Progression, and the Interpretation of Narrative.* Chicago: University of Chicago Press, 1989.

Phipson, Emma. *The Animal-Lore of Shakespeare's Time.* 1883. Repr., New York: AMS, 1973.

Pollard, Alfred F. "Pendleton, Henry." In *Dictionary of National Biography,* vol. 15, ed. Sir Leslie Stephen and Sir Sidney Lee, 737. Oxford: Clarendon, 1917.

Pollock, Sir Frederick, and Frederic William Maitland. *The History of English Law before the Time of Edward I.* 2 vols. 1898. Repr., Cambridge: Cambridge University Press, 1968.

Porter, H. C. *Reformation and Reaction in Tudor Cambridge.* Cambridge: Cambridge University Press, 1958.

Prendergast, Guy Lushington. *A Complete Concordance to the Iliad of Homer.* Ed. Benedetto Marzullo. Hildesheim: Georg Olms, 1971.

Price, Martin. *Forms of Life: Character and Moral Imagination in the Novel.* New Haven, Conn.: Yale University Press, 1983.

Pulton, Ferdinand. *De Pace Regis et Regni.* 1609. Facs., New York: Garland, 1978.

Quilligan, Maureen. *The Language of Allegory: Defining the Genre.* Ithaca, N.Y.: Cornell University Press, 1979.

———. *Milton's Spenser: The Politics of Reading.* Ithaca, N.Y.: Cornell University Press, 1983.

Randall, Michael. "On the Evolution of Toads in the French Renaissance." *Renaissance Quarterly* 57.1 (Spring 2004): 126–64.

Ravelhofer, Barbara. *The Early Stuart Masque: Dance, Costume, and Music.* Oxford: Oxford University Press, 2006.

Redfern, Walter. *French Laughter: Literary Humour from Diderot to Tournier.* Oxford: Oxford University Press, 2008.

Regan, Tom. *The Case for Animal Rights.* Berkeley: University of California Press, 2004.

Revard, Stella. "Lycidas." In *A Companion to Milton,* ed. Thomas N. Corns, 246–60. Oxford: Blackwell, 2003.

Riggs, David. *Ben Jonson: A Life.* Cambridge: Harvard University Press, 1989.

Ringler, William A., Jr. "*Beware the Cat* and the Beginnings of English Fiction." *Novel: A Forum in Fiction* 12 (1979): 113–26.

Ringler, William A., Jr., and Michael Flachmann, eds. *Beware the Cat: The First English Novel.* San Marino, Calif.: Huntington Library, 1988.

Roberts, Jeanne Addison. *The Shakespearean Wild: Geography, Genus, and Gender.* Lincoln: University of Nebraska Press, 1991.

Robinson, J. W. "The Art and Meaning of *Gammer Gurton's Needle*." *Renaissance Drama* n.s. 14 (1983): 45–77.

Rodriguez, Ronald L. "Two Odysseys: Rinaldo's Po Journey and the Poet's Homecoming in *Orlando furioso*." In *Renaissance Transactions: Ariosto and Tasso*, ed. Valeria Finucci, 17–55. Durham, N.C.: Duke University Press, 1999.

Rogers, Katharine M. *The Cat and the Human Imagination: Feline Images from Bast to Garfield.* Ann Arbor: University of Michigan Press, 1998.

Rorty, Amélie Oksenberg. *Mind in Action: Essays in the Philosophy of Mind.* Boston: Beacon Press, 1988.

Rosenberg, D. M. *Oaten Reeds and Trumpets: Pastoral and Epic in Virgil, Spenser, and Milton.* Lewisburg, Pa.: Bucknell University Press, 1981.

Ross, Gordon. "Enobarbus on Horses: *Antony and Cleopatra* 3.7.7–9." *Shakespeare Quarterly* 31.3 (Autumn 1980): 380–89.

Rubinstein, Frankie. *A Dictionary of Shakespeare's Sexual Puns and Their Signification*. London: Macmillan, 1984.

Ruskin, John. *Modern Painters*. Ed. David Barrie. London: André Deutsch, 1987.

Russell, Joycelyne G. *The Field of the Cloth of Gold: Men and Manners in 1520*. New York: Barnes and Noble, 1969.

Rusten, Jeffrey, and I. C. Cunningham, eds. and trans. *Theophrastus: Characters; Herodas: Mimes; Sophron and Other Mime Fragments*. Cambridge: Harvard University Press, 2002.

Sarasohn, Lisa. "A Science Turned Upside Down: Feminism and the Natural Philosophy of Margaret Cavendish." *Huntington Library Quarterly* 47.4 (1984): 289–307.

Sauval, Henri. *Histoire et recherches des antiquites de la ville de Paris*. 3 vols. 1724. Repr., Westmead: Gregg International Publishers, 1969.

Schelling, Felix. *Elizabethan Drama*. 2 vols. Boston: Houghton and Mifflin, 1908.

Schiesari, Juliana. "'Bitches and Queens': Pets and Perversion at the Court of France's Henri III." In *Renaissance Beasts: Of Animals, Humans, and Other Wonderful Creatures*, ed. Erica Fudge, 37–49. Urbana: University of Illinois Press, 2004.

Schorger, A. W. *The Wild Turkey: Its History and Domestication*. Norman: University of Oklahoma Press, 1966.

Scofield, Cora L. "Accounts of Star Chamber Dinners, 1593–4." *American Historical Review* 5.1 (October 1899): 83–95.

Sebillot, Paul. *Le folk-lore de France*. 4 vols. 1905. Repr., Paris: Editions G. P. Maisonneuve et Larose, 1968.

Sells, A. Lytton. *Animal Poetry in French and English Literature and the Greek Tradition*. Bloomington: Indiana University Press, 1955.

Semenza, Gregory M. Colón. "Sport, War, and Contest in Shakespeare's *Henry VI*." *Renaissance Quarterly* 54.4.1 (Winter 2001): 1251–72.

Sims, James H. "*Orlando Furioso* in Milton: Heroic Flights and True Heroines." *Comparative Literature* 49.2 (Spring 1997): 128–50.

Singer, Peter. *Animal Liberation*. New York: Ecco, 2002.

Smith, Bruce. *The Acoustic World of Early Modern England: Attending to the O-Factor*. Chicago: University of Chicago Press, 1999.

Snyder, Susan. *Pastoral Process: Spenser, Marvell, Milton*. Stanford, Calif.: Stanford University Press, 1998.

Spevack, Marvin. *The Harvard Concordance to Shakespeare*. 9 vols. Cambridge: Belknap Press of Harvard University Press, 1973.

Spiller, Elizabeth. *Science, Reading, and Renaissance Literature: The Art of Making Knowledge, 1580–1670*. Cambridge: Cambridge University Press, 2004.

Spivak, Bernard. *Shakespeare and the Allegory of Evil*. New York: Columbia University Press, 1958.

Stallybrass, Peter, and Allon White. *The Politics and Poetics of Transgression*. Ithaca, N.Y.: Cornell University Press, 1986.

Steadman, John. *Milton and the Paradoxes of Renaissance Heroism.* Baton Rouge: Louisiana State University Press, 1987.

———. *Milton and the Renaissance Hero.* Oxford: Clarendon, 1965.

Steiner, Gary. *Anthropocentrism and Its Discontents: The Moral Status of Animals in the History of Western Philosophy.* Pittsburgh: University of Pittsburgh Press, 2005.

Sterne, Laurence. *A Concordance to the English Prose of John Milton.* Binghamton, N.Y.: Medieval and Renaissance Texts and Studies, 1985.

Stone, Lawrence. *The Crisis of the Aristocracy, 1558–1641.* Oxford: Oxford University Press, 1967.

Thirsk, Joan. "Enclosing and Engrossing." In *The Agrarian History of England and Wales,* vol. 4, gen. ed. H. P. R. Finberg; ed. Joan Thirsk, 200–255. Cambridge: Cambridge University Press, 1967.

Thomas, Keith. *Man and the Natural World: Changing Attitudes in England 1500–1800.* London: Allen Lane, 1983.

———. *Religion and the Decline of Magic.* New York: Charles Scribner's Sons, 1971.

Tilley, Morris Palmer. *A Dictionary of the Proverbs of England in the Sixteenth and Seventeenth Centuries.* Ann Arbor: University of Michigan Press, 1950.

Todorow, Maria Fossi. *I disegni del Pisanello a della sua cerchia.* Florence: Leo S. Olschki, 1966.

Tomasik, Timothy J. "Fishes, Fowl, and *Le Fleur de toute cuysine*: Gaster and Gastronomy in Rabelais' *Quart livre.*" In *Renaissance Food from Rabelais to Shakespeare: Culinary Readings and Culinary Histories,* ed. Joan Fitzpatrick, ms. 27–71. Aldershot: Ashgate, 2010.

Toussaint-Samat, Maguelonne. *History of Food.* Trans. Anthea Bell. Oxford: Blackwell, 1992.

Traub, Valerie. *The Renaissance of Lesbianism in Early Modern England.* Cambridge: Cambridge University Press, 2002.

Turner, Henry S. *The English Renaissance Stage: Geometry, Poetics, and the Practical Spatial Arts 1580–1630.* Oxford: Oxford University Press, 2006.

Van Vechten, Carl. *The Tiger in the House.* New York: Knopf, 1920.

Wall, Wendy. "Renaissance National Husbandry: Gervase Markham and the Publications of England." *Sixteenth Century Journal* 27.3 (Autumn 1996): 767–85.

———. *Staging Domesticity: Household Work and English Identity in Early Modern Drama.* Cambridge: Cambridge University Press, 2002.

Wallace, Malcolm William. *The Life of Sir Philip Sidney.* Cambridge: Cambridge University Press, 1915.

Walters, Lori J. "Parody and the Parrot: Lancelot References in the *Chevalier du papegau.*" In *Translatio Studii: Essays by His Students in Honor of Karl D. Uitti for His Sixty-Fifth Birthday,* ed. Renate Blumenfeld-Kosinski et al., 331–44. Amsterdam: Rodopi, 1999.

Warwick, Henrietta Holm. *A Vergil Concordance.* Minneapolis: University of Minnesota Press, 1975.

Watson, Robert N. *Back to Nature: The Green and the Real in the Late Renaissance*. Phila-delphia: University of Pennsylvania Press, 2006.

———. "Horsemanship in Shakespeare's Second Tetralogy." *English Literary Renaissance* 13.3 (Autumn 1983): 274–300.

Watt, Ian. *The Rise of the Novel: Studies in Defoe, Richardson, and Fielding*. Berkeley: University of California Press, 1957.

Wayne, Don E. *Penshurst: The Semiotics of Place and the Poetics of History*. Madison: University of Wisconsin Press, 1984.

White, Hayden. *Metahistory: The Historical Imagination in Nineteenth-Century Europe*. Baltimore, Md.: Johns Hopkins University Press, 1973.

Willems, Michèle. "'Women and Horses and Power and War': Worship of Mars from *1 Henry IV* to *Coriolanus*." In *French Essays on Shakespeare and His Contemporaries: "What Would France with Us?,"* ed. Jean-Marie Maguin and Michèle Willems, 189–202. Newark: University of Delaware Press, 1995.

Williams, Sheila. "The Pope-Burning Processions of 1679, 1680, and 1681." *Journal of the Warburg and Courtauld Institutes* 21 (1958): 104–18.

Williams, Raymond. *Keywords: A Vocabulary of Culture and Society*. New York: Oxford University Press, 1976.

Wilson, F. P. *The English Drama, 1485–1585*. Oxford: Clarendon, 1968.

Wolf, William D. "Recent Studies in Early Tudor Drama: *Gammer Gurton's Needle*." *English Literary Renaissance* 8.1 (Winter 1978): 113–16.

Wolfe, Cary. *Animal Rites: American Culture, the Discourse of Species, and Posthumanist Theory*. Chicago: University of Chicago Press, 2003.

Wright, E. Perceval. *Animal Life: Being a Series of Descriptions of the Various Sub-Kingdoms of the Animal Kingdom*. London: Cassell, Petter, Galpin, and Co., 1879.

Yachnin, Paul. "Sheepishness in *The Winter's Tale*." In *How to Do Things with Shakespeare*, ed. Laurie Maguire, 210–30. Oxford: Blackwell, 2008.

Yates, Frances. *Astraea: The Imperial Theme in the Sixteenth Century*. 1975. Repr., London: Ark, 1985.

Yates, Julian. "Counting Sheep: Dolly Does Utopia (again)." *Rhizomes* 08 (Spring 2004). http://www.rhizomes.net/issue8/yates2.htm.

Zanon, Antonio. *Dell'agricoltura, dell'arti, e del commercio . . . lettere*. 3 vols. Venice, 1763.

Index

Acknowledgments

Among those who have contributed their time, effort, and expertise to the completion of this project, my first and deepest thanks go to Jerry Singerman, humanities editor at the University of Pennsylvania Press, with whom I have now had the privilege to work repeatedly, and ever more rewardingly, over a period of nearly twenty years. I am also grateful to Caroline Winschel and Erica Ginsburg for their efforts in preparing the book manuscript for print.

Erica Fudge and Karen Raber read the entire book manuscript, and their suggestions have improved it in ways that range from the massive to the minute. Other colleagues have been kind enough to read single chapters, offer research suggestions, respond to queries, or facilitate public presentation of parts of the manuscript. These individuals include Anne Coldiron, Mary Crane, Peter Edwards, Jody Enders, Ronald Hutton, Elizabeth Spiller, Henry Turner, Daniel Vitkus, and Paul Yachnin. As my irreplaceable research assistant of many years' standing, Trish Thomas Henley did me one last favor by helping to organize the paperwork for the volume's illustrations.

Portions of this book were presented orally at the 2007 meeting of the Modern Language Association of America, the 2007 meeting of the Group for Early Modern Cultural Studies, the Department of English of the University of Western Ontario, the Department of English of Rutgers University, and Roehampton University's 2009 Conference on the Renaissance and Early Modern Horse. In addition, a draft chapter was presented in writing to my home department's Renaissance Discussion Group, and the book's contents arguably owe something to discussions arising from the Shakespeare Association of America's seminar on "Nature and the Environment in the Early Modern English Drama," which I directed for that organization's 2006 annual meeting. An excerpt from the Introduction appeared in *PMLA* for

March 2009; most of Chapter 2 was printed in *Genre* for spring and summer, 2009; and a shortened version of Chapter 3 was published in *English Literary Renaissance* for spring 2009. I am grateful to these journals for granting me permission to reprint the material in question.